FOUNDATIONS OF
WOODWORKING

FOUNDATIONS OF
WOODWORKING

MICHAEL PEKOVICH

The Taunton Press

This book is dedicated to Rachel.

Thank you for your companionship, inspiration, and support on this journey we have been traveling together for so many years.

The Taunton Press
Inspiration for hands-on living®

63 South Main Street
Newtown, CT 06470-2344
Email: tp@taunton.com

Editor: Peter Chapman
Copy Editor: Elizabeth Knapp
Art Director: Michael Pekovich
Jacket/Cover Design: Rita Sowins
Interior Design: Michael Pekovich
Design Template: Rita Sowins
Layout: Michael Pekovich
Illustrator: John Hartman
Indexer: Peter Chapman
Photographers: Michael Pekovich and Rachel Barclay

The following names/manufacturers appearing in *Foundations of Woodworking* are trademarks:
Brusso®, Domino®, Earlex®, Festool®, Forstner®, SawStop®.

Library of Congress Cataloging-in-Publication Data

Names: Pekovich, Michael, author.
Title: Foundations of woodworking : essential joinery techniques and
    building strategies / Michael Pekovich.
Description: Newtown : The Taunton, Press, Inc., 2021. | Includes index. |
    Summary: "Foundations of Woodworking gets to the very core of the craft
    of woodworking: laying out, cutting, and assembling joinery for
    furniture and other treasured wood objects. After an introductory
    chapter on the basic woodworking strategies that apply to anything you
    might build, Pekovich dives into a step-by-step, project-by-project
    description of the essential wood joints, from rabbets and dadoes
    through mortise and tenons to dovetails and miters. Master these
    joints--with a combination of hand tools and power tools--and the door
    is open to create just about any design you can think of"-- Provided by
    publisher.
Identifiers: LCCN 2021021829 | ISBN 9781641551625 (hardcover)
Subjects: LCSH: Woodwork.
Classification: LCC TT180 .P3885 2021 | DDC 684/.08--dc23

LC record available at https://lccn.loc.gov/2021021829

Printed in the United States of America
10 9 8 7 6 5 4 3 2

"So Mike, what is the book about?"
In short, if my first book, The Why and How of Woodworking, *inspired you to get out in your shop and make something, then with this book in hand, I hope that you'll have the confidence and knowledge to actually go and make it.*

ACKNOWLEDGMENTS

Any book written on the subject of woodworking has by its nature many authors. While I am indebted to the generations of makers who have come before me, there are a handful of woodworkers who have touched my life directly through their mentorship, guidance, and friendship. Your fingerprints can be found throughout this book: Bob Van Dyke, Andrew Peklo, Steve Latta, Will Neptune, Roland Johnson, Marc Adams, Chris Becksvoort, Garrett Hack, Michael Fortune, and Chris Gochnour.

Special thanks to my *Fine Woodworking* family for your friendship and support: John Tetreault, Anissa Kapsales, Jon Binzen, Betsy Engel, Liz Knapp, Ben Strano, Barry Dima, Tom McKenna, you actually made me miss coming into the office this past year.

Thanks also for the support and trust of Peter Chapman, Mark Peterson, and Renee Jordan who have made this book possible.

This book would not be what it is without the editing efforts of Liz Knapp, the illustrations of John Hartman, or the photo-editing genius of Bill Godfrey. I am truly grateful for your contributions.

Finally, thank you to Rachel, Anna, Eli, and Belle for your love, support, and patience in putting up with an often-distracted and always-working housemate.

CONTENTS

INTRODUCTION

The seeds of this book were planted in the writing of my first book, *The Why & How of Woodworking*. While my initial intent with that effort was to include everything I felt important in relation to the craft, I quickly discovered that I would fall far short of that goal in the space I had to work with. So instead, I attempted to offer guidance on making meaningful work and getting the most from our time in the shop. As I worked on the book, I began to catalog the information that, while not fitting neatly within those themes, was still integral to the success of our efforts. That information is at the heart of this book. In it, I propose a path. It's not the only path by any means, but it is one that I am confident will lead you to doing the work you want to do.

We start with the building blocks, the notes in the melody, the basic joinery that becomes the means to achieve our goal. By developing a working knowledge of joinery, we create a tool kit of options to tackle the challenges along the way. Rabbets and dadoes are the most elemental of the joints, but they're incredibly powerful nonetheless. I'll show some time-tested techniques to execute them, and then we'll move on to the other essential joints from there. Each is simple enough to master, but when used in combination, they give us the power to build any project we can imagine.

I'll break down common examples of furniture construction to help illustrate the joinery options at your disposal. Once you begin to view a project through the lens of the joinery of its components, you've taken another big stride down the path of building the furniture you want to make. The final key to success lies in crafting a strategy to get you from start to finish in the most efficient way possible.

Any missteps, and you can find yourself halfway through a project having invested a lot of time and money but without a clue how to make your way to the finish line. That's about the worst place to be when trying your hand at this craft. I'll cover not only what to do and when to do it, but also why it makes the most sense to approach it that way. With that information in hand, my hope is that you can create a smart path through the building of any project you wish to tackle.

Learn how to make basic joints, and then how to combine them into a working plan. Finally, learn how to plot a path that gets you to the finish line with the least amount of effort and the best results. That's it. Let's go.

CHAPTER 1

BUILDING STRATEGIES

The advice in this chapter boils down to a few simple concepts: Pay attention to the grain when you're selecting lumber and breaking out parts. Start with parts that are flat and square. Have a system for organizing and marking your parts within a project. Have a clear idea about where to cut joinery (and where not to) before you pick up a hand tool or head to a machine. Understand the difference between *exact* and *equal* and why one is more important than the other. Finally, learn when to put plans aside and let the project dictate the dimensions of the parts.

Most, if not all, of these concepts are probably familiar to you. While each represents a piece of sound advice on its own, together they combine to create the stepping stones that point to a sure path toward a successful project. While the steps are simple enough to follow, skip any of them and you'll probably have a tougher time building. In addition, you're less likely to be satisfied with the end result.

For instance, not taking the time to choose lumber carefully will compromise the time and effort you invest in the project the rest of the way. Doing a poor job of getting flat and square makes cutting joinery a nightmare later. Not having a clear way to identify your parts and their orientation within a project will lead to miscut joints, patches, and remade parts. Cutting all of the parts in a project to size at the beginning will inevitably lead to trouble later (and more remade parts). Not having a grasp on the concept of why *equal* is more important than *exact* will not necessarily lead to poor results, but it will mean spending more work than necessary to get the results you want.

All of those scenarios may sound a little scary, though I didn't intend them to be. However, my guess is that you've suffered some of these difficulties if you've ever attempted to build a piece of furniture. I know that I have. I also know that as I've become more experienced and have come to understand how these things are interrelated, my time in the shop has become more enjoyable and my projects have tended to look closer to the way I had envisioned them.

CHOOSE AND USE LUMBER WITH CARE

This is where the journey begins. So much of our fate is decided by the lumber we start with that any misstep or lack of consideration at this point will compromise the efforts we invest in the remainder of the build. If we think in terms of "oak" or "walnut" or "cherry" when designing a piece, that's a start. Often, as we are getting our feet wet with the craft, we may put off any thought as to the type of wood we're going to work with until later in the decision-making process. But the more we work with different woods and get to know them—how they work, and the effect they have on the finished piece—the more we begin to design with specific woods in mind. Even then, there are variables to consider when mentally mapping out a project. When people say they don't like ash, it's probably because they're thinking of the wild grain of a baseball bat. Red oak gets put in the doghouse as well if '80s office furniture, or the large cathedrals of kitchen-cabinet door panels, come to mind. However in rift- or quartersawn form, both woods have a beautifully quiet, linear strength to them, and this points to the other aspect of choosing lumber. It's not only the species we're working with, but also how we go about ordering the grain within a project. This consideration can have as big an impact on the success of a piece as the type of lumber we choose.

Loud or quiet, the wood you choose plays a big role in creating the effect you're after. The table in figured shedua on the facing page makes a big splash, while the straight-grained ash of the cabinet above highlights the linear elements and offers a calm sense of order.

THE LOCATION DETERMINES THE GRAIN

Boards from the same tree can have a variety of personalities depending on where they were taken from the log. The orientation of the circular rings and the way they intersect the flat surfaces of a board are what constitutes wood grain. It is primarily the grain that gives a board its characteristic look, though it can vary depending on the species. The contrast between the earlywood and latewood that make up the rings can be very striking in some woods, creating prominent grain lines, and almost nonexistent in others, resulting in a featureless surface. Understanding how grain plays a role in the look of the lumber we choose is an important factor in taking control of the finished look of a project.

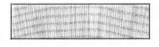

PLAINSAWN STOCK HAS PERSONALITY

Boards with rings parallel to the faces will yield striking patterns on the surface. While this undulating grain can be the perfect thing to enliven a broad surface like a door panel or drawer front, it can have a chaotic effect on more linear parts like table legs and door frames.

QUARTERSAWN CAN BE LOUD OR QUIET

A board with rings perpendicular to its faces yields tight, straight grain lines that can enhance the linear nature of parts like face frames, door frames, and dividers. It can also provide a decorative effect due to the medullary rays that radiate out from the center of the log. In a quartersawn board, these rays are almost parallel to the face of the board, and depending on their size, they can have a dramatic impact. The large rays in white oak (1) can result in tiger stripes across the surface, whereas the smaller rays of sycamore create an iridescent bee's-wing effect (2). In woods like ash that have inconspicuous rays, quartersawn stock can yield a quiet, ordered look to parts (3).

RIFTSAWN STOCK HAS STRAIGHT GRAIN ON EVERY FACE

When the grain runs at a diagonal to the surface, it is referred to as riftsawn stock. This grain orientation has neither the wild figure of a plainsawn board nor the prominent medullary rays of a quartersawn board, but it does have an important quality. The diagonal orientation of the stock creates tight, straight grain on all four faces of a part. This is especially important on square parts like table legs where adjacent faces are viewed at the same time. Like quartersawn stock, it can also be used to good effect on other thin parts, creating an ordered appearance that accentuates the lines of a piece (**1**). While boards are rarely sorted for rift grain, it can easily be had by taking parts from the edges of plainsawn boards where the rings tend to dive at an angle to the faces (**2**).

COMBINING GRAIN FOR BEST EFFECT

Plainsawn stock provides dramatic effect on the door panels and drawer fronts.

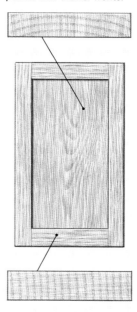

Quartersawn stock frames the figured wood and provides order to the cupboard parts.

Used in combination, stock with different grain patterns can add interest as well as order to a piece of furniture. On this cherry chimney cupboard, a highly figured plainsawn board was used to good effect on the door panels and drawer fronts, and it provides a lively focal point to an otherwise simple piece. Quartersawn and riftsawn stock was then used to frame the dramatic panels and provide order to the piece while enhancing the linear quality of the design. When combining woods, we often think in terms of different species, but even within the same wood, the combination of grain patterns is an important design tool.

DIFFERENT LOOKS FROM THE SAME BOARD

The log diagram on p. 8 is commonly seen in woodworking books. While it can be useful in understanding the various grain patterns that can be had depending on where a board is taken from the log, it can be misleading as well. Looking at such a drawing, you'd be forgiven if you came away with the notion that you'd need to buy a number of boards in order to have the ability to control the grain orientation of the parts within a project. The truth is that even within a single board, you can exercise a good deal of control over how the grain runs in individual parts, and that can have a big impact on the look of a finished piece. The board shown at left is sold as an 8/4 (2-in.-thick) plainsawn piece of cherry. However, by being mindful of where you are cutting your parts from, you can end up with plain-, rift-, or even quartersawn stock, which can be used to highlight the different aspects of the parts within the design.

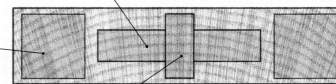

True plainsawn stock can be taken from the center portion of the board.

Parts requiring riftsawn stock can be taken from the edges of the board.

Narrow quartersawn parts also can be taken from the center.

A TABLE'S WORTH OF LUMBER FROM A BOARD

A favorite class that I teach is one where we begin with a single roughsawn board and end up with an elegant little table. While the class offers good lessons in table construction and shaping parts to invest some personality, it also offers the opportunity to try our hands at breaking down a board to get the appropriate grain for each part. To be successful when making the table, or any other project for that matter, it is important to know what look you're after for each part and keep it in mind when choosing and breaking down your lumber.

GIVING THE PARTS THE GRAIN THEY DESERVE

A 2-in.-thick, 8-in.-wide by 8-ft.-long board can yield all of the stock you need to build this side table with plenty to spare. While it might seem like a waste, having the extra lumber affords you the flexibility to get the grain exactly where you need it when building a project.

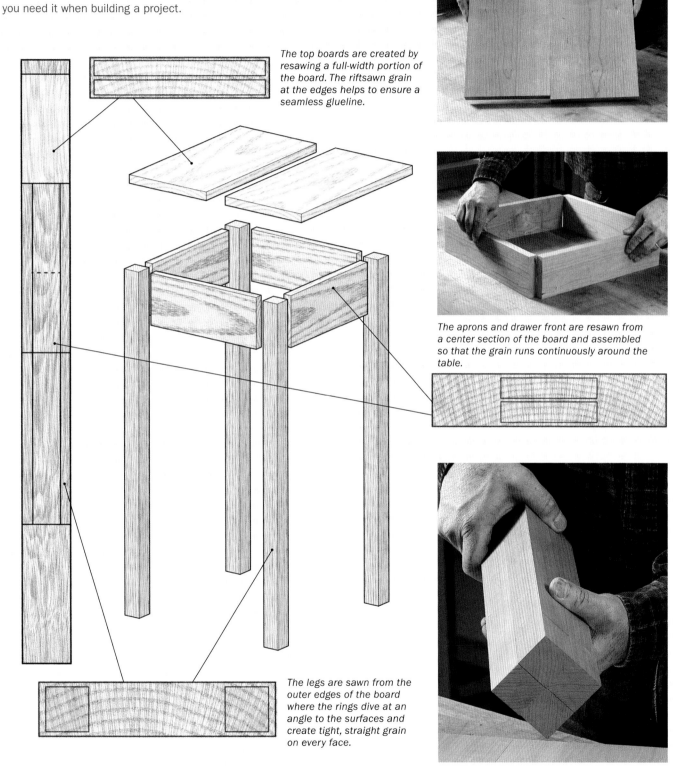

The top boards are created by resawing a full-width portion of the board. The riftsawn grain at the edges helps to ensure a seamless glueline.

The aprons and drawer front are resawn from a center section of the board and assembled so that the grain runs continuously around the table.

The legs are sawn from the outer edges of the board where the rings dive at an angle to the surfaces and create tight, straight grain on every face.

FLAT AND SQUARE:
THE FOUNDATION THE HOUSE IS BUILT ON

If you don't take the time to get the stock flat and square, nothing else will go well or easily the rest of the way.

My first assignment in my first woodworking class in college was to take a rough length of 2x4 and create a precisely dimensioned block 1 in. thick by 3 in. wide by 12 in. long, with flat faces and square edges. For the task we used machines—jointer, planer, and tablesaw—though hand tools could have done the job as well. That precisely dimensioned block was one of the most important lessons in my woodworking career, not just because it gave me an understanding of the order of the steps necessary to get there, but also because it opened my eyes to the notion that accurate milling is the foundation for doing good work. If you don't take the time to get there, nothing else will go well or easily the rest of the way. Working with warped lumber or boards with edges and ends out of square is just ensuring headaches later. Even if you execute everything perfectly from that point on, it will still be a frustrating process. The fact that I attempted this exercise with machines instead of hand tools is not really relevant; knowing how to get there either way is important. Each method has its challenges. Machines are a big investment, one that you may not be able or willing to make if you're just starting as a woodworker. Hand tools, while more affordable, have a pretty steep learning curve in regard to sharpening and setup before you can even think about squaring up your stock. There's no easy way into the craft, but those of us with a certain sensibility and perseverance will find our way in spite of that. There are a lot of ways for the journey to begin, but learning to get flat and square is always the first step.

BREAK IT DOWN

The first step in milling lumber is to cut the parts to rough size. This has a number of benefits. First, the smaller parts are easier to handle when jointing, planing, or sawing at the tablesaw. You can also increase the yield of the stock by reducing the amount of cup or bow you need to remove by cutting the parts to size first. But the most important reason for breaking down the stock first has to do with the tensions within the board. As the lumber dries, there is a lot of stress created in the wood. At its full size, the stresses in the board are at equilibrium, but as you cut it into separate pieces, those tensions are released, causing the individual parts to cup or bow. Because of that, I handle all of the crosscutting with a circular saw (1) and the rough ripping and resawing at the bandsaw (2). The boards are not yet flat enough to run safely through the tablesaw. Any cupping during the cut isn't a problem using the circular saw or bandsaw (3), but at the tablesaw the kerf can close up and pinch the back of the blade, causing a dangerous kickback.

EXTRA STOCK LETS YOU STRAIGHTEN THE GRAIN

I've learned that in order to have enough lumber for a project, I have to buy more than I need. I know that lumber can be expensive and the idea of spending more than necessary on a project can be tough to swallow. Starting out, I'd try to buy just enough lumber to get by, only to have to work around knots and figure out the best way to hide sapwood or other defects. Worse yet, any mistake would often lead to a second (or third) trip to the lumberyard. WIth a little more wood, these problems are easier to avoid.

Having extra stock on hand also offers the opportunity to dial in the ideal grain that you'd like on each part. The board shown here is a good example of that. The grain was fairly parallel to one edge, but dramatically angled to the other (**1**). Without the extra width I'd be left with a part with angled grain that could compromise the overall look of the piece. Working with wider stock allowed me to saw the board in such a way that I got straight grain on each part (**2 & 3**).

FINE-TUNE THE GRAIN ON TABLE LEGS

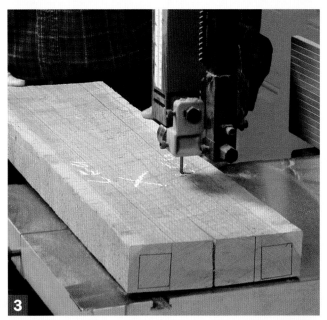

Cutting legs from the outer edges of a board will result in roughly riftsawn stock, but if the grain is too far off of diagonal, you can end up with some problematic grain and will spend time trying to figure out the best way to hide it. If I have the extra thickness, I try to dial in the grain direction even further to get the grain as straight as I can on each face. I still end up having to choose the best faces, but at least the decisions are a little easier to make. I start with a cutout in a piece of cardboard slightly larger than the blank I need. I use this window to orient the ends of the legs exactly diagonal to the grain (1). From there, I mark (2) and saw out each rough leg blank (3). To cut the finished blank, I tilt the bandsaw table so that one layout line is parallel to the blade and make a cut (4). After that, level the table and, using the freshly cut face as a reference, cut an adjacent face square (5). Then square up the remaining faces and you have a nice start to a table leg (6).

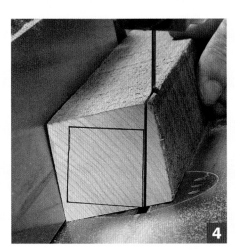

FACES FIRST, THEN EDGES AND ENDS WHEN MILLING STOCK

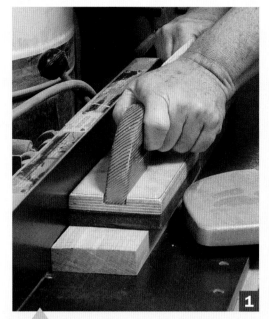

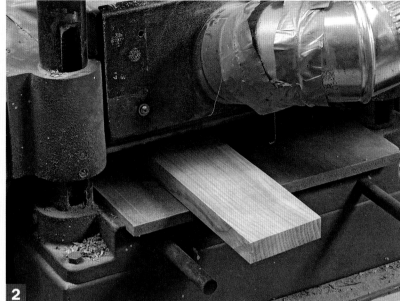

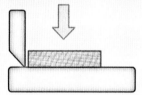

When flattening the first face, the jointer bed is the reference surface. Once the stock has passed the cutter, apply pressure against the outfeed table.

Whether milling by hand or machine, the first task is to get one face flat. I trust my jointer to handle that job (**1**). The next step is to take the stock to final thickness while making the opposite face parallel to the first. This is where the planer takes over (**2**). People often wonder if they need both machines, but they perform very different tasks. A jointer won't get a second face parallel to the first, and a planer won't get a first face flat (actually you can get it to do just that, but that's a different story). For the next step, we head back to the jointer to render one edge of the board flat and square to the faces (**3**). With that work done, we can finally turn on the tablesaw, rip the stock to width (**4**), and cut it to length (**5**). While the tablesaw seems like an instrument of brute force, I treat it as a final dimensioning and joinery-cutting tool. Properly tuned and equipped with a sharp blade, it handles that job quite well. Not all that different than a hand tool, I suppose.

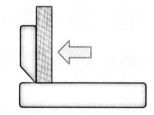

When flattening an adjacent edge, the fence becomes the reference surface, so keep the stock tight against it as you make a pass to ensure a square edge.

SKIP THE TABLESAW WHEN MILLING SQUARE STOCK

For square stock (and even narrow stock up to 3 in. wide), I use the planer to get the final faces square. At the jointer, square up two adjacent faces (1) and mark the square corner to use as a reference when planing (2). Then head to the planer and run the stock through with the jointed faces against the bed (3). This way you'll end up with consistently dimensioned square stock without the risk of tablesaw-blade marks.

A MEDITATION ON MILLING

I want to pause for just a moment because we've gotten off to a really fast start. Before we leave the subject of milling behind, I think it would be good to give it one more look. The focus of the discussion on selecting and milling lumber was about going from rough lumber to dimensioned stock. While it can feel like loud and dusty grunt work at times, that's where we create the foundation for everything to follow. The trick is to start with the finished design and determine how you would like the grain to run in each piece. From there, you can select boards at the lumberyard based on the grain you need, and then begin to plan how to cut up those boards to get the parts looking the way you want. I often say that a good finish begins at the lumberyard, and this is exactly what I'm referring to—the more care you give to lumber selection, the more likely you'll be to end up with the piece you envisioned before building.

With this in mind, the seemingly mundane task of milling becomes critical to the success of the project, both in regard to the ease and accuracy of building as well as the final look. Get this part right, and woodworking just got a little easier and more rewarding.

"Can't you pay someone to do the milling for you?" The answer to that reasonable-sounding question is no, because a really important thing happens at the milling stage. It's where you get to know your lumber. Planing and jointing, whether by machine or by hand, will quickly get you acquainted with the grain, where it changes direction, where it's likely to tear out. You begin to catalog the best faces as well as the knots and defects and slivers of sapwood, and you begin to plan the placement of parts around them. At the lumberyard, I aim to find "perfect" boards, but the reality always falls short of that ideal. Wood is an organic material, and though its random nature is part of its appeal, it can still be frustrating when you're searching for the exact grain for each part in the project. In the end, I pick the best boards I can find, then call it good. When I get to the shop, I do the best job I can to get the best wood where it matters most, and hide the defects where they are not easily seen. At the end of this selection and milling process it can feel as though I've spent the time making a series of least-bad choices, and my hopes for the ideal project I had envisioned have been beaten up a little bit. The funny thing is, as frustrated as I may feel at the time, the result once I take a step back is usually pretty nice. It's happened enough that I've begun to trust that as long as I do my best at each task and move on to the next with the same intent, I'll get the results I'm hoping for.

TRIANGLES KEEP YOUR PARTS IN ORDER

Without a system for quickly identifying and orienting all those otherwise indistinguishable parts, you're inviting mistakes.

They say that good joinery starts with good layout. I'd add that good joinery and good layout require clear orientation marks. If you've ever spent half a day dovetailing a drawer only to cut the last set of pins in the wrong direction, you know how important it is to mark parts clearly and refer to the marks often.

As your projects become more ambitious, and doors and drawers multiply, so do the opportunities for mix-ups. Without a system for quickly identifying and orienting all those otherwise indistinguishable parts, you're inviting mistakes.

To avoid the pain and suffering of miscut joinery, I use the carpenter's triangle, a deceptively simple mark that magically unravels the DNA of every part I'm working with and heads off mistakes before they happen.

Unlike more complicated marking systems that use matching numbers, letters, or hieroglyphics, the simple triangle gives you all the information you need for every part—which face and edge go out and up, and which joints go where. Whether you're doing a simple tabletop glue-up or making a complicated case piece with lots of parts, using the triangle is the easiest, most intuitive way to keep track of all of the parts.

EVERY PART GETS A PIECE OF A TRIANGLE

There are a lot of ways to go about marking the parts within a project, but I find a triangle to be the simplest and most effective. With a triangle in place, I can pick up any part from a jumble on my benchtop and know immediately where it lives within the project, which face is the front, the rear, the top and bottom. The first step in marking the parts is to position them the way you want them. On a frame-and-panel door, lay out the parts with their fronts facing up and then gang up the pairs of parts and mark a triangle across them. Once the parts are reassembled, all of the triangles should point in the same direction.

NAVIGATING A SMALL TABLE

Even a seemingly simple project like this side table by Christian Becksvoort has a fair number of parts and a fair number of opportunities to mix them up. It helps to organize the parts in groups—tabletop boards, aprons, drawer front and stretchers, and legs—and mark triangles to locate each part within its group.

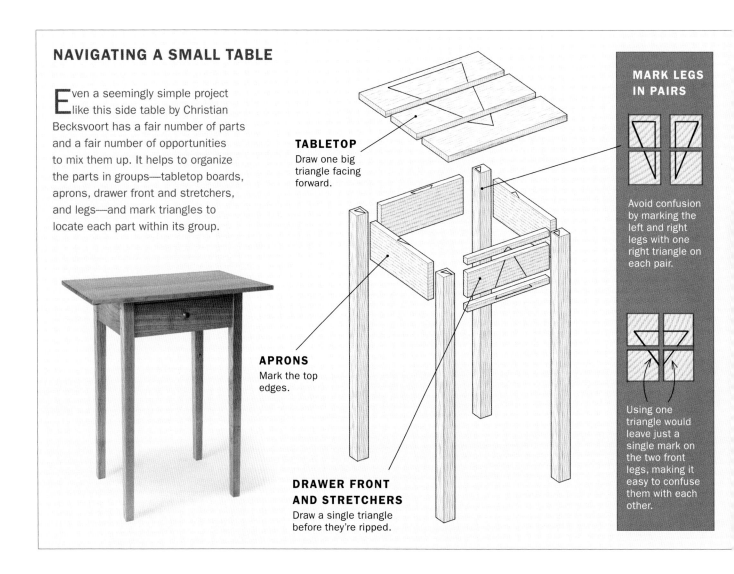

TABLETOP
Draw one big triangle facing forward.

MARK LEGS IN PAIRS

Avoid confusion by marking the left and right legs with one right triangle on each pair.

Using one triangle would leave just a single mark on the two front legs, making it easy to confuse them with each other.

APRONS
Mark the top edges.

DRAWER FRONT AND STRETCHERS
Draw a single triangle before they're ripped.

A few seconds spent marking triangles really pays off when you lay out and cut your joinery.

Every part gets marked with a partial or complete triangle on its face or top edge, with points facing forward or up. For a frame-and-panel door, for example, you'd start by ganging up the stiles. Mark one triangle, pointing up, across the front face of both pieces. Then gang up the rails and mark them with another triangle that points up. Finally, mark the panel. Each part now has a mark to identify its placement on the door, its front face, and its vertical orientation.

Instead of marking their faces, drawers get triangles across their top edges, pointing forward. Draw one across the tops of the sides, then another across the tops of the front and back. Treat case assemblies and table aprons the same way, with triangles on the front and top edges.

Table legs get a different approach. If you mark one triangle across the top of all four, the front two legs will get just a slash each, making it easy to confuse them. Instead, mark the tops in pairs, using right triangles to distinguish the left legs from the right. This way, you have enough information to taper the legs and cut the joinery with confidence. Right triangles also come in handy anytime you have two of the same elements in a piece, as with drawers or doors. If you have more than two, number them in the most straightforward, systematic way possible.

A few seconds spent marking triangles really pays off when you lay out and cut your joinery. No matter how patient you are setting up your machines and dimensioning stock, no two pieces of wood will ever be identical. The dimensions of any piece can vary

LOTS OF COMPONENTS IN A CASE PIECE

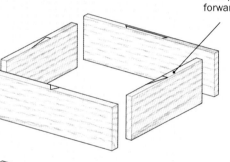

CASE PARTS
Sides and shelves get marks on the front edges with the triangles pointing up.

DRAWER
Draw a triangle across the top edges of the sides and one across the back and front, both pointing forward.

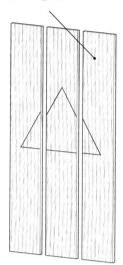

BACK PANEL
Mark the front face with a triangle pointing up.

Front-facing case parts like the back splash and toekick get a triangle on their front face.

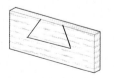

DOOR
Draw one triangle across the rails and one across the stiles, both pointing up. A door panel would get a triangle as well.

MARKING MULTIPLES

Multiple doors or drawers can add to the confusion when marking parts. For a pair of doors, I turn to right triangles. Orienting the vertical face of the triangle toward the center gives each piece a unique mark. I use the same approach for a pair of drawers, but for more than that, I mark each drawer as I would a single drawer and add a number to each part.

CONSISTENT MACHINE JOINERY

Keeping track of reference faces when machining parts can result in more consistent work, and triangles can help with that. At the tablesaw, place the triangle against the fence when cutting grooves (**1**). When cutting tenons, cut the first cheek with the front face down and adjust the blade height to the edge of the groove (**2**). Keep the front face against the fence when mortising as well (**3**). All of this should result in parts that are flush on the show face even if the thicknesses vary or the grooves or mortises are off center.

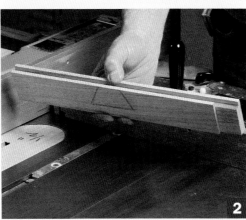

Before you plane or sand off the triangles, be sure to re-mark them on the joinery where they'll be out of the way.

slightly over time. By referencing off your triangles you can make sure that at least one face (usually the front) of each assembly ends up flat and flush.

Here's how it works. To get all the joints of a frame-and-panel door flush on the front face, orient the show faces of the rails and stiles against the rip fence when you cut the panel groove, and orient those same faces against the fence of the mortiser when you cut the mortises. This orientation ensures that the distance from the show face to the panel groove and from the show face to the mortise are the same. Any variations in the thickness of the parts will be apparent on the back of the door, not the front. The same goes for cutting tenons. Make the front-facing cheek cuts first, at that same distance from the face of the rail. Then, if you need to make any adjustments for fit, make them on the back-facing cheek.

I pay attention to the triangles when hand-cutting joinery as well. When dovetailing a drawer, I first look to the triangles to lay out the dovetails on the drawer sides. Once the tails are cut, the triangles play their most important role, ensuring that the parts are properly oriented when scribing the pins on the drawer front and back. I'll turn to the triangles once again when cutting the grooves for the drawer bottom at the tablesaw.

It's important to locate and orient your parts correctly during glue-ups, too. So before you plane or sand off the triangles, be sure to re-mark them on the joinery where they'll be out of the way.

AVOID WASTED HANDWORK

Bench work can be tough enough without wasting an afternoon re-milling parts because you cut dovetails in the wrong place. It happens at least once in just about every class I teach, and it's always frustrating for the student. Even in my own shop, I live in fear of wasting a good dovetail, and I keep a vigilant eye on my triangles when laying out joinery.

RE-MARK PARTS AS YOU GO

Triangles tend to disappear during surface prep, and if you're not careful you can be left trying to figure out where all the parts go. So before starting, I re-mark them in an inconspicuous location like a tenon cheek. You can also lessen the stress of a glue-up by clearly marking the triangles with tape on each part.

MAKE A ROAD MAP

Now that each part in the project is locked in with a cabinetmaker's triangle, there's one more equally important task before we get down to work. I call it a joinery road map. Take a few minutes and mark the approximate location of the joinery on each part. No squares, rulers, or marking knives, just a pencil squiggle to mark a rabbet, mortise, or dovetail. Later, when you get down to precise layout or cutting joinery, you can follow the map to ensure that everything is happening in the right place. Dividing the tasks of locating the work and doing the work might seem counterintuitive, but turning your attention to each task in turn is a lot more efficient than doing both at once.

This way of working is important for handwork, where we can invest a lot of time and effort for naught if the parts or their orientation gets mixed up, but it's just as critical at a machine, where a lot of things can go wrong quickly. Standing at a tablesaw with a dado blade spinning and the dust collector roaring is not the time to second-guess where to make the cut. That quick pencil line takes a lot of stress out of the situation and gives you a running chance at getting everything in the right place.

While the marking goes quickly, the process is deliberate. The point is to trust that the marks are where they need to be later in the game when your attention is turned to other tasks. For through-joinery, mark its location on each face of the part. When it comes to machine work or layout, if there's a mark, something goes there; if not, leave it alone. A rabbet gets a mark on each adjacent face; a stopped dado or groove has a

Take a minute to make a rough road map of all of the joinery on each part of a project (facing page). These rough marks will then guide the way for final layout. It's easier to concentrate on the accuracy of your layout if you're not worried about whether or not you're marking the correct face or end of a part (above).

prominent stop line. If the part will be curved or tapered, indicate that. The first Shaker nightstand I made was supposed to have tapers on the inside faces of the legs. After a miscut, it had four-sided tapers on each leg. I still have that table and I look at those legs every time I pass. While failure is a good teacher, it's nice not to learn all of our lessons that way.

I've made a lot of furniture, and while I've cut joinery where it didn't belong on occasion, I can't remember a time when I've had a misstep after laying out a road map first. At the start of a project class, the first task is always to get a triangle on everything and the second is to get the road map in place. This is such a critical thing that we don't turn on the machines until I've taken a look at everyone's parts. It's challenging enough when I'm working on my own, but to have a dozen projects take flight in a classroom takes it to another level, and I would be lost without the process.

DO LESS MEASURING TO DO BETTER WORK

Hitting exact measurements on a plan isn't that critical. As long as pairs of parts are of equal lengths, you'll end up with a square case.

Getting better results by measuring less might not make sense at first, but there's a lot to the notion. If you've ever taken a look at a furniture plan with its hundreds of dimensions, you'd be forgiven for assuming that you have to get them all right for your project to be a success. One of my jobs at *Fine Woodworking* is to assemble all of those dimensions and get them onto a drawing. The biggest challenge is actually getting the dimensions from the author in the first place. The reason is that they don't actually know all of them. How can that be? Every great woodworker I know follows two really important practices in their work. Both revolve around the idea of measuring less to do faster, more accurate work. And both are concepts that you can put to use right away.

The first concept I'll call "equal, not exact." If you take a look at the plans for the Arts and Crafts cabinet on pp. 114–15, you'll see a lot of dimensions. The good news is that you don't need to hit them exactly; you can be off here and there and you'll still end up with a nice piece. What is critically important, though, is that each set of like-minded parts be exactly the same length. If one side or shelf differs from the other by ¹⁄₁₆ in. or even less, you'll begin to build problems into the project before you really get started. Uneven case parts will result in a case that isn't square, or one with gaps at the joints.

BUILD IN SQUARE FROM THE START

Crosscutting parts can seem mundane enough, but the job you do now can have a big impact later. What's important at this point is not the exact length of the parts you are cutting, but whether or not related parts are equal to each other. A stop clamped to the crosscut fence is your best friend at this stage (**1**). While it's apparent that the sides of the case need to match (**2**), as well as the top and bottom, a closer look will reveal that the other horizontal parts share the same shoulder-to-shoulder dimension as the top and bottom. The easiest way to get everything to match up later is to cut them all to the same length now (**3**).

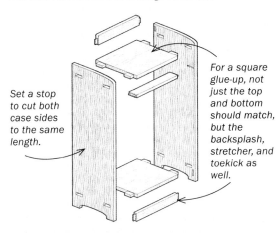

Set a stop to cut both case sides to the same length.

For a square glue-up, not just the top and bottom should match, but the backsplash, stretcher, and toekick as well.

SHOULDER-TO-SHOULDER DISTANCE IS THE KEY TO A SQUARE CASE

On p. 29, I mentioned that, even though parts may end up with different lengths, those with the same shoulder-to-shoulder dimension should start out at the same length. Here is where that strategy pays off. When cutting the tenons on the parts, you can set the fence once and then get to work (**1 & 2**). Afterward, you can cut the tenons to their final lengths (**3**) and end up with accurate parts without a lot of work (**4**). I know that we're just cutting a couple of tenons here, but this represents a really important concept in building where it's possible to improve your work while taking an easier approach to it. I learned of this concept from the brilliant Steve Latta many years ago, and it is one I put to use on just about every project I make.

CUT JOINERY BEFORE RIPPING PARTS TO WIDTH

This idea goes hand in hand with the shoulder-to-shoulder concept, but in this case, parts to be joined are first ripped to the same width. A common feature in my work, and one that I picked up from making Arts and Crafts furniture, is to offset parts where they meet. This often results in a number of parts with slightly different widths. If I were to cut all of those parts to their final dimensions prior to cutting the joinery, it would present a daunting task, one that I would most likely fall short in executing. On this cabinet, for instance, the top and bottom are joined to the sides with through-tenons. Starting with parts of the same width simplifies the joinery layout dramatically (1), and ripping the parts to their final width later is an easy task (2).

BUILDING FROM THE OUTSIDE IN

Fitting a door is a perfect example of putting the plans away after a point and letting the project dictate the dimensions of the components you're making. In this case, the strategy is to build the door slightly larger than the opening, and then trim it down to size. In spite of doing your best to build a square case, in reality it's likely to be a little off. Fortunately, this is not a big problem. As long as the gaps around the door are even, everything will look great, and an oversize door will give you the opportunity to get there. Fitting a door is a step-by-step process. The first task is to create a clean edge on the bottom of the door at the tablesaw (**1**). Next, set the door in place and, holding the door tight to the hinge side of the opening, check the gap along the bottom (**2**). If it's uneven, use a shim to angle the door slightly and take another pass at the tablesaw (**3**). Once the gap is even, repeat the process at the top of the door. Your goal is an even ⅛-in. gap along the top edge (**4**). The gap may look a little wide, but once the door is centered, it should be fine. To mark the hinge locations, shim the bottom of the door until it's centered vertically in the opening and make a knife mark at the top and bottom of each hinge mortise in the case (**5**).

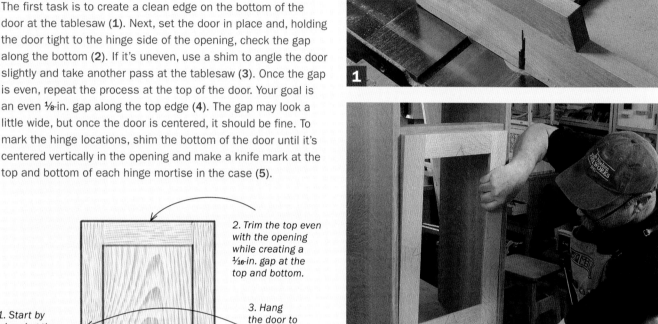

1. Start by trimming the bottom so that the door sits flush while held tight against the hinge side of the opening.

2. Trim the top even with the opening while creating a 1/16-in. gap at the top and bottom.

3. Hang the door to determine how much to trim off the pull side of the door.

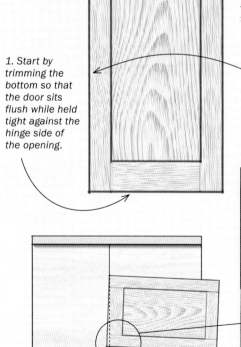

Use a shim to adjust the angle of the door bottom when crosscutting.

The key to getting parts to the right size is to have a smart way to get there. It sounds as though you need to be precise, which is true, but using a tape measure isn't the answer. A better method is to build in consistency by the way you go about milling the parts. For instance, I plane all of the parts at the same time so that even if I'm a little over or under the ideal thickness, all the parts will be consistent. If I have to match additional stock to parts that are already planed, I'll usually shoot for a little thinner dimension and run both the new and existing parts at the same time.

When it comes to ripping and crosscutting the parts, it's important to have a strategy here as well. Cutting parts to specified lengths or widths listed on a plan can actually make life more difficult for you right now. A better approach is to look for the key dimensions in the piece first. On a case piece or table, the shoulder-to-shoulder dimensions of the parts are what determines how well it comes together, even if the overall lengths of the parts may differ. So regardless of whether a piece has long through-tenons or short blind tenons, or dovetails for that matter, I will start by cutting those parts to the same length. That way I can use the same setting to cut the shoulders of the joints, and then trim the parts to final length later. This is a much easier way to get consistent dimensions than cutting the parts to their various final lengths and trying to dial in the shoulder dimensions on each with the hope that everything will come together at the same time. The same concept goes for ripping parts to width. It is easier to join parts of the same width and trim them to final width once you're done.

The second concept that minimizes the need for measuring is "working from the outside in." The idea is to hold off on making internal parts until the outside has been cut to size. For a cabinet this means waiting for the case to be assembled before cutting door and drawer parts to size. Yes, those dimensions will be listed on the plan, but there's no guarantee they'll be accurate once everything comes together. While a measured drawing is a good thing to have, it's pretty clear that at some point it's best to put it aside and begin to build around what you've already made.

CHAPTER 2

RABBETS, DADOES, AND GROOVES

This is where the building begins. We've spent some time and care milling our lumber into flat and square boards, and with a rabbet or a groove, we begin to transform those boards into furniture parts. A good place to dive into joinery is with a trio of simple joints that are sure to be familiar to you. They say that familiarity breeds contempt, and the risk here is that it may prevent us from giving these joints our proper attention. If so, we'd be missing out on an important piece of the puzzle. Together they form the fundamental joinery that finds its way into just about everything we make. While rabbets, dadoes, and grooves are not difficult to execute, the method you use to make them may vary depending on the situation at hand. Because of that, a good portion of this chapter presents options for cutting each joint and attempts to offer guidance on which to pick for the particular challenge you are facing.

Just as important as knowing how to make the joints is knowing how to incorporate them into your work. While simple and sometimes limited on their own, they can combine to offer a powerful and versatile way to build. Learn how to cut these three joints and put them to use in your work, and you're off to a good start.

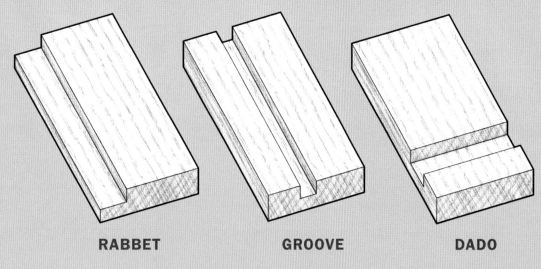

RABBET   **GROOVE**   **DADO**

COMBINATIONS THAT WORK

Here is a small sampling of the many forms these joints can take. In deciding what to include, I started with the combinations that I put to use most often. They have gotten me out of a few jams over the years, and there isn't a single one that I'd want to do without.

CORNER JOINTS

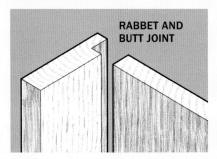

RABBET AND BUTT JOINT

Provides a simple way to register parts while concealing the edge of one part.

A PAIR OF RABBETS

A second rabbet reduces the width of each rabbet and offers a second reference edge.

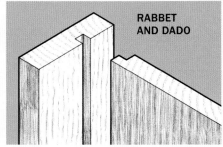

RABBET AND DADO

Adding a dado provides better registration and increases the glue surface.

SHELF JOINTS

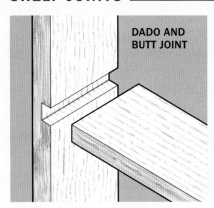

DADO AND BUTT JOINT

Requires precise shelf thickness and doesn't offer a lot of glue strength.

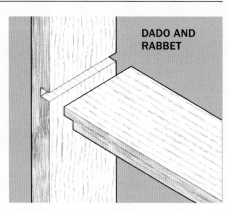

DADO AND RABBET

Shelf can be of any thickness, which makes it easier to fit.

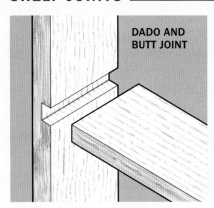

DADO AND TONGUE

Allows both sides of the shelf to be surfaced without changing the fit.

STOPPED DADO AND TONGUE

The dado and tongue are concealed on the edges of the case side.

CORNER JOINTS

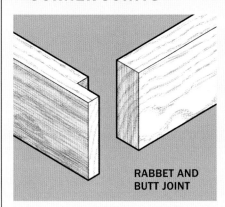

RABBET AND BUTT JOINT

Offers better registration than a butt joint but still creates a weak glue joint.

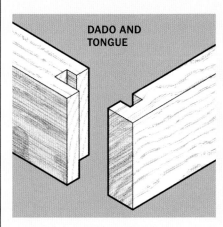

DADO AND TONGUE

Provides increased glue surface and better registration; good for plywood.

PANEL JOINTS

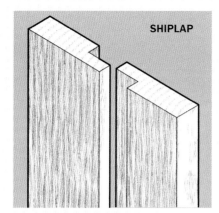

SHIPLAP

Mating rabbets allow for seasonal movement and conceal gaps.

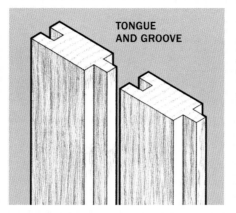

TONGUE AND GROOVE

Better registration than a shiplap but more effort to cut.

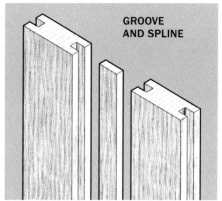

GROOVE AND SPLINE

Spline replaces tongue, making the joint easier to construct.

FLAT JOINTS

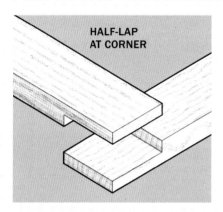

HALF-LAP AT CORNER

Provides some registration; broad glue surface makes it a strong joint.

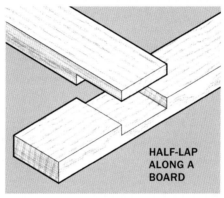

HALF-LAP ALONG A BOARD

Cross-member must be sized to fit dado; strong glue joint.

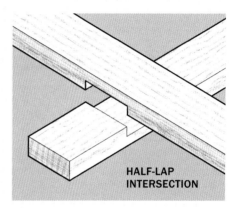

HALF-LAP INTERSECTION

Requires careful fitting of both parts; strong glue joint.

VERTICAL JOINTS

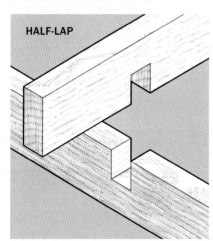

HALF-LAP

Can create weak short grain if near the end of a board.

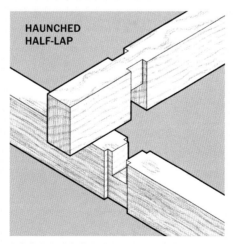

HAUNCHED HALF-LAP

Stronger than half-lap and eliminates short-grain issues.

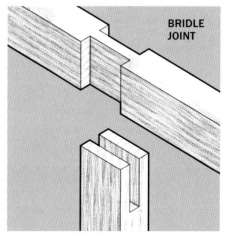

BRIDLE JOINT

Better registration and double the glue surfaces of a half-lap.

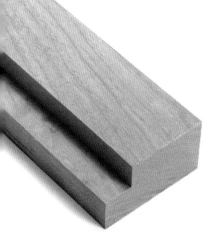

THE HUMBLE YET MIGHTY RABBET

Rabbet: An open groove or dado along the edge or end of a board.

As the illustrations on the previous pages prove, a rabbet can take many forms. Unfortunately, those different forms may require a different approach to cutting the joint. In short, I use a tablesaw where I can, and I turn to a router when it makes more sense.

If the rabbet runs the entire length of the edge or end of a board and the workpiece is small enough to hoist onto a tablesaw, that's the way I'm going to go. For stopped, or noncontinuous, rabbets, I'll turn to a router, using it handheld or mounted in a router table depending on the task.

Even when settling on the tablesaw to cut a rabbet there are still a couple of ways to go. Using a standard blade will require a pair of cuts, one with the workpiece flat on the table and one with the workpiece on edge. However, a dado set consisting of two outer blades with any number of chippers in between can handle any rabbet up to ¾ in. wide in just a single pass. Spoiler alert: A dado set can easily handle tenons as well, which makes it even more worth adding to your tool kit.

TACKLE FULL-LENGTH RABBETS AT THE TABLESAW

Begin by adjusting your dado set for a cut wider than the intended rabbet (**1**). Then clamp an L-fence to your rip fence, positioning it just above the blade (**2**). You don't want the blade to contact the L-fence, but it should be low enough to support the workpiece along the entire cut. Make sure that it is level front to back as well. It's easiest to set the height of the blade before sliding the fence into its final position. Use a combination square to set the blade height, which will determine the depth of the rabbet (**3**). It is important that the square sits on the tablesaw top and not the insert, which may not be level with the table. Then reset the square to the width of the rabbet and use it to set the fence location (**4**). Now you're ready to cut a rabbet (follow the layout steps on p. 26 to help ensure that you're cutting it in the correct location). For long, narrow parts, use a long push stick to keep downward pressure along the length of the part (**5**).

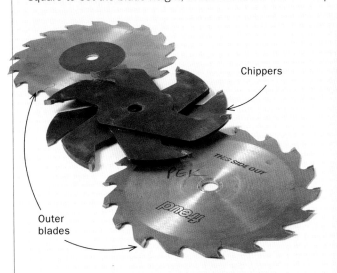

A dado set consists of a pair of outer blades and a set of chippers of varying thickness. By stacking them in combination, you can cut a dado from ¼ in. to ¹³⁄₁₆ in. wide.

Chippers

Outer blades

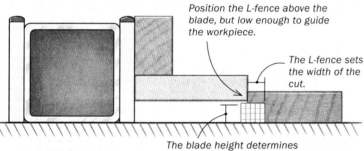

Position the L-fence above the blade, but low enough to guide the workpiece.

The L-fence sets the width of the cut.

The blade height determines the depth of the rabbet.

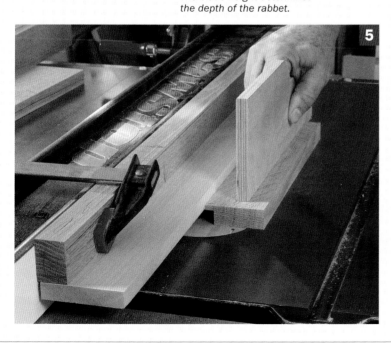

USE A PUSH PAD FOR PANELS

For wide stock, use a push pad to keep the part flat against the tablesaw top. The wide cut made by a dado set creates more upward force than a regular blade, which can cause the part to lift up during the cut, resulting in a rabbet that's too shallow.

TAKE A MINUTE AND MAKE A ROUTER TABLE

A router table in its simplest form is a router mounted upside down below a work surface that has an opening in the center for the bit. This transforms the router into a very different machine and allows you to do a lot of work that you can't with a handheld router. There are a lot of benchtop and floor-standing router tables on the market, but this is one of those fixtures that can be made easily and cheaply. The base of the router can be screwed directly to the underside of the table, or you can purchase a router lift that holds the router motor (see facing page). I have a router lift now and I love it, but for many years, I got by with a fixed-base router screwed to a simple plywood benchtop table. To change bits, it's easiest to remove the motor from the base (**1**). Setting the bit height can be cumbersome with one hand above the table and one below, but it can be done (**2**). A clamp-on fence can be adjusted easily and accurately by securing one end and pivoting it to the setting you want, and then clamping the opposite end in place (**3**).

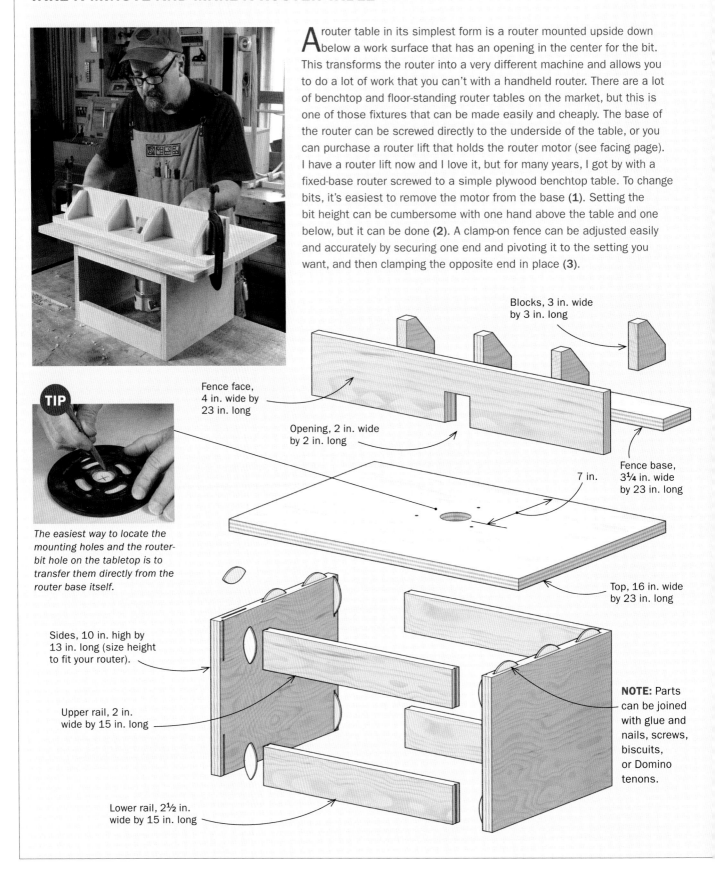

TIP

The easiest way to locate the mounting holes and the router-bit hole on the tabletop is to transfer them directly from the router base itself.

Blocks, 3 in. wide by 3 in. long

Fence face, 4 in. wide by 23 in. long

Opening, 2 in. wide by 2 in. long

7 in.

Fence base, 3¼ in. wide by 23 in. long

Top, 16 in. wide by 23 in. long

Sides, 10 in. high by 13 in. long (size height to fit your router).

Upper rail, 2 in. wide by 15 in. long

Lower rail, 2½ in. wide by 15 in. long

NOTE: Parts can be joined with glue and nails, screws, biscuits, or Domino tenons.

ROUTER LIFTS ADD CONVENIENCE

A router lift can set you back hundreds of dollars, and that's not including a router motor to power it or a router table to house it. That said, they do offer some nice benefits. Most lifts allow you to change bits from above the table. Height adjustments can be made from above the table as well, and many lifts have very accurate micro-adjustment features.

STOPPED RABBETS ON THE ROUTER TABLE

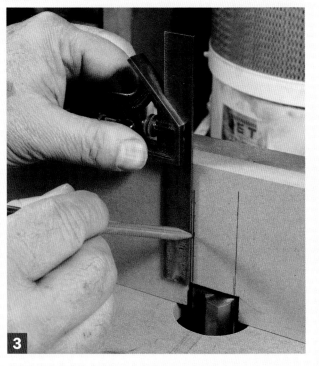

For a simple stopped rabbet, start by marking the end of the rabbet on the workpiece (1) and transferring the mark to the top face. A rabbeting bit with a guide bearing is a must for curved edges, but I use a straight bit inset into the fence for straight stock. To get ready for routing, adjust the fence to the desired rabbet width (2), and then draw vertical lines on the fence to mark the cutting area of the bit (3). When routing the rabbet (always rout from right to left when the bit is buried in the fence), align the stop line on the stock with the left line on the fence and pivot the stock into the bit to begin the cut (4). Take a slow, steady pass, keeping the stock against the tabletop and fence (5). When teaching, I'll often clamp a stop to the fence both at the beginning and the end of the cut, which makes the cuts safer and more consistent. For rabbets wider or deeper than ¼ in., it's best to make the cut in multiple passes, raising the bit ⅛ in. after each cut (6). A chisel makes quick work of squaring up the stopped end (7).

A large-diameter straight bit works well in a router table equipped with a fence. Shown here is a pattern bit, but the bearing is not used during routing.

A good strategy for cutting a rabbet is to set the dado blade for a cut that is wider than the rabbet, and then use just a portion of the blade to make the cut. An L-fence attached to your rip fence allows you to do just that. Clamp the L-fence just above the blade and set the width of the rabbet by moving the rip fence. The workpiece can now ride against the edge of the L-fence for quick rabbeting.

For stopped rabbets, a router is often the better choice. While you can cut rabbets using a handheld router, I prefer to use a router mounted in a router table when I can. Both floor-standing and benchtop models are available for sale, but it's easy to make your own. A router table allows you to cut rabbets safely and accurately, and can handle many other routing tasks, making it an important addition to your shop. Router bits designed for rabbeting often come equipped with a guide bearing. The bearing is essential for rabbeting with a handheld router, but when using a router table, I like to guide the cut using the router-table fence instead. This has the added benefit of allowing you to easily adjust the width of cut by moving the fence.

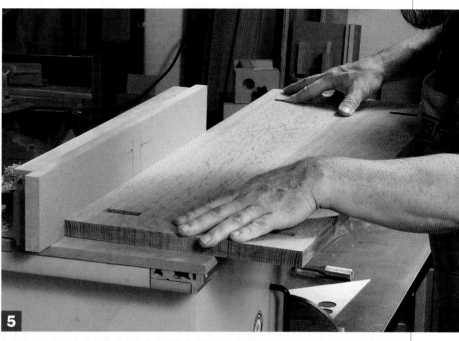

ONE BIT, MANY RABBETS

There are times when a bearing-guided router bit is the best option; rabbeting a picture frame is a great example. Some bits come with a number of bearings, and by changing them out, you can change the width of the rabbet. Rout clockwise as you go. Working against the rotation of the bit helps to keep it in the cut and the router under control.

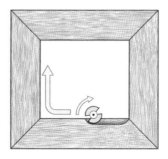

CUT THROUGH-GROOVES AT THE TABLESAW

Cutting through-grooves is a straightforward task: Just adjust your dado set to the width, set the blade height for the depth you want, and align your rip fence for the desired inset. However, the width and location of the groove have to be dialed in precisely. A dado blade can yield a groove of an exact width in a single pass, but if a perfectly centered groove is called for (or you just don't feel like installing a dado blade), it might make more sense to use a narrower blade and cut the groove in two passes, rotating the stock after the first cut.

For flat stock, push pads are handy. For grooves on the edge of a board (right), It's a good idea to add a featherboard to help keep the stock against the fence, because if the stock comes away from the fence during ripping, you'll end up with a wavy groove. You can make a featherboard and clamp it to the tabletop or buy one with a magnetic base. Another option, which I like, is a featherboard that rides in the miter-gauge slot.

GROOVES EXPAND YOUR OPTIONS

A groove is a useful thing. Grooves show up in a lot of places in furniture projects and assume different forms based on the task at hand. Because of that, it's good to have a few ways to go about cutting them. Through-grooves can be handled easily enough on the tablesaw with a dado blade. For stopped grooves, I turn to the router table or a handheld router depending on the location of the groove and the size of the part to be grooved.

Like rabbets, grooves are simple to cut and useful enough on their own, but when you use them in combination, you can begin to do some serious work. Add a dado to the mix, and the possibilities become even greater. It's a mistake to think that "fine" work must consist of complicated techniques or difficult-to-cut joinery. The real challenge is in understanding how to combine simple joints to perform the task you wish to accomplish. While mortises, tenons, and dovetails are necessary to round out your joinery options, focusing first on utilizing basic joinery to solve your construction challenges will go a long way toward making you a better woodworker.

USE A ROUTER FOR STOPPED GROOVES

When routing a stopped groove on the edge of a board, such as a panel groove, I like to use a wing cutter (far left) and run the stock flat on the table. It's more efficient because the larger diameter of the cutter offers a smoother cut than a straight bit, but it leaves rounded ends. On door-frame parts this isn't a problem because you can run a through-groove in the rails, and start and stop the cut in the stile at the mortise locations. Set the height of the bit by centering it on the mortise (**1**). Adjust the fence to set the depth of the groove and mark its cutting area on the fence. Mark the mortise locations on the face of the board and pivot the stock into the cutter at the mortise (**2**). Continue routing until you hit the second mortise. Use a push stick to keep the stock flat and your hands away from the bit (**3**). The result should be a clean groove from mortise to mortise (**4**). For grooves farther from the edge, a straight bit is your only option. In this case, hold the workpiece against the fence and drop it onto the bit (**5**). If the groove runs between mortises at each end, there's no need to square the ends (**6**).

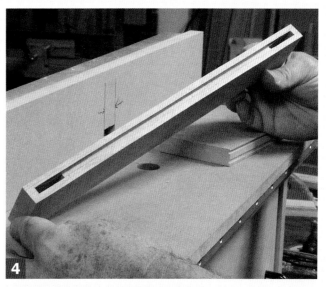

When routing stopped grooves on larger pieces like case sides, I bring the router to the workpiece. While you can use a fixed-base router and carefully tilt the bit into the stock, a plunge router is a better way to go. Attach a fence and set the distance from the edge of the board to the bit (**1**). I upgrade my router fences by adding a longer hardwood strip, which offers more support and a flat reference surface to guide the router. I also prefer a spiral straight bit (far left), which cuts smoother and plunges easier than a bit with straight flutes. Start by defining the ends of the groove with a full-depth plunge at each end (**2**). When routing the groove, be sure to rout in the direction where the rotation of the bit helps to pull the fence against the stock (**3**). Start with a light pass (**4**) and continue with progressively deeper cuts until you reach full depth. To finish the groove, chisel the ends square (**5**).

A TIP FOR ROUTING IN THE RIGHT DIRECTION

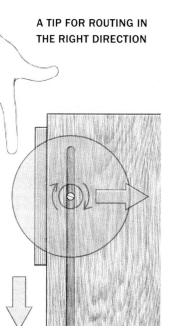

It's important to rout so that the rotation of the bit is helping to pull the fence against the stock. A quick way to determine which way to go is to make an "L" with your right hand. Your thumb indicates which side of the stock you're routing on, and your finger points you in the right direction.

3

4

5

DADOES COMPLETE THE TRIO OF BASIC JOINTS

A dado is just a cross-grain groove, but the orientation has an impact on what we can do with the joint and the way we go about cutting it. Dadoes are a useful joint for tasks like securing shelves in a bookcase or drawer runners in a dresser. They can also be combined with rabbets and grooves to do some pretty amazing things (see the illustration plate on pp. 36–37). However, because a dado runs perpendicular to the grain of a board, its side walls consist of end grain, which doesn't yield a lot of glue strength if you're relying on glue alone to hold the parts together. That doesn't mean it's not a good joint to use, but it does mean that you need to be strategic about how you use it. The chimney cupboard project on p. 68 offers a good example of how dadoes can be combined with rabbets and grooves for a rock-solid assembly.

For through-dadoes, a tablesaw equipped with a dado blade and a crosscut sled is my preferred choice. For dadoes on panels too wide to cut comfortably on my saw, a router is a better option. If I'm cutting multiple dadoes across a board, for bookcase shelves, for example, I'll add a stop block to the fence to ensure that the dado ends up

A DEDICATED SLED FOR DADOES

While you can use your everyday sled for dadoes, the wide blade will leave a big kerf behind (see p. 62 for a sled that's been patched a few times!). I made a batch of small sleds that I can use with anything other than a standard blade at 90°. Rather than going through the trouble of adding runners, I keep a pair of miter gauges around and screw them onto the sled I need.

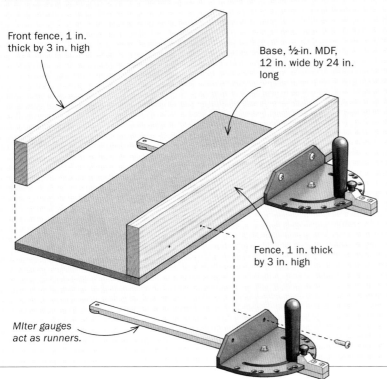

Front fence, 1 in. thick by 3 in. high

Base, ½-in. MDF, 12 in. wide by 24 in. long

Fence, 1 in. thick by 3 in. high

MIter gauges act as runners.

ADD STOPS FOR CONSISTENT CUTS

For dadoes in large projects, I'd need a larger sled, or I might skip the tablesaw altogether and break out a router. But for smaller wall shelves and cabinets, this 12-in. by 24-in. sled with a 3-in.-high fence can handle the job just fine. Typically, I clamp a stop block along the fence and register the end of the workpiece against it when dadoing (1 & 2), but for stock that's longer than the sled,

I use a hook stop instead. A hook stop is simply a long board with a tab at one end. Clamping it to the crosscut-sled fence allows me to set the stop beyond the length of the sled (3 & 4). To help keep the hook stop level, screw a cleat along the top edge. The cleat rests on the top of the fence and keeps the stop level when clamping.

ROUTING STOPPED DADOES

Stopped dadoes are a common feature in furniture, and a router is a good way to tackle them. While it's possible to use a fixed-base router and carefully pivot the bit onto the stock to begin the cut, I much prefer a plunge router. Depending on the location of the dado and the size of the workpiece, there are a few ways to go about cutting it. With all of the techniques, though, the routing process is the same: Start with full-depth plunges at the ends of the dado and then rout the length of the dado, taking progressively deeper passes until you reach full depth. Follow by squaring the ends with a chisel, if needed. For a dado near the end of a board, you can attach a fence to your router and proceed as you would for a groove (**1**).

For a dado farther from the end of a board, clamp an edge guide to the stock to control the path of the router. Measure from the edge of the router base to the bit to determine the required offset for the edge guide (**2 & 3**). While some router bases have a flat, I prefer to register the rounded portion of the base against the guide (**4**). If the flat is against the guide and the router pivots during use, the dado will not be straight. This isn't a concern with the round portion of the base against the fence. However, I do make a mark on the base that I align with the guide to ensure consistent spacing in the event that the bit isn't perfectly centered on the base. One benefit of using an edge guide is that you can clamp parts together and rout both at once to save setup time and ensure that the dadoes in each piece are aligned with each other.

The walls of a dado consist of end grain, which doesn't yield a lot of glue strength if you're relying on glue alone to hold the parts together.

in the same location on each board. For stock longer than your sled, use a hook stop, which as the name implies is a long board with a hook on the end. By clamping it to the crosscut-sled fence, you can set up for accurate, repeatable dadoes near the center of a longer board.

For stopped dadoes, I typically turn to a router (though there are situations where a tablesaw makes sense as well; see p. 52). When routing a stopped dado near the end of a board, I treat it like a stopped groove and use a fence to guide the router. Be careful as you move farther from the end because it can be more difficult to keep the router fence against the stock without pivoting during the cut. A better solution when routing farther from the end is to clamp an edge guide to the workpiece to guide the router. This has the added benefit of allowing you to gang up parts side by side and rout them at the same time, ensuring that the dadoes in each board line up.

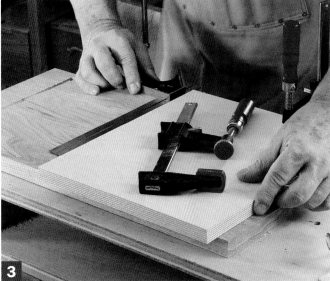

DESKTOP ORGANIZER:
STOPPED DADOES AT THE TABLESAW

While I typically cut stopped dadoes with a router, there are times when it makes more sense to handle them at the tablesaw. The dadoes for the shelves on this desktop organizer are a good example. While the dovetails may be the first thing you notice, it's the thin shelves and divider that turn the project from an ordinary box to an interesting and useful addition to a home office. The reason I use the tablesaw has to do with the size of the parts. It would be difficult to clamp an edge guide to these short case sides, and they wouldn't provide a base to support a router. However, the small scale of the parts makes them easy to handle using a crosscut sled at the tablesaw.

On typical projects I cut the dadoes narrower than the thickness of the shelves and rabbet the shelves to fit. On thin stock like this, I let the shelf's full thickness into the dado. I cut the dadoes using a box-joint blade set, which is basically a two-piece dado set that cuts a groove with a flat bottom. I stack the blades for a ¼-in. cut

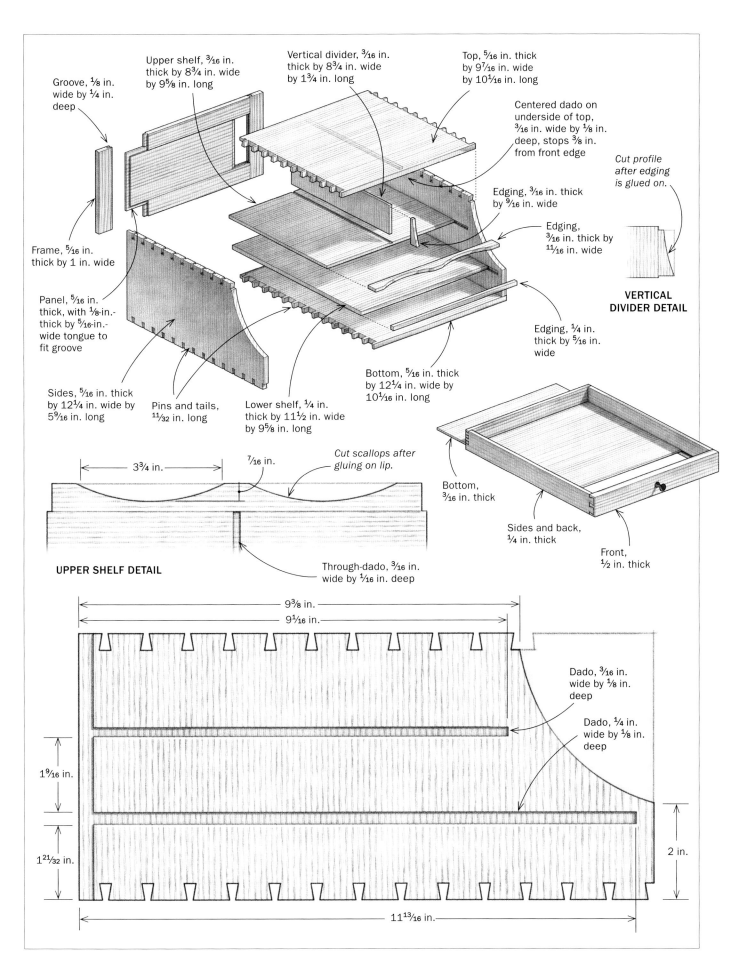

Groove, ⅛ in. wide by ¼ in. deep

Upper shelf, ³⁄₁₆ in. thick by 8¾ in. wide by 9⅝ in. long

Vertical divider, ³⁄₁₆ in. thick by 8¾ in. wide by 1¾ in. long

Top, ⁵⁄₁₆ in. thick by 9⁷⁄₁₆ in. wide by 10¹⁄₁₆ in. long

Centered dado on underside of top, ³⁄₁₆ in. wide by ⅛ in. deep, stops ⅜ in. from front edge

Cut profile after edging is glued on.

Edging, ³⁄₁₆ in. thick by ⁹⁄₁₆ in. wide

Edging, ³⁄₁₆ in. thick by ¹¹⁄₁₆ in. wide

VERTICAL DIVIDER DETAIL

Frame, ⁵⁄₁₆ in. thick by 1 in. wide

Panel, ⁵⁄₁₆ in. thick, with ⅛-in.-thick by ⁵⁄₁₆-in.-wide tongue to fit groove

Sides, ⁵⁄₁₆ in. thick by 12¼ in. wide by 5⁹⁄₁₆ in. long

Pins and tails, ¹¹⁄₃₂ in. long

Lower shelf, ¼ in. thick by 11½ in. wide by 9⅝ in. long

Bottom, ⁵⁄₁₆ in. thick by 12¼ in. wide by 10¹⁄₁₆ in. long

Edging, ¼ in. thick by ⁵⁄₁₆ in. wide

Bottom, ³⁄₁₆ in. thick

Sides and back, ¼ in. thick

Front, ½ in. thick

3¾ in.

⁷⁄₁₆ in.

Cut scallops after gluing on lip.

UPPER SHELF DETAIL

Through-dado, ³⁄₁₆ in. wide by ¹⁄₁₆ in. deep

9⅜ in.

9¹⁄₁₆ in.

Dado, ³⁄₁₆ in. wide by ⅛ in. deep

Dado, ¼ in. wide by ⅛ in. deep

1⁹⁄₁₆ in.

1²¹⁄₃₂ in.

2 in.

11¹³⁄₁₆ in.

STOPPING A DADO AT THE START OF A CUT

Dropping a workpiece down onto a spinning blade may not sound like the wisest thing to do, but with the right setup, it's a safe and efficient way to cut a stopped dado. The key to safety is controlling the position of the stock as you drop it onto the blade. If it moves backward, it can get away from you quickly, and a lot of bad things can happen before you have a chance to react. The best way to prevent this and make it a safe operation is to use a crosscut sled. To keep the sled from moving backward at the beginning of the cut, clamp a stop block to the rip-fence rail flush with the back of the sled. The only real trick is locating the stop so that the blade begins the cut where you want it to.

Start by marking the end of the dado on the workpiece and raising the tablesaw blade to the desired depth of cut. Then lay the workpiece on the sled and slide it forward until the mark on the workpiece aligns with the point where the blade teeth are even with the base (**1**).

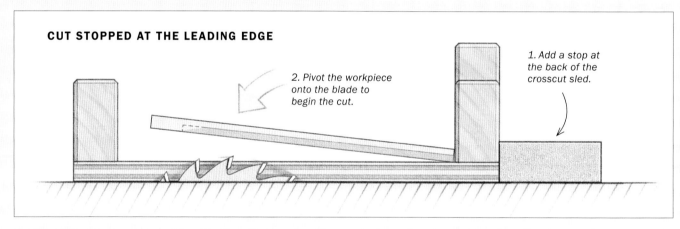

CUT STOPPED AT THE LEADING EDGE

2. Pivot the workpiece onto the blade to begin the cut.

1. Add a stop at the back of the crosscut sled.

Because I use the same stop for both case sides, half of the dadoes must be stopped at the leading edge when sawing and the others at the trailing edge.

to handle the lower dado and switch to a single blade for the ³⁄₁₆-in. upper shelf and divider dadoes.

Making stopped cuts at the tablesaw can be tricky, but there are a few steps to ease the process. The main challenge is introduced by registering the workpieces against a stop block to ensure that the dadoes in the case sides align. Because I use the same stop for both case sides, half of the dadoes must be stopped at the leading edge when sawing and the others at the trailing edge.

For the dadoes that stop at the leading edge, I drop the workpiece down onto the blade to begin the cut. To make this safer, clamp a stop at the rear of the sled. The stop determines where the cut starts and prevents the sled from moving backward during the plunge cut. The remaining dadoes stop short of the trailing edge. To set the stop block for this cut, move the sled forward until the stop mark is aligned with the point where the blade stops cutting. Then clamp a block to the tablesaw at the front of the sled. Start the cut in the same way you'd cut a through-dado and stop when the sled contacts the block. Let the blade come to a stop before removing the piece. Square up the ends of the dadoes with a chisel.

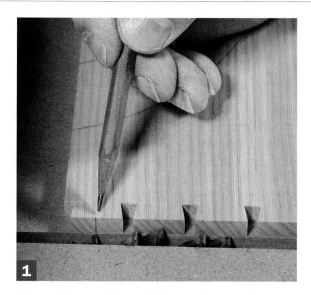

Keep the sled in position while you clamp a stop block flush to the back of the sled (**2**). Clamp a second stop to the crosscut-sled fence and position the end of the workpiece against it. Turn on the saw and drop the piece onto the blade, keeping it snug against the fence and the end stop (**3**). Once the stock is flat on the sled, move it forward to complete the cut.

STOPPING A DADO AT THE END OF A CUT

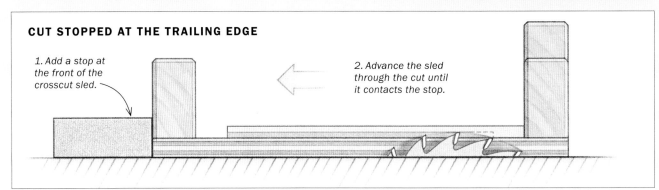

CUT STOPPED AT THE TRAILING EDGE

1. Add a stop at the front of the crosscut sled.

2. Advance the sled through the cut until it contacts the stop.

Stopping the dado at the end of the cut is a more straightforward affair. The operation begins as if you were cutting a through-dado, but a stop block at the front of the sled prevents the blade from exiting the workpiece at the back. To locate the block, start by marking where you would like the cut to stop on the workpiece, or in this case, on the sled itself. Then slide the sled forward until a tooth flush with the sled top at the rear of the blade is aligned with the mark (**1**). Clamp the stop in place (**2**) and make the cut. When the sled contacts the stop, hold the workpiece in place as you turn off the saw and wait for it to come to a stop (**3**).

Extend the side walls of the dado to the stop line with a wide chisel. Then use a narrow chisel to establish the end of the dado and excavate the bottom.

AN ALTERNATIVE TO NOTCHING THE SHELF

Rather than sawing a notch into the shelf (see p. 74), a simpler approach is to add a shorter strip to the front edge that forms the notches. To size the strip for a gap-free fit, slide the shelf in place (**1**). Cut a strip slightly thicker than the shelf and trim the ends for a snug fit in the case (**2**). With the shelf still in place, glue on the strip using tape as a clamp (**3**). When the glue is dry, remove the shelf and plane the strip flush.

MIRRORED WALL CABINET:
BUILDING WITH JUST DADOES AND RABBETS

The dado construction in this project allows a good deal of freedom when designing. Because the sides can extend beyond the top and bottom you can have a lot of fun with the design. On this cabinet the sides and back boards extend above the top to create an extra storage space. The top edges of the sides are also curved to take away from the boxy look of the cabinet. Below the cabinet bottom, the sides are coved to lighten the look and create a narrow exposed shelf for odds and ends.

The stiles glued to the front of the case, which serve as a partial face frame, are a really important design element. Visually, they add mass to the piece by hiding the narrow front edge of the sides. They are also an important structural element tying the sides to the shelves. In addition, they hide the dadoes on the front edge of the sides and offer an opportunity to add a door. The door itself consists of pinned half-lap joints at the corners and applied edging to house the mirror. The back slats are rabbeted or "shiplapped" where they meet to allow for seasonal movement without creating gaps between the boards. The slats also help tie the sides to the shelves at the back of the case, further strengthening the joinery. This cabinet is a great example of how staying with basic joinery doesn't mean sacrificing the look of the piece or limiting the design possibilities or the strength of the construction. If you told me that I could use only rabbet and dado joinery, I think I could make a lot of projects before running out of ideas.

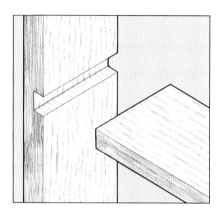

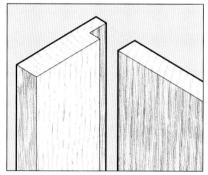

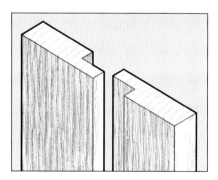

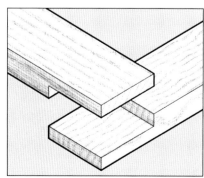

BUTTERNUT WALL CABINET

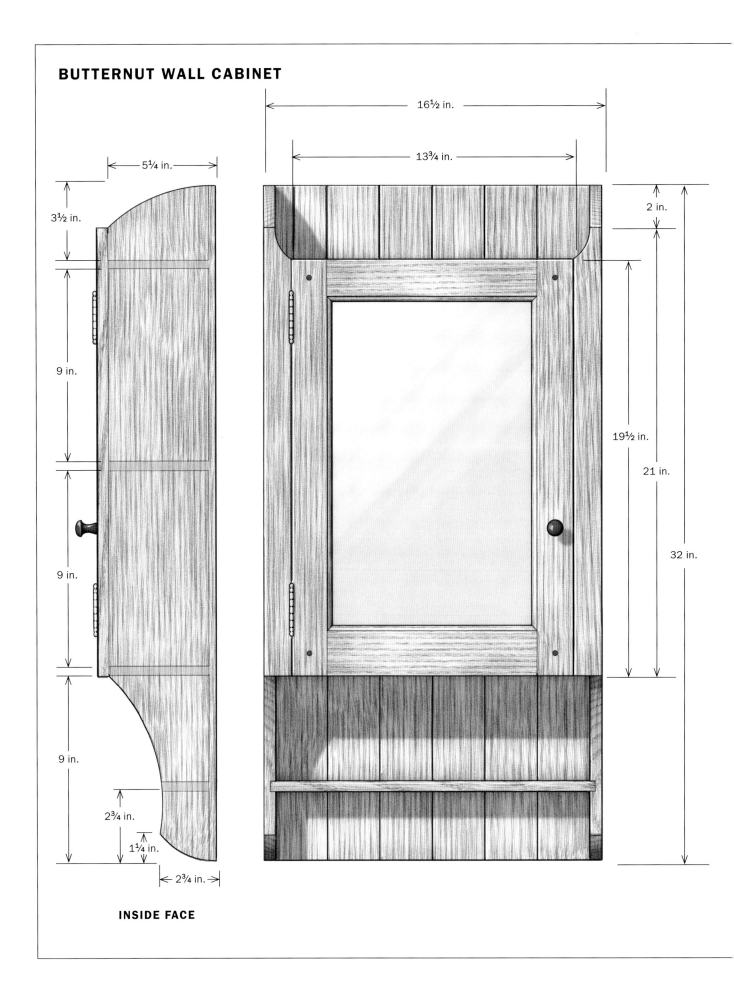

16½ in.

13¾ in.

5¼ in.

3½ in.

2 in.

9 in.

19½ in.

21 in.

9 in.

32 in.

9 in.

2¾ in.

1¼ in.

2¾ in.

INSIDE FACE

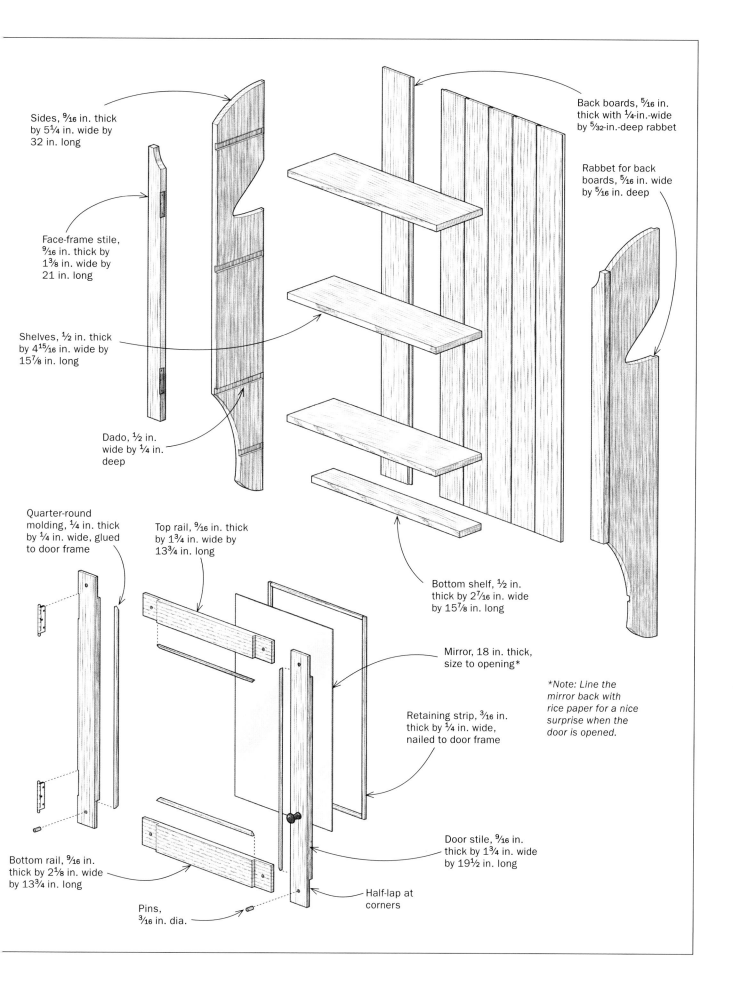

Sides, ⁹⁄₁₆ in. thick by 5¼ in. wide by 32 in. long

Back boards, ⁵⁄₁₆ in. thick with ¼-in.-wide by ⁵⁄₃₂-in.-deep rabbet

Face-frame stile, ⁹⁄₁₆ in. thick by 1³⁄₈ in. wide by 21 in. long

Rabbet for back boards, ⁵⁄₁₆ in. wide by ⁵⁄₁₆ in. deep

Shelves, ½ in. thick by 4¹⁵⁄₁₆ in. wide by 15⁷⁄₈ in. long

Dado, ½ in. wide by ¼ in. deep

Quarter-round molding, ¼ in. thick by ¼ in. wide, glued to door frame

Top rail, ⁹⁄₁₆ in. thick by 1³⁄₄ in. wide by 13³⁄₄ in. long

Bottom shelf, ½ in. thick by 2⁷⁄₁₆ in. wide by 15⁷⁄₈ in. long

Mirror, 18 in. thick, size to opening*

Retaining strip, ³⁄₁₆ in. thick by ¼ in. wide, nailed to door frame

*Note: Line the mirror back with rice paper for a nice surprise when the door is opened.

Door stile, ⁹⁄₁₆ in. thick by 1³⁄₄ in. wide by 19½ in. long

Bottom rail, ⁹⁄₁₆ in. thick by 2¹⁄₈ in. wide by 13³⁄₄ in. long

Pins, ³⁄₁₆ in. dia.

Half-lap at corners

A FAST WAY TO BUILD USING RABBETS AND DADOES

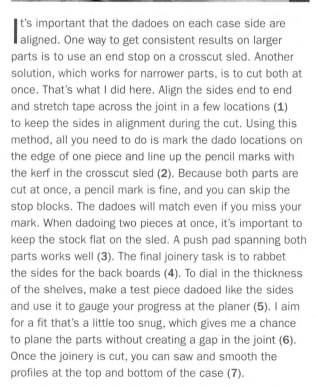

It's important that the dadoes on each case side are aligned. One way to get consistent results on larger parts is to use an end stop on a crosscut sled. Another solution, which works for narrower parts, is to cut both at once. That's what I did here. Align the sides end to end and stretch tape across the joint in a few locations (**1**) to keep the sides in alignment during the cut. Using this method, all you need to do is mark the dado locations on the edge of one piece and line up the pencil marks with the kerf in the crosscut sled (**2**). Because both parts are cut at once, a pencil mark is fine, and you can skip the stop blocks. The dadoes will match even if you miss your mark. When dadoing two pieces at once, it's important to keep the stock flat on the sled. A push pad spanning both parts works well (**3**). The final joinery task is to rabbet the sides for the back boards (**4**). To dial in the thickness of the shelves, make a test piece dadoed like the sides and use it to gauge your progress at the planer (**5**). I aim for a fit that's a little too snug, which gives me a chance to plane the parts without creating a gap in the joint (**6**). Once the joinery is cut, you can saw and smooth the profiles at the top and bottom of the case (**7**).

A STRATEGY FOR ALIGNING PARTS DURING GLUE-UP

The challenge when gluing up a dadoed case is to make sure the shelves are aligned front to back. The dadoes don't provide a lot of help with that, so I use two different methods to ensure good results. At the back of the shelves where their edges need to be flush with the rabbet, I tape a strip of wood into the rabbet that I can use to register them against (**1 & 2**). To guarantee that the shelves align with the front of the case, I rip them slightly overwidth and plane them flush after assembly. During glue-up, make sure the clamps are aligned over the dadoes (**3**). It's easy to rack the case out of square if you're not paying attention. Once the clamps come off, flush the front of the shelves with the case sides (**4**). Finally, glue on the face-frame stiles (**5**). I like to cut the hinge mortises before assembly.

A QUICK LESSON IN MAKING A SHIPLAPPED BACK

A shiplapped back consists of slats tacked or screwed to the back of the case. To allow room for seasonal movement, each board is rabbeted to overlap the adjoining one. As simple as it is, I have a couple of tips that can help you end up with a nice case back. The first challenge is calculating the width of the boards. You'll need to account for the width of the opening, the number of boards, the amount of overlap between each board, and finally the desired gap between the boards. It's a lot to keep track of, so I make a full-size drawing to ensure that the numbers add up. Even then, I leave the end slats a little wide and trim them to fit later. Arrange the slats and mark a triangle across their backs. Now mark the rabbet locations on the edges of the slats. You'll need a pair of rabbets at each joint, one on the front face of one piece and the other on the rear face of its mate. It can get a little confusing, so I mark an "O" on every edge that needs a rabbet and an "X" on those that don't (**1**). This reduces the head scratching at the tablesaw. I use a pair of push pads to ensure a rabbet of even depth along the length of the slat (**2**). The end slats play an important role in strengthening the case by tying the sides to the shelves, so I glue them in addition to nailing them in place. The center slats are nailed at each shelf, using shims between them to maintain even spacing (**3**). For larger cases, I'd opt for screws instead of nails.

A SIMPLE, STRONG DOOR FRAME

A half-lap may not seem like a joint suited for a door frame. Though not commonly used, the joint can handle the job quite well. The broad glue surface of the joint makes it very strong, and it's quick to make. I use a miter gauge and dado blade at the tablesaw in the same way that I would cut a tenon, but in this case there's just a single cheek to cut on each piece (**1**). The half-lap's shortcoming as a frame joint is that it needs a lot of clamps to keep it in alignment during glue-up. You'll need a pair of clamps oriented across the width of the frame and a pair along the length as well (**2**). In addition, you'll need to clamp the joint top to bottom (**3**). It's not absolutely necessary, but pinning the joint after glue-up adds mechanical strength and creates a nice visual detail.

MITERED EDGING CREATES A RABBET FOR THE MIRROR

DOOR DETAIL

Mitered molding glued to door frame

Mirror

Retaining strips nailed in place

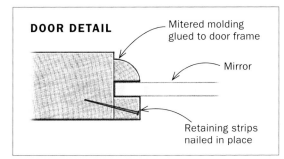

Instead of rabbeting the frame for the mirror, you can create a rabbet by gluing mitered molding along the inside edge of the frame. On this piece the molding has a quarter-round profile, which creates a thumbnail profile when installed just below the frame surface. Start by routing a roundover on both edges of a wide piece of stock. Then rip a strip off each edge to create the molding (**1**). I find it best to miter and fit the molding by hand. Saw a rough miter on each end, leaving the piece overlong. Then use a handplane and shooting board to fine-tune the angle and take it to final length (**2**). Aim for a snug fit at the corners, but not so tight that the molding bows out at the center (**3**). I place a tape-covered piece of medium-density fiberboard (MDF) in the opening to register the molding at the right height on the frame edge for gluing. To secure the mirror, I make square strips and nail them in place without glue, which allows the mirror to be removed later if necessary (**4**). Gluing rice paper to the back of the mirror offers a nice surprise when the door is opened.

CHIMNEY CUPBOARD:
A SMART USE OF SIMPLE JOINERY

While rabbets and dadoes may be simpler to execute than dovetails or mortise-and-tenon joinery, I want to stress that they still constitute a versatile and powerful combination when it comes to building furniture. This is not a "dumbed-down" way of building or a compromise for the sake of ease of construction. The classic Shaker chimney cupboard is a great example of how you can make sturdy, elegant furniture using simple joinery. Most of the case joints on this project are rabbets and dadoes. The subtop rails are connected with half-blind dovetails, but I've substituted a rabbeted dado joint for those on occasion. (You can also replace the dovetails on the drawers with pinned rabbets.)

We face the same challenge here as on the previous wall cabinet, in that a dado joint offers no mechanical means to hold parts together like a dovetail does. It also provides no long-grain glue surfaces, which results in a weak glue joint. It sounds like a nonstarter, but with a smart building strategy we can provide the strength to the case joinery that the dado alone lacks. As on the wall cabinet, we're adding vertical stiles to create a partial face frame to tie the shelves into the sides. Because this is a larger floor-standing piece and will encounter more racking stresses, we're fortifying the glue joint with some mechanical help. On this piece, the sides connect to the face-frame stiles with a tongue-and-groove joint. In addition, the stiles are secured to the shelves with pins. A frame-and-panel back ties the shelves to the sides at the rear of the case.

The dadoes that connect the shelves to the sides also get an upgrade. Whereas the wall cabinet employed dadoes the full width of the shelves, on this project the shelves are rabbeted to fit narrower dadoes. It's a little more work, but adding a rabbet to the process actually solves some challenges and makes for more accurate work. The idea is to cut a dado narrower than the stock and then rabbet the end of the stock to create a tongue that fits into the dado. A big advantage of this approach is that it saves you from having to mill your stock to an exact thickness to match a dado. The other benefit has to do with ending up with square work. On a full-width dado, the stock bottoms out in the joint, so any inconsistency in the depth of the dado (which is not all that uncommon) will affect the dimensions of the case. When you rabbet the stock that fits into the

dado, the shoulder of the joint becomes the determining factor in how it comes together. So the aim is to cut the dado a little deeper than you need in order to ensure that the rabbeted part doesn't bottom out before the shoulder seats. This is a lot easier than trying to nail an exact dimension.

Understanding how something as simple as adding a rabbet to a joint can lead to more accurate work is important to your woodworking journey. This one step does away with worrying about exact thicknesses and exact depths and makes your life easier at the same time. As you become more experienced, the craft will become easier and more enjoyable, not just because your skills will improve but because your approach and strategy will improve as well. The more effectively you can navigate through a project, the more you can build accuracy into your work without adding effort.

It's also a good illustration that sound construction doesn't rely solely on the strength of the joinery you choose but in the application of those joints. While we often think of design in terms of how a piece looks, determining how something will go together and whether it will stand the test of time is an equally important part of the design process.

CHERRY CHIMNEY CUPBOARD

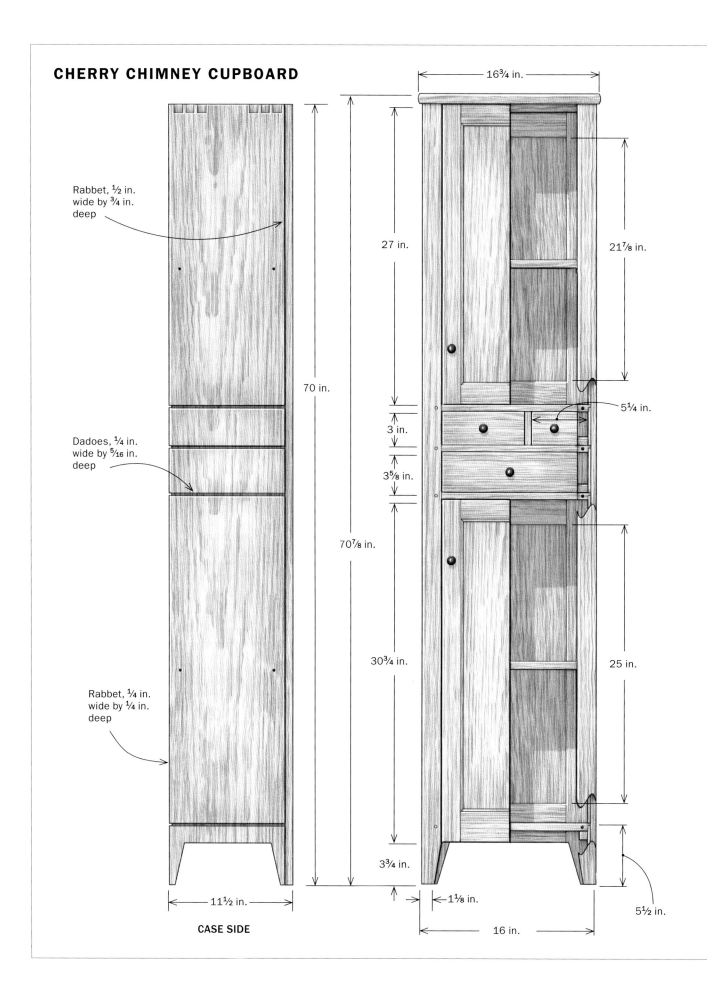

Rabbet, ½ in.
wide by ¾ in.
deep

Dadoes, ¼ in.
wide by ⁵⁄₁₆ in.
deep

Rabbet, ¼ in.
wide by ¼ in.
deep

70 in.

70⁷⁄₈ in.

11½ in.

CASE SIDE

16¾ in.

27 in.

21⁷⁄₈ in.

5¼ in.

3 in.

3⁵⁄₈ in.

30¾ in.

25 in.

3¾ in.

1⅛ in.

16 in.

5½ in.

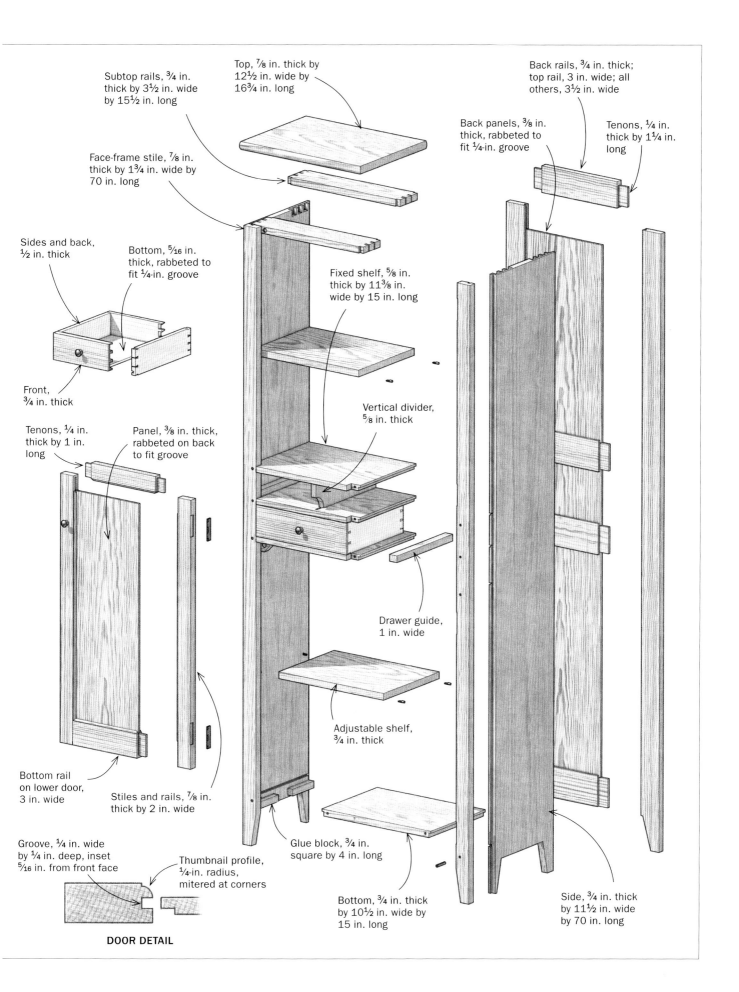

Subtop rails, ¾ in. thick by 3½ in. wide by 15½ in. long

Top, ⅞ in. thick by 12½ in. wide by 16¾ in. long

Back rails, ¾ in. thick; top rail, 3 in. wide; all others, 3½ in. wide

Face-frame stile, ⅞ in. thick by 1¾ in. wide by 70 in. long

Back panels, ⅜ in. thick, rabbeted to fit ¼-in. groove

Tenons, ¼ in. thick by 1¼ in. long

Sides and back, ½ in. thick

Bottom, 5⁄16 in. thick, rabbeted to fit ¼-in. groove

Fixed shelf, ⅝ in. thick by 11⅜ in. wide by 15 in. long

Front, ¾ in. thick

Vertical divider, ⅝ in. thick

Tenons, ¼ in. thick by 1 in. long

Panel, ⅜ in. thick, rabbeted on back to fit groove

Drawer guide, 1 in. wide

Bottom rail on lower door, 3 in. wide

Stiles and rails, ⅞ in. thick by 2 in. wide

Adjustable shelf, ¾ in. thick

Groove, ¼ in. wide by ¼ in. deep, inset 5⁄16 in. from front face

Thumbnail profile, ¼-in. radius, mitered at corners

Glue block, ¾ in. square by 4 in. long

Bottom, ¾ in. thick by 10½ in. wide by 15 in. long

Side, ¾ in. thick by 11½ in. wide by 70 in. long

DOOR DETAIL

RABBETS AND DADOES JOIN THE CASE

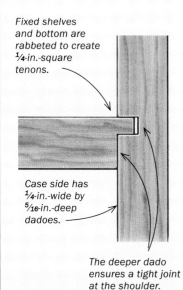

Fixed shelves and bottom are rabbeted to create ¼-in.-square tenons.

Case side has ¼-in.-wide by ⁵⁄₁₆-in.-deep dadoes.

The deeper dado ensures a tight joint at the shoulder.

Combining a rabbet with a dado on the case joints has big benefits. First, rabbeting a part to fit a dado is much easier than milling a part to a precise thickness to fit a full-width dado. Second, the rabbet creates a shoulder on the shelf that registers against the inside face of the case side. This makes for much more accurate glue-ups because it doesn't rely on the bottom of the dado being perfectly even (which is difficult to pull off on a wide case side). And

because the joint registers off the shoulder, you can cut the dado a little deep, which allows room for excess glue to gather and prevents squeeze-out. The face frame and back panel hide any gap at the bottom of the joint.

To cut the dadoes in the case sides for the shelves, dividers, and case bottom, I used a crosscut sled and a ¼-in.-wide dado blade on the tablesaw. The long sides create a bit of a challenge when dadoing. To cut the three dadoes

The ends of the vertical divider are rabbeted on each face to create a centered tenon, which is notched at the leading edge.

Stopped dado for vertical divider

near the center for the shelf and drawer dividers, I clamped a long hook stop to the crosscut-sled fence (1 & 2). The dado for the case bottom is trickier because the long side can pivot during the cut. For that dado, I made a stop block with hold-down clamps and attached it to the sled (3). Clamping the piece in place kept it tight against both the fence and the sled base (4). The vertical drawer divider required a stopped dado in the top and center shelves. Clamping them together and routing both dadoes at once ensured that they would line up once assembled and result in a truly vertical divider (5). The ends of the shelves and case bottom were rabbeted to create a tab sized to fit the dadoes in the case sides (6). A featherboard clamped to the rip fence provided downward pressure to keep the part from lifting during the cut, resulting in tabs of consistent thickness. Aim for a snug fit and fine-tune it as necessary with a shoulder plane.

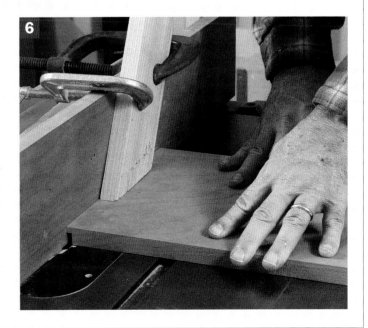

CASE ASSEMBLY GOES QUICKLY

FACE FRAME STRENGTHENS THE CASE JOINERY

Case side

Shelves joined to case with dadoes

Face-frame stile attaches to the case side with a tongue-and-groove joint, which has the added benefit of keeping the sides from bowing along their length.

Shelf

Face-frame stile

After assembly, a pin is driven through the face-frame stile into the shelf. This locks the case side, shelf, and stile together for a strong joint that won't come apart over time.

Normally the face frame is the last thing I add when building a case, but it was the first thing I tackled on this project. Use a narrow caul to direct clamp pressure over the joint and use a square to check that it sits flat (**1**). Gluing the frame first eased construction in a couple of ways. First, it allowed me to plane the edges flush to the case sides while the side assemblies were easy to deal with. It also made it easier to mark and notch the shelves to fit around the stiles.

The case bottom and the front subtop rail butt against the back of the face frame and act as door stops. The fixed shelf and dividers, on the other hand, end up flush with the front of the face frame, so you need to notch them to fit around it. With the stiles already glued to the case side, it's easy to scribe the notches (**2**). Cut the notches a little deep so the shelves end up protruding a bit from the front of the case. That will let you plane them perfectly flush later. Cut just outside the line with a handsaw or on the bandsaw, and pare the remaining waste with a chisel.

Continue the assembly by gluing up the sides, shelves, and bottom and top rails (**3**). Once all the clamps are on, add glue blocks under the bottom shelf. Apply a thin coat of glue on two faces and rub the block back and forth until it grabs. The vacuum will hold it in place without clamps. To allow for seasonal

movement, apply multiple short blocks along the joint rather than one long one. The drawer guides are glued in the same way, but because the guides are long, glue the front half only. Afterward, drill through the face frame at the shelf, divider, and bottom locations and pin the joints. This really locks the assembly and adds a little visual interest.

After the case has dried, flush up the shelf and dividers with the face frame (**4**). Then slide in the vertical divider (**5**) and plane it flush (**6**). This is much easier than trying to plane all of the parts flush at once. All that's left of the casework is to glue the top in place and add the frame-and-panel back (**7**). The back has two center rails aligned with the fixed shelf and lower divider, allowing you to screw the back to them as well as the sides, further strengthening the case joinery. The back plays an important role in keeping the case square and tying the horizontal members to the sides.

CHAPTER 3

MORTISES AND TENONS

While the dovetail may take top billing as the iconic woodworking joint, when it comes to essential joinery the mortise-and-tenon has it beat by a mile. This joint finds its way into most pieces we make for good reason. It offers a lot of mechanical strength, and it does a good job of keeping parts aligned during assembly. A mortise-and-tenon joint can be completely concealed, or it can extend through the workpiece and become a decorative element as well as a structural element. It can be pinned or wedged and can incorporate a rabbet or a miter. It can be found on casework, doors, beds, tabletops, chairs, wall cabinets...I'm sure I'm forgetting something. Some projects, like the small Arts and Crafts cabinet shown later in the chapter, are constructed almost entirely of mortise-and-tenon joinery. In short, it's a versatile and valuable joint to have in your tool kit. In its simplest form, it consists of a tenon shouldered on all four sides that fits into a mortise in the mating workpiece, but that's just the beginning. Learn its variations, how to make them, and when to use them, and you'll have gone a long way toward mastering this craft.

MORTISE-AND-TENON VARIATIONS

There are a lot of ways to adapt a mortise-and-tenon joint to a specific task. The aim of many of these is to increase glue-surface area when working in a limited space in order to provide more strength to the joint.

SIZING

A general rule of thumb when sizing a tenon is to make it $\frac{1}{3}$ as thick as the stock. This provides a good balance of strength between the tenon and the walls on either side of the mortise.

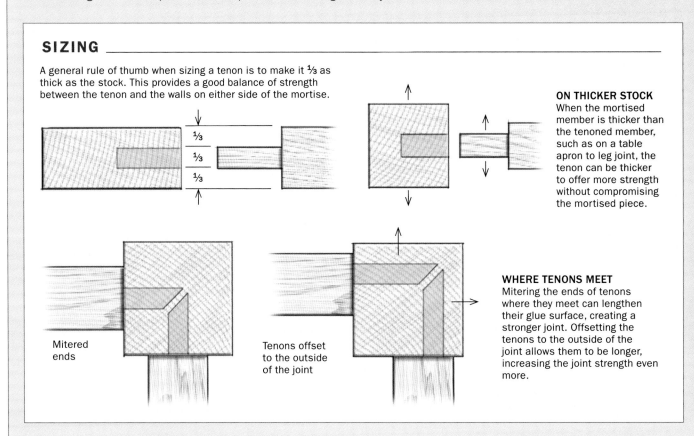

$\frac{1}{3}$
$\frac{1}{3}$
$\frac{1}{3}$

ON THICKER STOCK
When the mortised member is thicker than the tenoned member, such as on a table apron to leg joint, the tenon can be thicker to offer more strength without compromising the mortised piece.

Mitered ends

Tenons offset to the outside of the joint

WHERE TENONS MEET
Mitering the ends of tenons where they meet can lengthen their glue surface, creating a stronger joint. Offsetting the tenons to the outside of the joint allows them to be longer, increasing the joint strength even more.

TABLE-BASE JOINTS

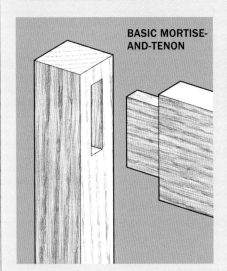

BASIC MORTISE-AND-TENON

Even in its most basic form, the mortise-and-tenon joint offers tremendous strength.

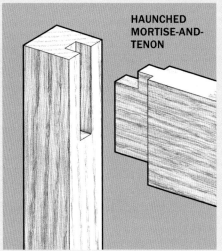

HAUNCHED MORTISE-AND-TENON

Adding a haunch at the top eliminates the weak cross-grain section above the mortise in the leg and offers better racking resistance.

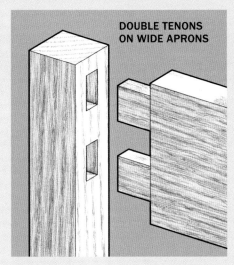

DOUBLE TENONS ON WIDE APRONS

On wide aprons, a single long mortise can weaken the leg. A better option is to use two tenons paired with shorter mortises that have solid stock in between them.

DOOR-FRAME JOINTS

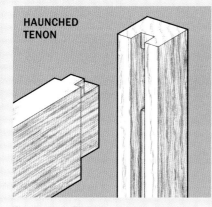

HAUNCHED TENON

The haunch fills the panel groove and allows you to cut through-grooves in all of the frame stock before assembly.

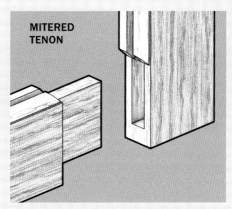

MITERED TENON

Mitering the inside corner of the joint allows you to rout a profile on the inside edge.

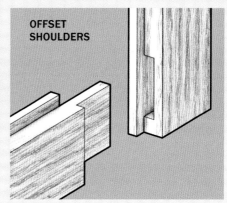

OFFSET SHOULDERS

By offsetting the shoulders, you can make a frame with a built-in rabbit, which is useful on doors with glass panels.

ADDING STRENGTH

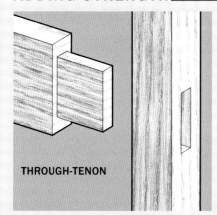

THROUGH-TENON

A through-tenon offers greater glue surface. The joint can be wedged from the outside to strengthen it further.

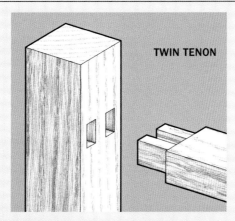

TWIN TENON

Twin tenons are useful on horizontal pieces like drawer rails. The multiple tenons double the vertical glue surface.

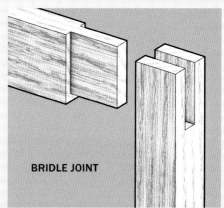

BRIDLE JOINT

A variation on the through-tenon, this joint has the added benefit that it can be clamped across the joint during glue-up.

CASE AND TABLETOP JOINTS

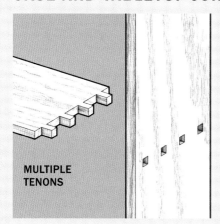

MULTIPLE TENONS

Multiple through-tenons offer greater glue surface; through-tenons can also be wedged in place.

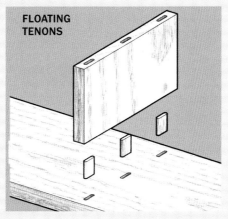

FLOATING TENONS

Floating tenons such as those used with a Domino joiner hold well and simplify construction on non-through case joinery.

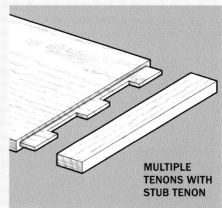

MULTIPLE TENONS WITH STUB TENON

The perfect joint for breadboard ends. Long tenons provide strength, while the stub tenon helps to keep the top flat.

DRILL AND CHOP A MORTISE

Because it's usually easier to fit a tenon to a mortise, the mortise is a good place to start. I have a hollow-chisel mortiser that makes quick work of the joint, but I drilled and chopped mortises for years (and actually still do when the need arises), so I'll show you that method first. A plunge router is also a good choice for mortising, and though I don't use it as often, it does have its place.

As a rule of thumb, handwork requires careful layout to be successful, while machine work requires careful setup. What that means for us is that we need to pull out a marking knife, square, and marking gauge when drilling and chopping mortises, but we can skip all of that when we head to the tablesaw to cut the tenons.

To cut a mortise, first scribe its outline, then drill out most of the waste, and finally pare the faces square. While it sounds like a lot of work, it's not difficult to cut an accurate mortise.

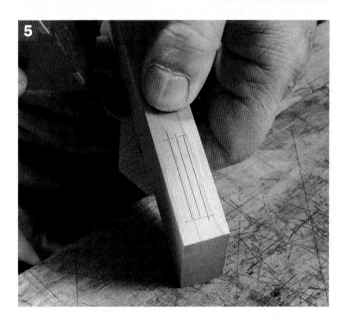

LAYOUT FIRST

Start by marking the ends of the mortise; a sharp pencil works well here (**1**). Then scribe the ends using a square and marking knife (**2**). Because this face is typically hidden by the tenoned piece, I don't worry about stopping exactly at the corners of the mortise. Hold the square tight against the fence and try scribing a single full-width line. After that, scribe the width of the mortise with a marking gauge (**3**). For a centered mortise, register the gauge against each edge of the workpiece. The width is not critical, but I try to size the mortise to fit my chisels (and the drill bit, for that matter), aiming for a mortise just a little wider than the chisel. A rule of thumb for sizing mortises on the edge of a part, such as a door frame, is to make the mortise one-third of the thickness of the frame. To aid in drilling, also scribe a line along the center of the mortise (**4**). WIth the layout complete (**5**), you're ready to head to the drill press.

DRILL OUT THE WASTE

At the drill press, set the workpiece in place and align the centerline of the mortise with the bit, then clamp a fence to the drill-press table behind the workpiece (1). Attach a piece of plywood or MDF to your drill-press table to act as an oversize tabletop and make it easier to support long stock. Drill bits are one of the less expensive pieces of tooling in the shop, though we tend to live with dull bits longer than we should. A new sharp brad-point bit is a wonderful thing. My favorite bits are sold by Lee Valley and Fuller. They have long, sharp spurs that cut a clean entry and exit hole.

With the fence in place, set the depth of the bit. If there's room, I like to cut a mortise that's a little deeper than the tenon so that I don't have to worry about the tenon bottoming out (2). Begin by drilling a hole at each end of the mortise (3), and then work your way along the mortise with holes that just touch (4). If they overlap too much, the bit will tend to wander. As you near the opposite end of the mortise, it's common that the bridge of waste between the last two holes is a little narrower than your bit. Center the point of the bit on the waste and take a very slow cut, which will help to keep the bit from wandering. With most of the waste drilled out, a chisel can handle the rest of the job quickly.

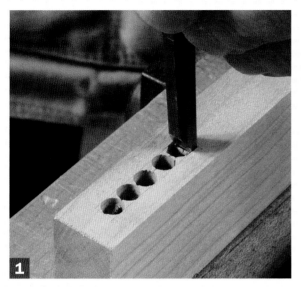

CHISEL THE MORTISE SQUARE

The first task when chiseling is to cut the square ends of the mortise (**1**). Rather than placing the chisel right at the scribe line, start at the wide part of the hole where the end grain is almost completely severed. Then work your way back to the scribe line, taking thin cuts. By the time you get to the scribe line there should be just a sliver of waste to remove. It's important that the end walls of the mortise are vertical, and the drilled holes can help act as a guide. As you're chopping, if the hole appears wider toward the bottom of the mortise, then the mortise wall is angled in toward the bottom, which could cause a problem when fitting the joint. Start at the top and try to pare straight down until what remains of the hole is parallel top to bottom and then finally disappears as you reach the scribe line.

Next, pare the side walls of the mortise (**2**). Use a wide chisel and start toward the center of the mortise, beginning your paring cuts at the peaks of the waste (**3**). Again, the drilled holes come in handy as a guide here. Work your way back to the scribe line, keeping an eye on the width of what remains of the drilled holes as you go (**4**). The aim is to end at the scribe line with vertical walls. Any inconsistencies between mortises will make fitting the tenons a little more difficult later. With an accurately scribed mortise, a centered row of cleanly drilled holes, and careful paring with sharp chisels, a good mortise is painlessly quick and simple to execute. Get the little stuff right and the rest is easy.

GIVE MORTISING A POWER ASSIST

I hadn't actually planned on addressing the hollow-chisel mortiser. It's a single-use machine, and floor-standing models can get expensive. However, it was such a game changer for me, both in speed and accuracy, that I thought it was worth a mention.

The hollow-chisel mortiser, as its name implies, has a drill bit that spins inside of a square chisel. As you pull the handle, the drilling and chopping of a mortise is accomplished in a single action. It cuts a mortise quickly, but there are benefits beyond speed. The chisel creates a mortise of consistent width, which makes fitting tenons easier later. Another great thing about the mortiser is that you can do away with most of the layout. The bit takes care of the width of the mortise, and the fence determines the distance from the edge of the stock, so all that's left to do is to set the depth stop and mark the ends of the mortise so that you know where to start and stop.

While it resembles a drill press, a mortiser has a longer handle to help with the extra force needed to drive the chisel through the cut. Mortisers also have a hold-down to keep the workpiece in place as you lift the chisel out of the cut. On most benchtop machines, the workpiece is slid side to side under a fork-style hold-down on a stationary base. Floor-standing models (and recently a few benchtop models as well) have an XY table that allows you to clamp the stock securely while you move the table side to side with a handwheel. No matter which type you choose, the most important task is to sharpen the bit and chisel before use. That will have the greatest impact on the performance of the tool. In addition, the chisel must be mounted parallel to the fence, and there needs to be enough clearance between the bit and the chisel to prevent it from overheating during use.

Hollow chisel is installed in mortiser.

Drill bit spins inside hollow chisel.

DRESS THE CHISEL AND DRILL BIT

Begin by polishing the faces of the chisel. You can use a sharpening stone or sandpaper on a flat surface; just be careful to use a light touch so that you don't change the outer dimension of the chisel. Diamond-coated cones are commonly available to remove any burrs on the inside of the chisel. Finally, touch up the point and spur of the bit with a slip stone or fine file.

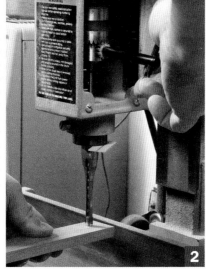
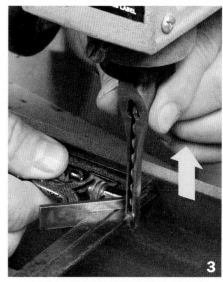

SET IT UP AND GET TO WORK

Temporarily lock the chisel in place, using a shim to leave a
¹⁄₁₆-in. gap between the machine and the shoulder of the chisel
(**1**). Position the bit against the bottom of the chisel and chuck it in
place (**2**); be careful, the bit is sharp. I like to use a block of wood
to hold it in place. Finally, loosen the chisel and slide it up until it
fully seats. This creates the necessary gap between the bit and
chisel at the bottom. Use a square to align the chisel with the fence
and lock it in place (**3**). Adjust the fence to center the bit on the
layout marks (**4**), and then set the bit depth slightly below the tenon
length (**5**). This saves the hassle of having to clean out the bottom
of the mortise. Begin cutting at one end of the mortise layout lines
(**6**). The chisel can stick in the first hole, so take short passes,
withdrawing the bit as you go until you reach final depth. Then work
your way across the mortise in slightly overlapping passes. Leave
a bridge of waste when cutting the last hole to prevent the bit from
wandering and to ensure a vertical mortise wall (**7**). Then go back
and drill out the remaining waste.

ROUTING A MORTISE:
BRING THE MACHINE TO THE WORK

Woodworkers who graduate from chopping mortises by hand usually take one of two paths. I chose to go with a hollow-chisel mortiser for most of my work, but a lot of woodworkers end up routing their mortises. It isn't a technique I use often, but there are times, especially on large pieces, when a router is the best choice for the job at hand.

While I still drill and chop through-mortises on case construction (p. 117), a router works well to handle non-through-mortises on parts that are too big to hoist onto my mortiser. I go about them in the same manner that I'd rout a dado or groove (see pp. 46–47).

For mortises parallel to an edge, think of it like a short stopped groove and use a fence to guide the router. For mortises across the grain, especially those inset a ways from the end of the board, treat them like a short stopped dado and use an edge guide. Rather than clamping a board to the stock to act as a guide, taking the time to make a T-square guide can make the job easier.

MORTISING PARALLEL TO AN EDGE

I treat mortises parallel to the edge of a piece as a stopped groove, so the technique is about the same as that described in the previous chapter. Use a plunge router equipped with a fence and work left to right along the board so that the rotation of the bit pulls the fence tight against the edge (1). Start by plunging a full-depth hole at each end of the mortise (2), and then work along the length in ⅛-in. increments until you reach full depth (3). Use a chisel to square the ends of the mortise (4).

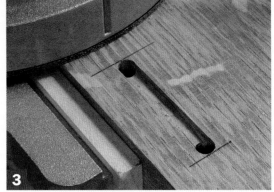

A T-SQUARE GUIDE MAKES ALIGNMENT EASY

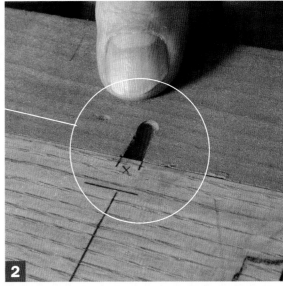

A T-square guide consists of a fence that the router rides along and a cleat perpendicular to the fence that registers against the workpiece and ensures a square cut. The benefit over a simple edge guide is that the T-square is not only easier to square to an edge but also easier to align. The key is to rout a notch in the cleat with the same bit you'll be using (**1**). To use the guide, start by marking the mortise location on the edge of the workpiece. Then align the notch in the guide with the layout marks and clamp it in place (**2**). When routing the mortise, begin by establishing the ends with a full-depth plunge cut. Then, starting with a shallow pass, take successively deeper cuts to complete the dado (**3**). The result should be a mortise exactly where you want it, and that's a good thing (**4**).

A FAST, ACCURATE JIG FOR HINGE MORTISES

Making a jig is fast and a good fit is just about automatic. The key is to build the template around the hinge itself.

There are a lot of ways to go about cutting a hinge mortise. One option that I wasn't really interested in for a long time was using a routing template. My reasoning was that I never knew what hinge I would use for a project and it didn't seem worth it to make a new template for every project. Second, I assumed it would be a pain to make, and last, I doubted the accuracy of the template. Once again, teaching had a way of changing my view. In trying to figure out a way to get a class through the process of hanging a door at the end of a long week, I decided to give the router a look. It turns out that making a jig is fast and a good fit is just about automatic. The key is to build the template around the hinge itself. From there, a short pattern bit makes quick work of the mortising, leaving just the rounded inside corners to take care of with a chisel. It's important to use a good quality hinge (which you should do anyway) because the sizes are more consistent from hinge to hinge, which makes for a more consistent fit. I've had good luck with hinges from Horton Brasses, Brusso, and Whitechapel Ltd.

MAKING THE TEMPLATE

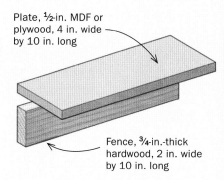

Plate, ½-in. MDF or plywood, 4 in. wide by 10 in. long

Fence, ¾-in.-thick hardwood, 2 in. wide by 10 in. long

Start by marking the width of the hinge on the plate (**1**). The notch needs to account for the thickness of the fence as well, so butt the plate and fence against a vertical surface when marking. Then mark the length of the notch. On a normal butt hinge, mark at the center of the barrel. On a ball-tip hinge, shown here, mark at the inside edge of the barrel. Then cut the side walls of the notch at the tablesaw, sneaking up on a snug fit (**2**). Bandsaw out most of the waste and cut to the line with a skim cut at the tablesaw (**3**). When you're done, the hinge should just fit into the notch (**4**). The final task is to glue and pin the plate to the fence (**5**). Be sure to keep the parts flush as you go.

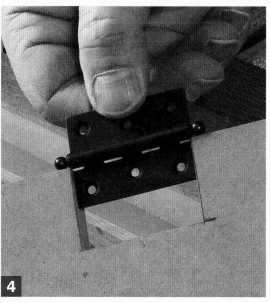

ROUTING A HINGE MORTISE

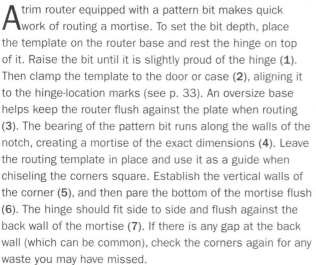

A trim router equipped with a pattern bit makes quick work of routing a mortise. To set the bit depth, place the template on the router base and rest the hinge on top of it. Raise the bit until it is slightly proud of the hinge (**1**). Then clamp the template to the door or case (**2**), aligning it to the hinge-location marks (see p. 33). An oversize base helps keep the router flush against the plate when routing (**3**). The bearing of the pattern bit runs along the walls of the notch, creating a mortise of the exact dimensions (**4**). Leave the routing template in place and use it as a guide when chiseling the corners square. Establish the vertical walls of the corner (**5**), and then pare the bottom of the mortise flush (**6**). The hinge should fit side to side and flush against the back wall of the mortise (**7**). If there is any gap at the back wall (which can be common), check the corners again for any waste you may have missed.

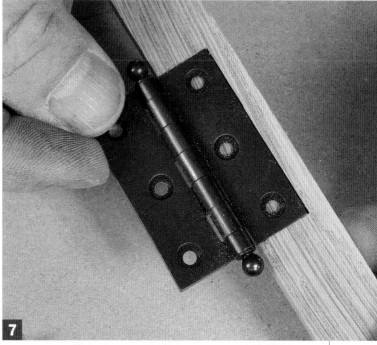

FAST TENONS AT THE TABLESAW

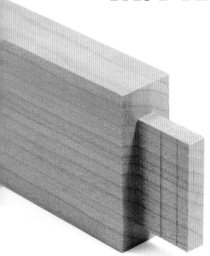

There are a lot of ways to go about cutting a tenon. You can cut them by hand, or tackle them on the router or bandsaw. For the most part, I use the tablesaw, but even then there are multiple ways to go about it. A dado blade does a really good job and it's a technique I've used for quite a few years, so it's a good place to start. Using a dado blade with the stock flat on the table has a couple of advantages. First, you are guaranteed a tenon that has parallel cheeks and is parallel to the face of the board. That goes a long way toward ensuring square glue-ups later. In addition, as long as your stock is of consistent thickness, the tenons will be consistent as well. Finally, the dado blade cuts the cheeks and shoulders of the tenon with a single pass, which saves time and machine setups.

This technique is not limited to a simple tenon with even shoulders. With just a little extra work you can cut haunched tenons, which are perfect for frame-and-panel construction. You can also offset the shoulders to create a joint with a built-in rabbet, which is ideal for picture frames or doors with glass panels.

ONE PASS OR TWO? SETTING THE WIDTH OF THE DADO SET

TAKE MULTIPLE PASSES ON LONG TENONS

For tenons longer than ¾ in., stack the dado blade for a narrower cut and adjust the fence to the tenon length. Cut the tenon in multiple passes.

Dado set

BURY THE BLADE FOR SHORT TENONS

L-fence

For tenons under ¾ in. long, stack the dado set wider than the tenon's length. Clamp an L-fence to your rip fence to overlap a portion of the blade, and cut the tenon in a single pass.

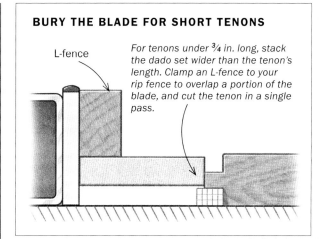

When using a dado blade to cut a tenon, start with a blade set to cut a dado that is either narrower than the finished tenon or wider. It may sound odd, but it's the easiest way to get the tenon length you're after. Most dado sets can be set up to cut a ¾-in.-long tenon. For tenons longer than that, I prefer to set up for a cut just over half the length of the tenon. This way, I can use the fence to set the tenon length without risk of the blade contacting it and still be able to cut the tenon in just two passes (above).

For tenons under ¾ in. long, I like to set up for a ¾-in. cut and bury a portion of the blade in the fence. You can add a sacrificial fence to your rip fence and raise the blade into it, or clamp on an L-fence so that it sits just above the blade. You can then cut the tenon in a single pass (right).

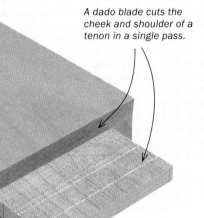

A dado blade cuts the cheek and shoulder of a tenon in a single pass.

SET UP SQUARE FOR EVEN SHOULDERS

Little things can make a big difference in the quality of the resulting cut, so let's spend a minute on setup. A typical miter gauge doesn't offer back support to the workpiece at the blade. Without it, you can be left with chipout on the trailing edge of the cut. So step one is to attach a hardwood fence to the miter gauge (**1**). It should be long enough to support the stack and should overlap the blade slightly. After your first pass, the resulting notch in the fence will act as a zero-clearance backer, preventing chipout. The next step is to square the gauge to the fence (**2**). Before doing this, make sure the fence is aligned to the miter-gauge slots in the table. Finally, use a combination square to dial in the fence setting to cut the tenon length you're after (**3**).

SNEAK UP ON A SNUG FIT

Start with the blade height set to cut a tenon that's a little too thick for the mortise (1 & 2). Then use a test piece to dial in the fit by raising the blade slightly and taking another pass. Be patient. Because you take a pass on each face of the tenon, each adjustment is effectively doubled and it's easy to go from too tight to too loose quickly. I aim for a fit where the tenon can just slip into the mortise but still be on the snug side (3). That way I can get a perfect fit at the bench with a shoulder plane. With the height set, cut the cheeks on all of the tenons (4) before moving on to the tenon sides.

TRIM AND FIT THE TENON

The final step at the tablesaw is to cut the tenon to its final width. It's not uncommon for a tenon to have a wider shoulder at one end than the other, so it's important to keep track of the orientation of the parts when cutting the shoulders. An easy way to determine where to trim the tenon sides is to measure from the mating mortise itself. Place the tenoned piece in position and make a tick mark at each end of the mortise (**1**). Keeping the fence in the same position, raise the blade to hit one of the marks and cut one end of all the pieces (**2**). Repeat the process for the second end and check the fit. The final fit doesn't need to be overly snug top to bottom (**3**). A little gap won't compromise the strength of the joint, and a little wiggle room can let you align the parts more easily during glue-up.

If you were close to a good fit off of the saw, it shouldn't take more than a few swipes with a shoulder plane to get the tenon to seat (**4**). A well-fitting tenon is one that can be assembled with hand pressure but won't fall apart when you lift it off the bench (**5**). The score marks left by the dado blade act as a good guide to make sure you are removing stock evenly when planing.

4

5

ADD A HAUNCH TO FILL A PANEL GROOVE

A typical frame-and-panel door is joined with mortises and has a groove along the inside edge of the frame parts to house the panel. While you can cut simple mortise-and-tenon joints at the corners and rout a panel groove that stops at the mortises, I find it easier to cut grooves the entire length of the parts at the tablesaw. This results in the groove being exposed on the end grain. To avoid leaving a void, I add a haunch to the tenon to fill it up. When cutting tenons, save this task for last since it requires repositioning the rip fence. To determine the size of the haunch, measure the depth of the groove and offset the fence the same amount. Start with a haunch that's a little long and trim it until the joint seats fully on the face of the door.

MORTISE-AND-TENON WITH A BUILT-IN RABBET

Mortise is flush with the inside face of the rabbet.

Shoulder offset equals the width of the rabbet.

This is a great joint for a door that has a glass panel. The offset shoulders accommodate a rabbet that is milled into the door-frame parts prior to cutting the joinery (**1**). The rabbet is then used to locate the mortises in the stiles, which are flush to the inner wall of the rabbet (**2**). After that, milling proceeds in a fashion similar to a regular tenon, with the exception of the offset shoulders. To cut the front face of the tenons, raise the blade even with the inside face of the rabbet (**3**). Set the fence for the mortise depth plus the width of the rabbet (**4**). To cut the rear face of the tenons, set the height of the blade even with the rear wall of the mortise (**5**). Offset the rip fence the width of the rabbet to cut the rear faces (**6**). Keep the fence in this position to cut the outer edge of the tenon. The inner edge is already defined by the rabbet (**7**). Test the fit; the front and rear shoulders of the tenon should seat without gaps (**8**).

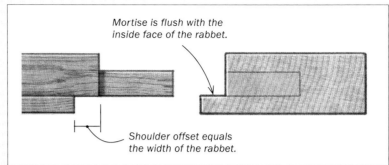

1

2

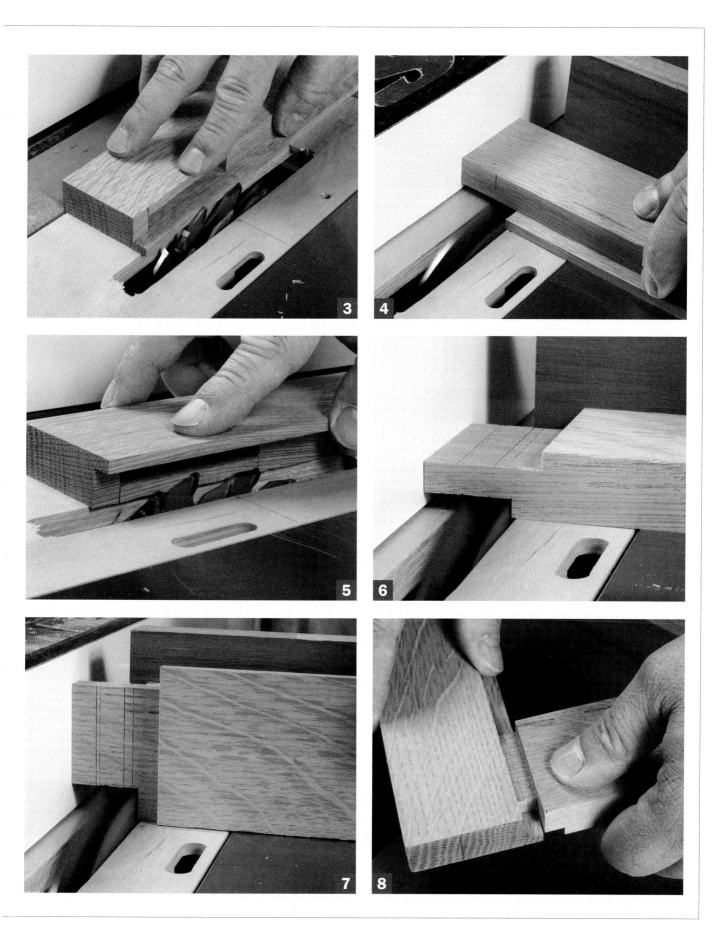

USE A SPACER FOR CONSISTENT TENONS

Cutting a tenon vertically requires a few more steps than using a dado blade, but when combined with a custom spacer the accurate results can be worth the extra work. Making a spacer for tenons is a little tricky because you need to account for the width of the blade as well as the tenon (below). Once you have it, however, you can make accurate tenons easily. Set the tenoning jig to cut the cheek farthest from the jig and cut the first cheek (**1**). Then, keeping the stock in the same orientation,

MAKING A TENON SPACER

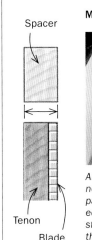

Spacer

Tenon

Blade

An easy way to determine the size of the spacer you need is to set your rip fence to the tenon size, make a partial cut in a test piece, and then measure from the edge of the board to the outside of the kerf. Start with a strip slightly thicker than you need, make test cuts, and then plane down the stock until you get a good fit.

WHEN TO GO VERTICAL WITH TENONS

Tenoning with the stock flat on the tablesaw works most of the time, but there are some situations where standing the workpiece on end makes sense. It requires more work than using a dado blade because cutting the cheeks and shoulders requires two separate setups, but it does have its advantages. Cutting double tenons and angled tenons are two tasks where going vertical makes the job easier (see pp. 128 and 262). Even with a simple tenon, going vertical can yield more consistent results. A shopmade tenoning jig is simple to make, and commercial jigs are easy to find. I often use a custom crosscut sled with a tall fence to cut vertical tenons as well (see p. 48 for how to make one). The deciding factor is usually the orientation of the tenon. If the tenon is parallel to the face of the board, I'll use a tenoning jig. If it's perpendicular to the face, such as a double tenon for a drawer stretcher, I'll use a sled.

A big advantage of cutting vertically is that you can use a spacer when cutting the cheeks. While you can cut one cheek and then rotate the stock in the jig to cut the second cheek, similar to the way you would cut a tenon with a dado blade, adding a spacer to make the second cut instead will yield a more consistent fit. This is because any variation in the thickness of the parts will result in tenons of different thickness when rotating the stock, whereas a spacer will create a consistent thickness regardless of the dimensions of the stock. It takes a few minutes to dial in the size of the spacer, but once you have it, you can use it on any project.

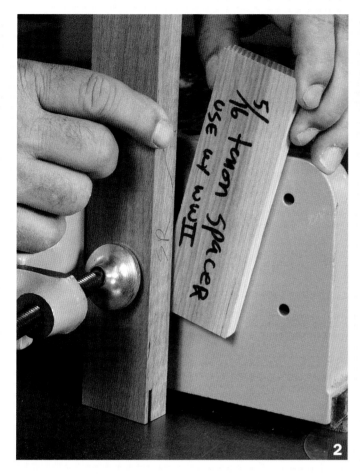

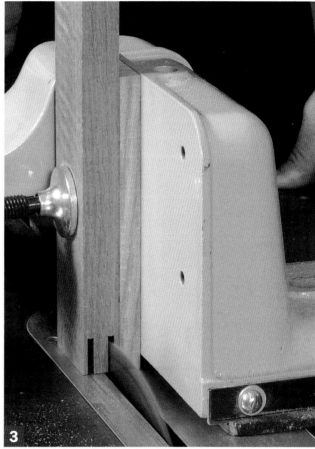

slip the spacer between the jig and workpiece (**2**) and cut the second cheek (**3**). Cut the shoulder with the stock flat on the saw (**4**). I like to bandsaw off most of the waste first to keep the offcut from getting trapped between the blade and the fence. I also make a cut on the edges to establish the shoulders on the sides of the tenon. Finally, I head to the bandsaw to trim the tenon to its final width (**5**).

A QUICK BRIDLE JOINT

Here's a fast, accurate way to cut bridle joints for a frame-and-panel door or chest lid. Be sure to use a blade with a flat-top grind. The bridle joint is exposed, so you want the slots to have flat bottoms. Start by cutting the panel grooves. They guide the rest of the cuts so it's important that they are centered on the stock. The best way to ensure that is to cut the grooves in two passes, flipping the workpiece for the second cut. Then cut the slots, aligning the blade with one side of the groove and making the first cut (**1**), then flipping the workpiece to cut the second side of the slot (**2**).

Cut the tenon cheeks in the same way, this time aligning the blade with the outside edge of the groove (**3**). To avoid trapping the offcut when cutting the shoulders, trim away most of the waste on the bandsaw, then cut the shoulder on the tablesaw (**4**). Finally, use a dado set to rabbet the panels to fit the groove.

1

2

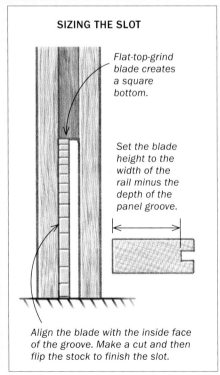

SIZING THE SLOT

Flat-top-grind blade creates a square bottom.

Set the blade height to the width of the rail minus the depth of the panel groove.

Align the blade with the inside face of the groove. Make a cut and then flip the stock to finish the slot.

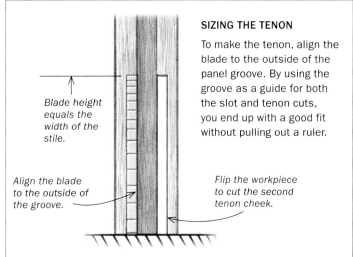

SIZING THE TENON

To make the tenon, align the blade to the outside of the panel groove. By using the groove as a guide for both the slot and tenon cuts, you end up with a good fit without pulling out a ruler.

Blade height equals the width of the stile.

Align the blade to the outside of the groove.

Flip the workpiece to cut the second tenon cheek.

CLAMP FROM THREE DIRECTIONS

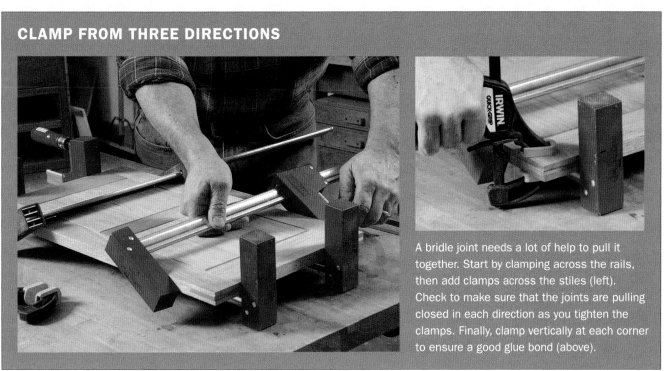

A bridle joint needs a lot of help to pull it together. Start by clamping across the rails, then add clamps across the stiles (left). Check to make sure that the joints are pulling closed in each direction as you tighten the clamps. Finally, clamp vertically at each corner to ensure a good glue bond (above).

LOCKING DOWN A MORTISE-AND-TENON

When we think of joint strength, there are actually two factors to consider. The first is glue strength, which is determined by the amount of long-grain-to-long-grain surface area. For example, an edge joint between two boards provides a great deal of glue strength. The second factor is mechanical strength, where the geometry of the joint provides strength as well. A mortise-and-tenon and a dovetail are good examples. Both can slip together along one axis, but the joint resists coming apart perpendicular to that. Whereas a dovetail provides good glue strength along the walls of the pins where there is long-grain-to-long-grain contact, a mortise-and-tenon joint can fall short depending on its orientation. A tenon that runs parallel to the grain, on a table apron for example, has good glue strength, but a horizontal or square tenon provides less long-grain contact and therefore less glue strength. Fortunately, there are a few ways to make up for that by adding a little more mechanical strength in the form of wedges or pins.

WEDGES ADD MECHANICAL STRENGTH TO THE JOINT

For through-tenons, a wedge is an effective way to keep the joint in place. Use a single wedge on square tenons and a pair on wide tenons. The wedges should be perpendicular to the grain to prevent splitting. While it's common to angle the outer walls of the mortise, I prefer to keep them square. Start by cutting the kerf prior to assembly (**1**). Then clamp the parts together while driving in the wedges (**2**); they will hold the joint together but won't pull it together, so clamps are a must. Saw off the excess and pare flush with a block plane or chisel (**3 & 4**).

FAST WEDGES AT THE BANDSAW

A simple sled lets you batch out wedges quickly. Start by milling stock to the thickness of the tenon and crosscut it into strips. The sled has an angled notch in the side that the stock fits into as you make the cut. Flip the stock after every cut to keep the grain aligned to the wedge.

1

DRAWBORE PINS PULL IT ALL TOGETHER

A traditional method for securing tenons is with a drawbore pin. The concept is simple: a pin driven into the joint through offset holes pulls the joint together snugly. This method has a few benefits. First, because of its clamping action, you can join curved or odd-shaped parts that would be difficult to join with clamps (**1**). Second, if your joints aren't tight, you don't need to worry about it. And finally, drawbore pins allow you to dry-fit parts and disassemble them as necessary when building. The first step is to drill a hole through the mortised part (**2**). A piece of scrap inserted into the mortise prevents blowout on the inside face. Then assemble the parts and use a drill bit to mark the center of the hole on the tenon (**3**). Use an awl to make a mark that is offset $\frac{1}{32}$ in. toward the shoulder of the joint (**4**). Align the bit to this mark and drill through the tenon (**5**). Again, use scrap underneath to prevent blowout. I make two sets of pins, one for use during dry-fitting and the second for final assembly, because the pins tend to get deformed during repeated use.

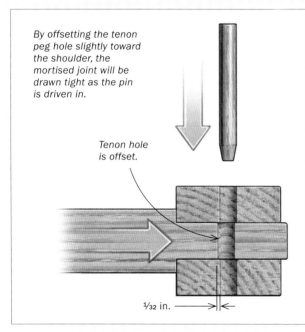

By offsetting the tenon peg hole slightly toward the shoulder, the mortised joint will be drawn tight as the pin is driven in.

Tenon hole is offset.

$\frac{1}{32}$ in.

FLOATING TENONS AREN'T CHEATING

There aren't a lot of new innovations in woodworking. The basic techniques really don't change, and hand tools, of course, haven't changed significantly in the last 100 years or so. Woodworking machines have been around for quite a while as well. The two major advances in machinery that I can think of, short of CNC gizmos, are the SawStop tablesaw brake technology and the addition of segmented cutterheads for jointers and planers. Regarding handheld power tools, I might list battery-powered tools, but they've been common for quite a while. Which brings us to the Festool Domino joiner. It's an odd machine that looks like a biscuit joiner at first, but instead of a spinning blade that creates a scallop-shaped slot, the Domino has a spinning end-mill bit that oscillates back and forth to create a deep mortise. Once floating tenons are glued in place, it becomes a very strong joint. The machine is not cheap, but it is a one-stop joinery solution. I've always liked my biscuit joiner for joining parts like internal dividers, and I use a Domino for those tasks now. I'd say it's a good solution for joinery that doesn't show. Unfortunately for me, I like joinery that is visible, so I get limited use from this machine. I do think it's worth covering, however, so here are some useful tips that will help you get the most out of the tool.

FAST CASE JOINERY

One of the advantages of using floating tenons is that you can cut pieces to exact size without worrying about accounting for the joinery (**1**). On case joints, you typically need to cut slots in the face of one part and in the end grain of the mating piece. When slotting the face of a board, clamp an edge guide with marks at the mortise locations to the workpiece. I'll often add a cleat on the end to register the guide for consistent insets (**2**). Align the center mark on the base of the joiner to your layout mark and *slowly* cut the mortise (**3 & 4**). Ramming the bit into the workpiece too quickly will cause it to chatter. For the mating part, transfer the tenon marks from the edge guide to the workpiece (**5**). Clamp it down and make the cut (**6**).

TURN IT INTO A STATIONARY TOOL

Much like installing a router in a router table, attaching the joiner to a base transforms it into a different tool. This setup makes tasks like joining door frames safe and accurate. It doesn't have to be fancy. I just screw blocks to a work base along the sides and back of the joiner and drop the joiner in place (**1**). In addition, I attach stops for locating the rails and stiles when mortising (**2**). A strategically placed hold-down clamp can handle parts in both orientations when mortising (**3 & 4**). I use floating tenons on doors that don't have panel grooves (**5**), but for those that do, I still use traditional mortises and haunched-tenon joinery (see p. 234).

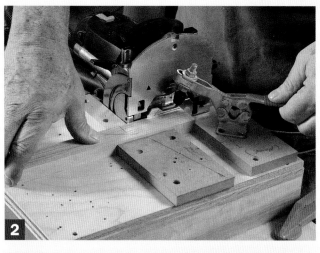

A TIP FOR EASIER ASSEMBLY

Unlike a biscuit joiner where you have extra room in the slots for adjusting side-to-side alignment, the Domino cuts mortises the same width as the tenons. If your layout marks are a little off on a joint with multiple tenons, it can make fitting the joint difficult. Fortunately, there's a width adjustment on the machine (**1**), but you need to be strategic in the way you put it to use. You could simply elongate all of the slots, but you would lose any side-to-side registration. Also, if the slots in both parts are elongated, it can make it hard to keep the tenons straight when assembling the parts. Instead, I like to cut slots the width of the tenon in all of the end-grain slots. On the face-grain slots, I'll cut the mortise nearest the front edge the width of the tenon. For the remaining slots, set the joiner to a wider mortise setting. This will provide registration where you need it but let the joint come together without a problem (**2**). When assembling the joint, start by gluing the tenons into the end-grain mortises (**3**) and then treat the part like a normal tenoned part when gluing the pieces together (**4**).

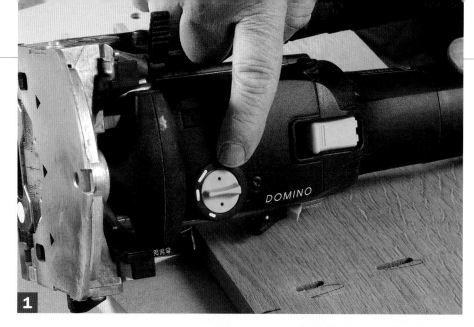

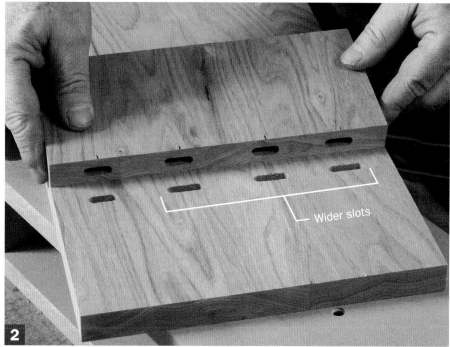

Wider slots

CRAFTSMAN CABINET:
A CASE FOR MORTISE-AND-TENON JOINERY

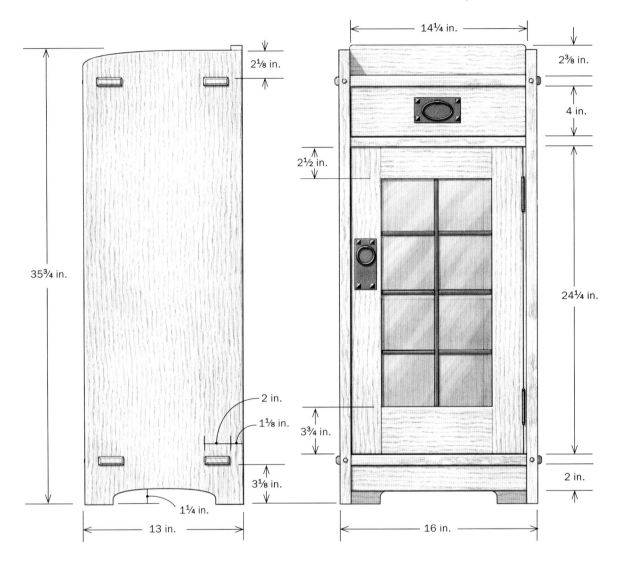

This cabinet is a smaller version of a display case I had made a while back (left), but even in its compact form it offers an example of the strength and versatility of mortise-and-tenon joinery. The major structural elements in the case are the through-tenons that join the case sides to the top and bottom. In addition to the through-tenons, there are non-through-tenons that connect the drawer stretcher, backsplash, and toekick. The case through-mortises are easiest to cut by hand, but I use a router for the remaining mortises (see p. 86). The door frame also features mortise-and-tenon construction, though with a twist. The frame has tenons with offset shoulders that create a built-in rabbet for the glass panel. Although the joints may seem complex, they are easily handled at the tablesaw (see p. 98).

Let's pause for a minute and take a look at the parts that comprise the case. While they appear quite different from each other, all of the parts other than the sides share a very important feature. They are all the same length shoulder to shoulder regardless

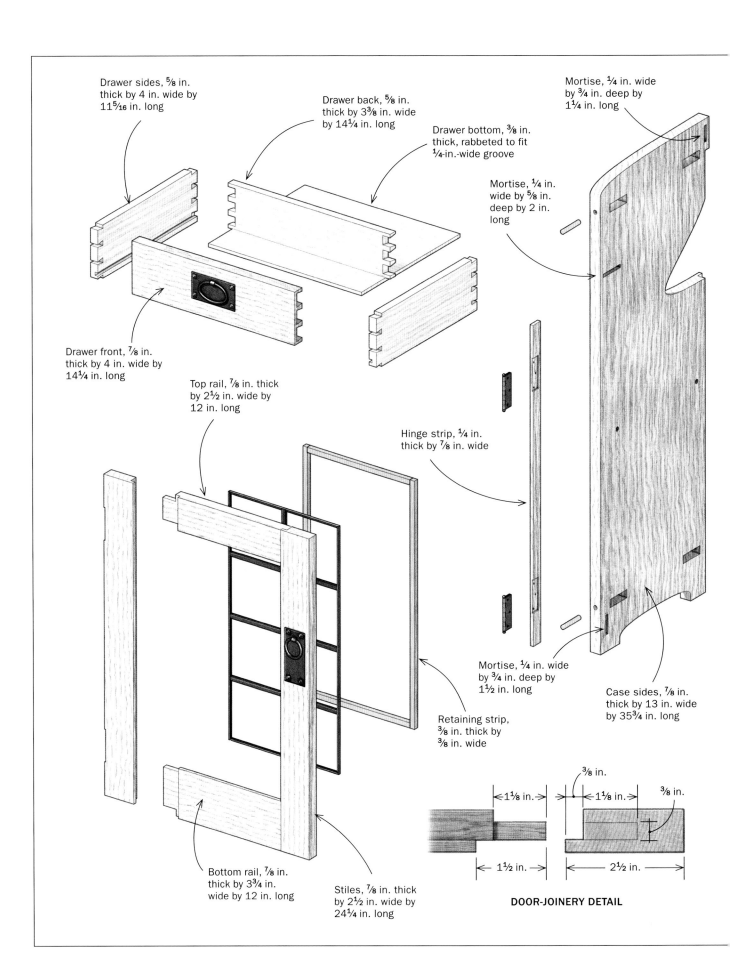

Drawer sides, ⅝ in. thick by 4 in. wide by 11⁵⁄₁₆ in. long

Drawer back, ⅝ in. thick by 3⅜ in. wide by 14¼ in. long

Drawer bottom, ⅜ in. thick, rabbeted to fit ¼-in.-wide groove

Mortise, ¼ in. wide by ¾ in. deep by 1¼ in. long

Mortise, ¼ in. wide by ⅝ in. deep by 2 in. long

Drawer front, ⅞ in. thick by 4 in. wide by 14¼ in. long

Top rail, ⅞ in. thick by 2½ in. wide by 12 in. long

Hinge strip, ¼ in. thick by ⅞ in. wide

Mortise, ¼ in. wide by ¾ in. deep by 1½ in. long

Case sides, ⅞ in. thick by 13 in. wide by 35¾ in. long

Retaining strip, ⅜ in. thick by ⅜ in. wide

Bottom rail, ⅞ in. thick by 3¾ in. wide by 12 in. long

Stiles, ⅞ in. thick by 2½ in. wide by 24¼ in. long

⅜ in.

1⅛ in.

1⅛ in.

⅜ in.

1½ in.

2½ in.

DOOR-JOINERY DETAIL

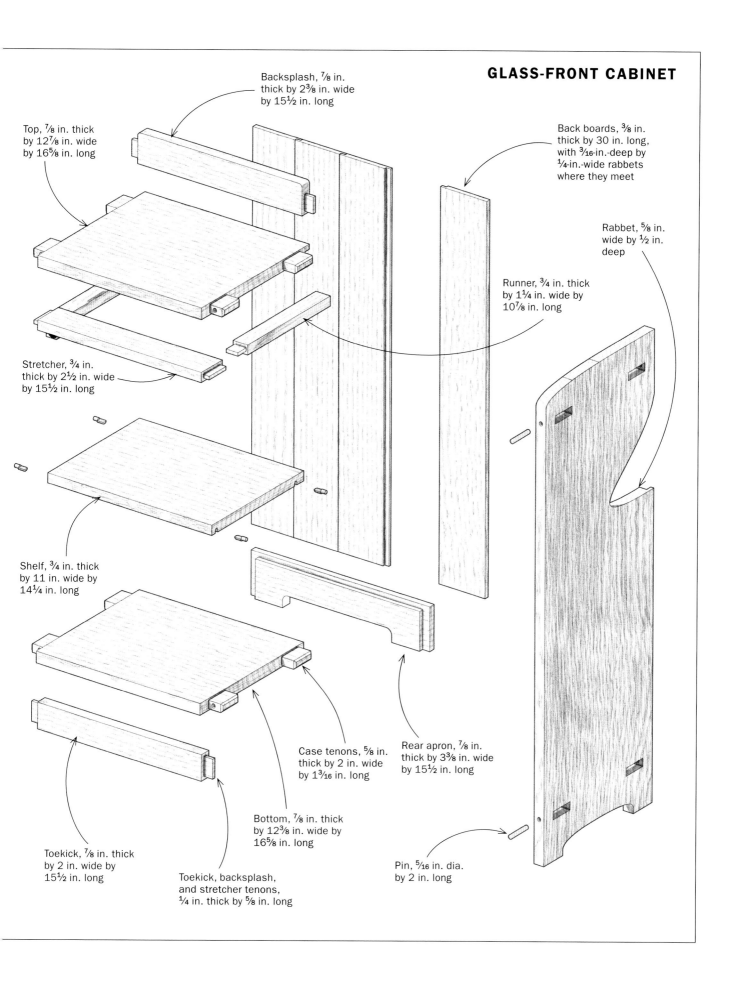

GLASS-FRONT CABINET

Backsplash, ⅞ in. thick by 2⅜ in. wide by 15½ in. long

Top, ⅞ in. thick by 12⅞ in. wide by 16⅝ in. long

Back boards, ⅜ in. thick by 30 in. long, with ³⁄₁₆-in.-deep by ¼-in.-wide rabbets where they meet

Rabbet, ⅝ in. wide by ½ in. deep

Runner, ¾ in. thick by 1¼ in. wide by 10⅞ in. long

Stretcher, ¾ in. thick by 2½ in. wide by 15½ in. long

Shelf, ¾ in. thick by 11 in. wide by 14¼ in. long

Case tenons, ⅝ in. thick by 2 in. wide by 1³⁄₁₆ in. long

Rear apron, ⅞ in. thick by 3⅜ in. wide by 15½ in. long

Toekick, ⅞ in. thick by 2 in. wide by 15½ in. long

Bottom, ⅞ in. thick by 12⅜ in. wide by 16⅝ in. long

Toekick, backsplash, and stretcher tenons, ¼ in. thick by ⅝ in. long

Pin, ⁵⁄₁₆ in. dia. by 2 in. long

ACCURATE LAYOUT IS A MUST FOR THROUGH-MORTISES

Begin by laying down a wide strip of tape in the general area of the mortises on each face of the board, then use a pencil to mark the rough width of the mortises (1). This gives you a starting and stopping point when scribing the top and bottom walls of the mortise. Set a marking gauge to the innermost edge of the mortise and scribe between the pencil lines (2). To mark the outer wall of the mortise, cut a piece of stock to the width of the mortise and use it as a spacer between the edge of the board and the gauge (3). This method yields mortises of a consistent width, which makes cutting the tenons easier later.

Next, scribe the sides of the mortise. For long mortises, I use a pair of gauges, each set to one end of the mortise

The idea is to build in accuracy by the way you go about building rather than relying on hitting a variety of dimensions precisely in order to end up with the results you want.

of the thickness, width, or length of the tenons. While you could cut each part to its final length and then measure out the tenons hoping for a consistent shoulder-to-shoulder dimension, an easier way to go about it is to start with all of the parts cut to the same length, and then trim them to their final dimensions only after the joinery is cut. I outline this method in the "Building Strategies" chapter (see p. 29). In essence, the idea is to build in accuracy by the way you go about building rather than relying on hitting a variety of dimensions precisely in order to end up with the results you want.

Although I tend to cut non-through-mortises with a hollow-chisel mortiser or a router, I find it easiest to drill and chop the through-mortises by hand. It may seem like more work than using a machine method, but the accuracy of the results is worth it. The big challenge in laying out a through-mortise is that you need to locate it in the same precise location on each face. When I put away my square and knife and picked up a marking gauge to handle the tasks, my results improved immediately. When you register the marking gauge along the edge or end of a workpiece, it's quick work to lay out a mortise on each face simply by flipping the board. The added benefit is that I can use the same marking-gauge setting to lay out the tenons for a perfect-fitting joint.

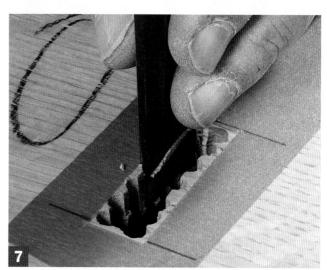

(4 & 5). For square mortises, I use the same spacer that I used for the top and bottom of the mortise. Save these gauge settings to use later when laying out the width of the tenons.

Drill and chop the mortise in the same way you handle non-through-mortises, but this time drill through the entire thickness of the stock. For wider mortises, I like to drill two rows of holes in order to remove more stock (6).

When chopping, start along the top and bottom edges. Take thin cuts, starting at the center and working back to the baseline (7). Then chop the sides square (8). Chop only halfway through the thickness of the stock, and then flip the board and chisel in from the other face. Working this way ensures that you have an accurate opening on each face and a better chance of ending up with a gap-free joint. The additional benefit of stopping halfway is that you can undercut the joint slightly to ensure that there isn't any waste in the center of the joint to prevent the tenon from fully seating.

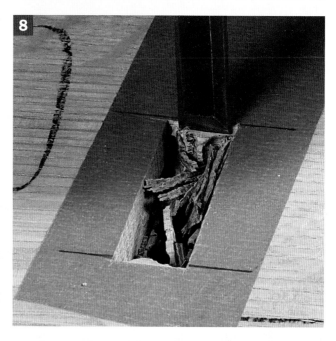

MATCH THE TENONS TO THE MORTISES

The multiple tenons begin as a single full-length tenon. Cut the cheeks using a dado blade with the stock flat on the tablesaw top (**1**). Start with a tenon that's too thick and slowly raise the blade, taking test cuts until the tenon fits snugly in the mortise (**2**). If you've had the foresight to save the marking-gauge settings from laying out the mortises, you can use them here to lay out the tenon sides as well. Apply tape along one cheek of the tenon and scribe through it (**3 & 4**). Then peel away the tape from the waste areas, leaving it just on the tenons. Check to see if the tenons are aligned with the mortises (**5**). If both parts are cut to the same width and the gauge setting didn't move, you should have a perfect match.

SAWING THE TENONS

W hile I often saw the tenons by hand, I can get accurate results at the tablesaw as well. That's why I applied tape to the tenon face rather than to the tenon end. If your crosscut sled is a little worn, tack down a layer of ¼-in. MDF and make a cut. The fresh kerf will offer a good guide for positioning the stock (**1**). Set the blade slightly lower than the tenon shoulder, align one end of a tenon to the kerf, and make a cut (**2**). After cutting all of the tenon sides, take a couple of extra passes on the waste side of one of the inside kerfs to create an access notch for the bandsaw blade when sawing out the waste (**3**). Before heading to the bandsaw, use a square to knife a line even with the shoulders on the edges of the stock (**4**). The scribe line will help to guide the chisel when cleaning up later. At the bandsaw, set the fence to trim the waste just outside of the tenon shoulder (**5**).

FINISH THE TENONS BY HAND

We began the process by chopping mortises at the bench. After that, the machines took over and made quick work of the tenons. Now we find ourselves at the bench once again, where hand tools take us to the finish line.

If you were brave in getting close to your shoulder line when sawing out the waste at the bandsaw, you should be left with just a sliver of waste that a chisel can handle with a single pass. Start by establishing a shoulder on the ends of the workpiece (**1**). This is where the time taken to scribe the edges before bandsawing pays off. Set the chisel in the scribe line and pare a shoulder about ⅛ in. wide. Then you can get serious about removing the waste. The shallow shoulder created at the tablesaw when cutting the tenon cheeks offers a solid backing for the chisel. Chop halfway through the thickness of the stock, angling the chisel just a little to slightly undercut the joint as you go (**2**). Undercutting the joint will ensure that there isn't any waste remaining in the center to keep the joint from seating. Then flip the board and continue from the opposite face (**3**). For final cleanup and test-fitting, clamp the board vertically in your vise to make paring easier.

A CHAMFER ON THE ENDS

It's nice to finish off a through-tenon with a chamfer along the end. The width of the chamfer can vary greatly and is directly related to how far the tenon protrudes. On some of my pieces, the tenons are proud of the surface by less than ¹⁄₁₆ in. In that case, the tenon usually gets a light single pass with a block plane. On other pieces, the tenons can stick out ¼ in. or more, in which case they usually receive a heavy chamfer. On this piece, the tenons protrude by ³⁄₁₆ in. To determine the width of the chamfer, dry-fit the case and draw a line at the base of the tenon (**1**). Disassemble the parts and draw a second line about ¹⁄₁₆ in. above the first (**2**). This is the line you'll plane to. Then draw lines around the edges on the end grain. When chamfering, the aim is to hit both lines (**3**). Keep an eye on your progress as you go and make any course corrections as needed before getting too close to the lines. The idea is to end up with a single full-width facet.

PIN THE TENONS AFTER ASSEMBLY

A through-mortise-and-tenon is very strong mechanically, but because the only structural glue surface is on the sides of the tenons, there's not a lot to keep the joint tight with glue alone. Wedging the tenon from the outside works very well, but it's not a detail you typically find in Arts and Crafts furniture. Instead, it's more common to pin the joint from the front and rear edges of the case side. To get a head start, I use a dowel jig to drill a hole in the edge at the mortise location, stopping short of drilling through the mortise itself, which could create chipout on the inside face. Start by drawing a centerline on the case side (**1**). Align the jig with the centerline and use a wooden depth stop to prevent the bit from drilling too deep (**2 & 3**). Once the case is assembled (**4**), continue the hole about halfway into the tenon using the predrilled hole as a guide to keep the drill square to the surface (**5**). Cut the pin to length and chamfer the end with sandpaper before driving it in (**6**). Leave the pin just proud of the surface.

CASE WITH A STURDY BASE: STRENGTH IN TIGHT SPACES

If I had to limit my furniture making to a single form, the cabinet on stand might just be it. For one thing, the design possibilities when combining a case and stand are almost endless, and it offers a versatile palette for exploring ideas. For another—and this is a pretty important one—the general scale of the components is a good size to work with. Anything smaller and venturing toward box territory can get fussy when working with small details. On the other hand, larger pieces like the cabinet on p. 112 present their own challenges in terms of the amount of material required and the size of the parts, which often require a different approach to joinery than smaller projects. And that's not to mention how a big project can suddenly make my shop feel smaller than it already does. A cabinet on stand fits comfortably between those two extremes and offers room to explore door and drawer combinations in an easy-to-manage project.

One of the biggest challenges, especially on a project like this with its substantial white oak case, is finding a way to support its weight in a sturdy fashion without it looking too heavy. One strategy is to break up horizontal elements into multiple rails. These offer the same support against racking that a single wide rail would, but with a lighter, more delicate look. To keep the thinner legs from deflecting, a lower stretcher assembly locks everything in place. A common feature shared by all of the components is that they are joined with through-tenons, which maximizes the glue surface in the thin parts. Most are straight-forward single tenons, but the case supports are attached to the front and rear rails with double tenons. These horizontal tenons offer more long-grain glue surface than a single tall tenon would, and it's worth the extra effort to cut them. Shown on the following pages is a technique I use that does away with a lot of measuring on what can be a fussy joint to lay out. The key is using spacers to help ensure that the mortises and tenons align right off of the machine.

MORTISE-AND-TENON BASE MAKES A STURDY FOUNDATION

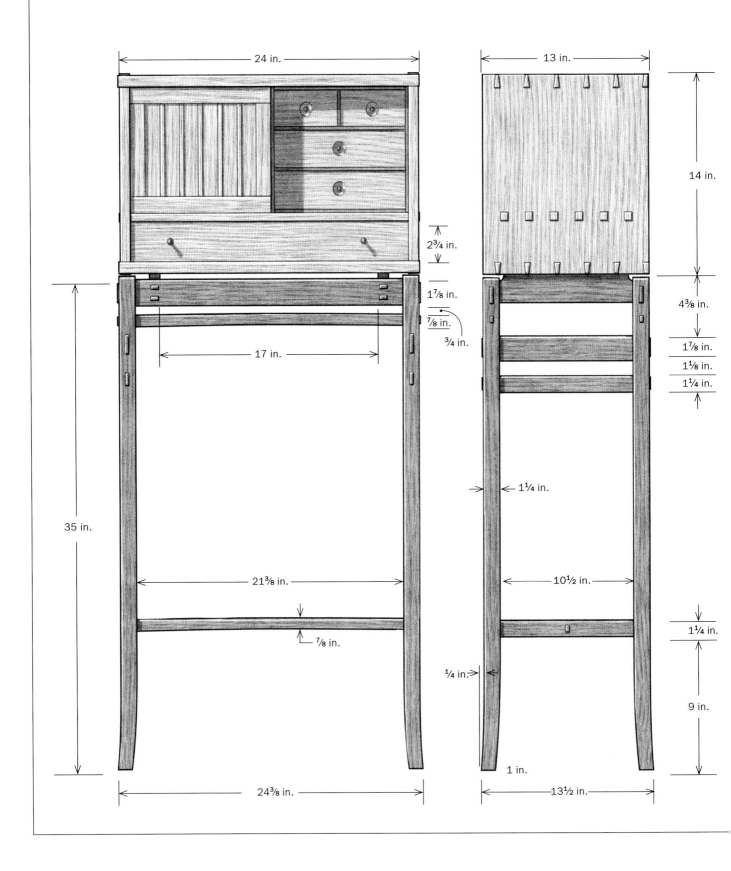

24 in.

13 in.

14 in.

2¾ in.

1⅞ in.

⅞ in.

¾ in.

4⅜ in.

1⅞ in.

1⅛ in.

1¼ in.

17 in.

35 in.

1¼ in.

10½ in.

21⅜ in.

1¼ in.

⅞ in.

¼ in.

9 in.

1 in.

24⅜ in.

13½ in.

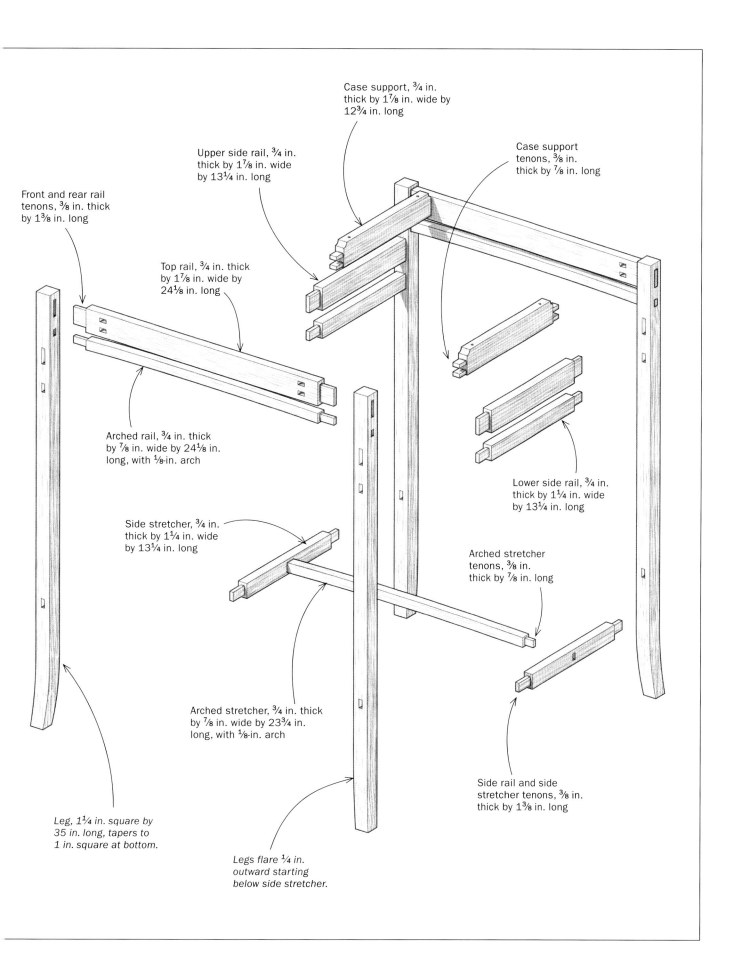

Case support, ¾ in. thick by 1⅞ in. wide by 12¾ in. long

Upper side rail, ¾ in. thick by 1⅞ in. wide by 13¼ in. long

Case support tenons, ⅜ in. thick by ⅞ in. long

Front and rear rail tenons, ⅜ in. thick by 1⅜ in. long

Top rail, ¾ in. thick by 1⅞ in. wide by 24⅛ in. long

Arched rail, ¾ in. thick by ⅞ in. wide by 24⅛ in. long, with ⅛-in. arch

Lower side rail, ¾ in. thick by 1¼ in. wide by 13¼ in. long

Side stretcher, ¾ in. thick by 1¼ in. wide by 13¼ in. long

Arched stretcher tenons, ⅜ in. thick by ⅞ in. long

Arched stretcher, ¾ in. thick by ⅞ in. wide by 23¾ in. long, with ⅛-in. arch

Side rail and side stretcher tenons, ⅜ in. thick by 1⅜ in. long

Leg, 1¼ in. square by 35 in. long, tapers to 1 in. square at bottom.

Legs flare ¼ in. outward starting below side stretcher.

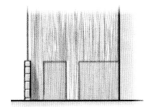

DOUBLE TENONS: A PAIR OF SPACERS HANDLE ALL OF THE CUTS

Sizing a double tenon can be tricky. Not only do the tenons need to fit the mortises, but they also must be spaced the same distance apart as the mortises. For multiple tenons on case joinery, I find it best to start with careful layout and then drill and chop (see p. 80). But for double tenons on the ends of rails, I skip the layout and use a pair of spacer blocks instead. One spacer determines the width of the tenon (see p. 100 for how to make it), and a second spacer determines the distance between the tenons (left).

Start by cutting the mortises. This technique works best when using a mortiser or a router, where the chisel or bit creates mortises of consistent widths. Set the fence to cut the outer mortise (**1**), and then insert the gap spacer between the workpiece and the fence to cut the second mortise (**2**).

To cut the tenons, set a stop on a crosscut sled to cut the outside face of the outer tenon (**3**). Then slip in the tenon spacer to cut the second cheek (**4**). Now replace the tenon spacer with the gap spacer to cut the next cheek (**5**). Finally, combine the tenon spacer and gap spacer to make the final cut (**6**).

Saw and chop out the waste between the tenons and you should have a joint that's close to fitting right off of the saw.

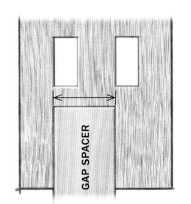

SIZING THE GAP SPACER
The width of the gap spacer equals the mortise/tenon width plus the desired distance between the mortises/tenons.

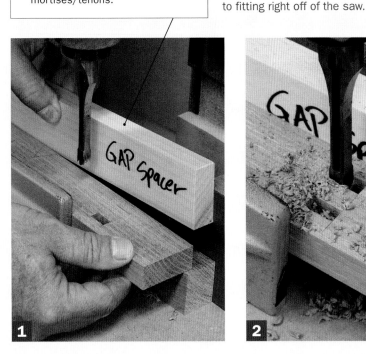

1

2

see p. 80 ... see p. 100 ... see p. 100

CUTTING SEQUENCE

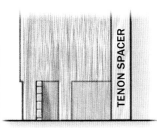

FIRST CHEEK
Set the fence to cut the farthest cheek and make a cut without a spacer.

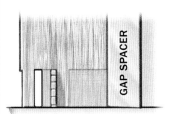

SECOND CHEEK
Add the tenon spacer (see p. 100) to cut the second cheek of the first tenon.

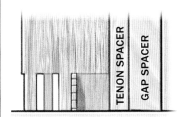

THIRD CHEEK
Replace the tenon spacer with the gap spacer to cut the first cheek of the second tenon.

FOURTH CHEEK
Combine both spacers to cut the final cheek of the second tenon.

CHAPTER 4

DOVETAILS

The dovetail has an odd place in woodworkers' hearts. We view it as a symbol of handcrafted work, yet, maybe because we also see it as a test of our mastery of the craft, we tend to dread cutting dovetails just a bit. First and foremost, the dovetail is a really useful joint and one of the most effective ways to join boards to form a corner. It provides a good deal of glue surface and a lot of mechanical strength as well. That's the primary reason we've been using dovetails since the Egyptians started cutting them 4,000 years ago. The biggest difference between the way they've been used historically and the way we think of them today is that in the past, dovetails were most often hidden from view. Today, we typically want to show them off, and that's where we begin to focus not just on how well they work but also on how good they look. I think that's where the stress begins to creep in, and the pressure to make them "perfect." You may be tempted to skip dovetails altogether, but doing so would limit the things that you can make. One of the biggest challenges is that cutting a dovetail is not a singular skill in and of itself. Instead, it requires a number of distinct skills, none of which are particularly hard to master. The real challenge is knowing how to link those tasks into a routine that will get you from start to finish with the least stress and the best results.

Another challenge with cutting dovetails, short of pulling out a router jig, is that the best way to go about them is by hand. Most of us learn that way—laying out, sawing, chopping, scribing, sawing, and chopping some more, followed by some careful paring for that "perfect" fit. I covered this process in my first book, but this time around I also want to talk about ways that I speed the process both when working in my own shop and when I'm teaching. In addition, I'll cover some common dovetail variations, particularly the ones I find useful when building. Finally, I want to talk about making a dovetailed drawer. It's a common component in furniture, but at its heart it's an odd beast, and it's important to have a strategy when making and fitting one.

DOVETAIL VARIATIONS

The dovetail joint appears in many forms and adds strength to a piece in a number of ways. Understanding how these variations work and where to use them will provide powerful solutions to your building challenges.

SIZING

Dovetails come in many shapes and sizes. Here are just a couple of considerations that I keep in mind while making them.

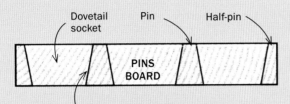

Dovetail socket · Pin · Half-pin

PINS BOARD

The important glue surfaces are the side walls of the pins and tails, so the greater the number of pins, the stronger the joint will be.

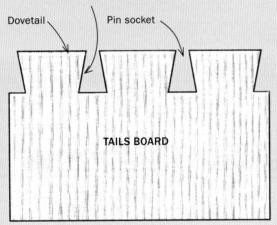

Dovetail · Pin socket

TAILS BOARD

The dovetail angle is typically described as a ratio. A 1:6 ratio is often recommended for softwoods, with a 1:8 angle used for hardwoods. However, I use a 1:8 dovetail for just about everything.

Typical joints combine wide dovetails with narrower pins, a layout that has become associated with hand-cut dovetails. Evenly spaced pins and tails have a machine-made look.

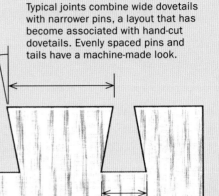

It's a good idea to size the pin sockets slightly wider than your chisel. For small work I'll aim for ¼ in., and on larger work ⅜ in.

The lap on half-blind dovetails can range from ⅛ in. wide on small parts to ¼ in. wide on larger parts. While wide laps can look clunky, a lap that's too thin can be fragile and break when chopping the dovetail sockets.

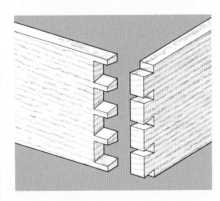

THROUGH-DOVETAIL

Visible on both faces, this joint was traditionally hidden at the back of a drawer or under molding on a case side. Today it's common to show them off.

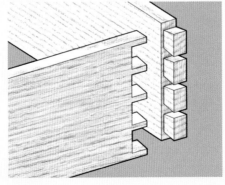

RABBETED SHOULDER

Adding a rabbet to the tails board creates a shoulder on the inside face that makes it easier to align parts when scribing (see p. 138).

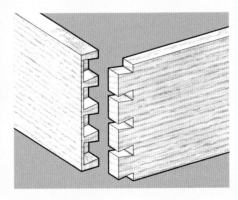

HALF-BLIND

With tails visible on only one face, this joint has become commonplace on drawers and case sides where you don't want the joinery to be seen.

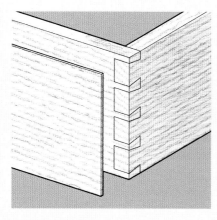

FAUX HALF-BLIND

Easier than a traditional half-blind dovetail. The through-dovetail is quick to cut, but the face veneer can be a little fussy to glue and trim.

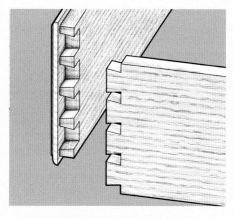

LIPPED HALF-BLIND

Seen on traditional high-style furniture, the rabbeted and molded lip conceals the gaps around the drawer and provides a built-in depth stop.

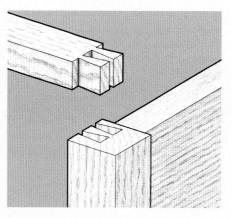

HALF-BLIND LEG JOINT

Though concealed by the tabletop, this joint is still worth adding to a table with drawers. The dovetails help keep the joint from failing when the legs get bumped.

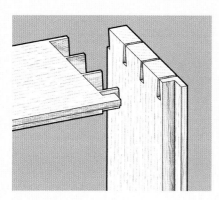

BUILT-IN RABBET

Useful on cases with an inset back or back boards. It's not much more work than a simple dovetail but allows you to rabbet the case parts before assembly.

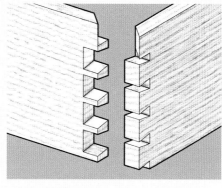

DOVETAIL WITH A MITER

This joint creates a mitered edge, which is a clean look for casework. It also allows you to cut a profile along the edge on parts like bracket bases.

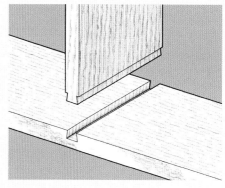

SLIDING DOVETAIL

Adds mechanical strength to a joint that a simple dado doesn't. It's a good joint for connecting horizontal and vertical drawer dividers on casework.

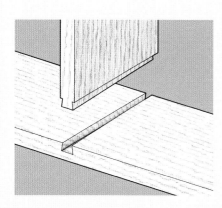

TAPERED SLIDING DOVETAIL

More difficult to cut, but a very good joint on casework with wide parts. The tapered dovetail starts loose and only tightens as the joint is seated.

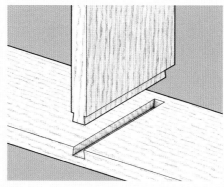

STOPPED SLIDING DOVETAIL

A stopped slot and key provide a clean look on a case front where you want the strength of a sliding dovetail but not the look.

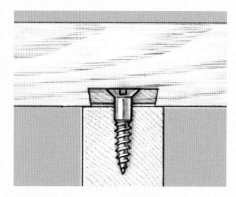

ADJUSTABLE SLIDING DOVETAIL

A good joint for attaching molding to a case or a tabletop to a base (see p. 156). A floating key can be adjusted by tightening or loosening screws along its length.

ONE GOOD METHOD FOR CUTTING DOVETAILS

I've been cutting dovetails for a long time, and over the years my methods have continued to change and evolve. When I came to *Fine Woodworking* magazine over 20 years ago, I knew how to cut dovetails. Or I thought I did. What I really knew was just one way to cut them. After working on my first article where the author used a different technique, a light went on. I realized then that not only did I know only one way to go about cutting dovetails, but there were probably a lot of other ways to go about it as well. Over the course of my tenure at the magazine, I've tried out many methods as I've continued to refine my technique, but the next big leap in my evolution was when I began to teach others to cut dovetails. As I worked with students and saw where they were struggling the most, I rethought my process and tried to come up with solutions to address their challenges. As commonly happens whenever I come up with a process to make it easier for students, I realized that it was a better way for me to work as well.

While I expect that my approach will continue to change and evolve over time, I want to a show you a method that works well for me now, and one that students have used with good success. Like anything in woodworking, there are many ways to approach a task and I don't mean to imply that this is the only method that will work for you, but I am confident that it's a good place to begin.

START WITH THE TAILS

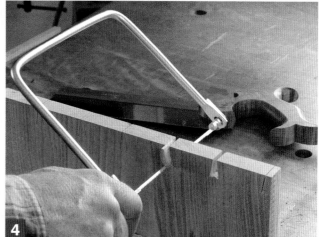

Though I typically turn to the tablesaw to cut the tails (see the following pages), I spent many years cutting them by hand, and that's where I'd like to start. Even if you end up at the tablesaw, I think you'll benefit from trying them by hand first.

The first step is to lay out the dovetail spacing (**1**). I like to use an expanding divider, which is easy to find online. Next, lay out the walls of the sockets (**2**). Two common angle ratios are 1:6 and 1:8, the steeper angle recommended for compressive softwoods and the shallower angle for hardwoods. I tend to go with a 1:8 angle for everything. When sawing, a lot of attention is given to hitting the angled line as you go, but more important is to start square to the face; this will have a much bigger effect on the ease of fitting the joint later (**3**). From there, it's a matter of removing the waste without cutting past the baseline. I like to give myself a head start by coping out most of the material (**4**), and then chopping to the baseline (**5**).

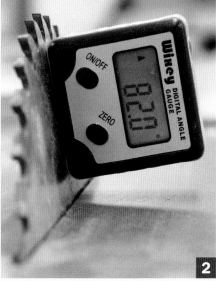

This technique requires a blade that is ground to the same angle as the tails you want to cut. At the time of publishing, you can buy a blade pre-ground for dovetails from Forrest Saw Blades or Ridge Carbide Tool Co. You can also have any flat-top blade ground by your local sawblade sharpener.

Cutting tails at the tablesaw is fast, but the real time savings comes in layout, where all you need to do is mark the center of each pin. You can also stack the parts and cut them both at once. The key is a specially ground blade that has all of the teeth sharpened at the same angle. This allows you to tilt the blade to that angle (anywhere from 8° to 14° is typical) and cut right into the corner of the pin socket (**1**). I use a digital angle gauge when tilting the blade (**2**). To set the height of the blade, first scribe the shoulder line on a piece of scrap (**3**). Then, starting with the blade lower than the shoulder, take successive cuts, raising the blade until you just hit the scribe line (**4**). From there the process goes quickly. For layout, all you need is a mark at the center of each pin socket. When making the cuts, align the pencil marks with the kerf in the sled (**5**). This will create one of the pin-socket walls. To finish the socket, rotate the board and align the kerf in the workpiece with the kerf in the sled (**6**). Depending on the height of the tails, there may be a triangle of waste to chisel out (**7**).

5

6

7

SCRIBE AND SAW BY HAND

ADD A RABBET OR FAKE IT

A great technique for keeping parts aligned when scribing that I learned from Steve Latta is to cut a shallow rabbet in the tails board (left). The downside is that the rabbet changes the dimensions of the parts and you need to account for that when scribing the baseline on the pins board. I found that I can get the same benefit of a rabbet by clamping a board along the scribe line (3). A fence on one end keeps the parts aligned from side to side as well.

Even with the aid of a tablesaw, and possibly a router later, I still consider this to be a hand-cut dovetail because the most important part of the process, scribing and sawing the pins, is handled with hand tools. This is not meant to add a challenge to the process, but it's simply the most efficient and accurate way that I know how to do it. Because it's a hand process, accurate layout is the key to good dovetails. A scribe line that you can't see well isn't very useful, so begin by applying masking tape to the end grain (**1**). I use a simple block with a fence glued on to set the height of the board in the vise (**2**). Then, to help register the parts when scribing, I use a shoulder guide, which consists of a grooved piece of pine glued to a piece of MDF. Align the guide with the scribe line and hold it in place with a spring clamp (**3**). Use the block to support the far end of the tails board when scribing (**4**). Peel away the tape for a clear guide to sawing (**5**). Pencil vertical lines from the tape to the baseline (**6**) to act as a guide when sawing (**7**). Finally, cope away most of the waste (**8**). (You're welcome to chop it all out, but your first project in white oak may have you looking for an alternative.) From here, you can chisel to the baseline or pull out your router; turn the page to find out how that works.

ROUT AWAY THE WASTE

The task I dreaded most when first learning to cut dovetails was chopping out the waste between the pins. Today, I skip the chisels and use a trim router equipped with a bearing-guided pattern bit instead. To support the stock vertically and provide a flat support for the router, I made a simple dovetailing stand (see p. 142). To use it, clamp an alignment board to the top of the stand (**1**) and register the workpiece against it while clamping it in place. I added a lip to the alignment board to recess the stock slightly below the surface to prevent the tape on the end grain from contacting the router base and peeling up (**2**). I also replaced the router's baseplate with a larger base, which allows me to put pressure over the stand when routing (**3**). Set the bit depth to split your scribe line (**4**) and rout away. The bearing rides along the pin wall and prevents the bit from cutting into it inadvertently.

TAKE YOUR TIME WITH THE FINAL FIT

Head back to the workbench to dial in the fit of the joint. The first step is to check that the pin walls are vertical (**1**) and pare any tapered walls as necessary (**2**). If the walls are angled out, they can cause the boards to split when fitting. Next, work on getting the joint to fit along its entire length. The tape can act as a guide when paring. If you did a good job with layout, you should be able to pare to the tape and end up with a good fit. If you get the joint to fit but it still doesn't seat fully, use a pencil to help determine where you still need to pare the waste. Rub some lead along the inside bottom edge of the pin sockets (**3**). Tap the tails board lightly in place and then remove it. Any graphite marks transferred to the pin walls indicate where the joint is still too snug (**4**). Take your time paring away those areas. At this point, it will take only a little work to get the joint to seat fully (**5**) (it's easy to go too far and create gaps in the joint).

A SIMPLE WORKSTATION FOR DOVETAILS

One technique I've adopted to speed the dovetailing process and save some wear on my chisels is to rout out the waste between the pins instead of chopping. To help with that, I made a simple stand to support the work vertically and provide a flat horizontal surface for the router to rest on. While this use alone makes it worth building, the stand can handle a number of other dovetailing jobs as well. In fact, if you don't own a bench with a vise, this stand can assist you throughout the entire process. If you have a sturdy worktable and a couple of clamps, you can cut dovetails.

This router stand is a smaller version of a design I've been using for years. When I began traveling frequently to teach, the original stand proved too heavy and bulky to bring along. So I set about making a smaller, lighter version. It performs the basic routing tasks just as well as the larger version, but its small size and lighter weight make it easy to reposition on the bench, and that in turn makes it easy to perform a number of additional tasks. If you flip the stand on its back, the stock can be secured parallel to the benchtop, which allows it to serve as a workstation not just for routing but also for scribing, sawing, and chopping.

Made from home-center materials, and requiring only a couple of rabbets and dadoes, the stand goes together quickly. The joinery is there to help keep the parts aligned during assembly, and you can skip it altogether if you wish. I used MDF for most of the stand because it is flat and stable, but I went with pine for some parts because of its nail- and screw-holding ability. You'll also need some toggle clamps and T-nuts, which secure the bars the clamps are attached to.

This stand can handle parts up to 6 in. wide between the clamp bars, and you can accommodate up to 10-in.-wide boards by removing one or both bars and using regular clamps to secure the work instead. If you regularly work with wider stock, you may want to size yours a little larger.

NO WORKBENCH? NO PROBLEM

While there's no sub-stitute for a stout workbench with a vise or two, if that's still something on your wish list, this stand can help out with other dove-tailing chores. Clamped to a sturdy surface, the stand can support stock vertically for sawing as well as routing. Laid flat on the tabletop, it can hold work for chopping tasks.

WORK STAND FOR DOVETAILS

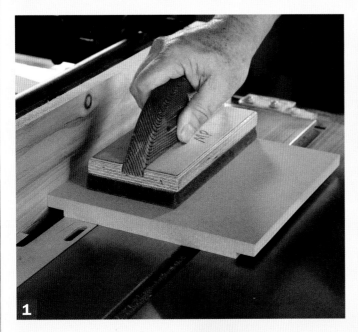

The stand goes together quickly without a big price tag. The only real joinery is the grooves and rabbets on the inside faces of the front and back (**1**). These serve to register the parts and make gluing up a little easier and more accurate (**2**). There is also a groove on the outer face of the front that accepts a cleat on the inside face of a spacer that I use to hold thinner stock. The clamping bars are made of hardwood for better holding power for the screws that secure the clamps. They bolt to the front through threaded inserts inset into the inner face to keep the bars from lifting when clamping pressure is applied (**3**). The top is attached with screws alone, so that it can be replaced later if necessary.

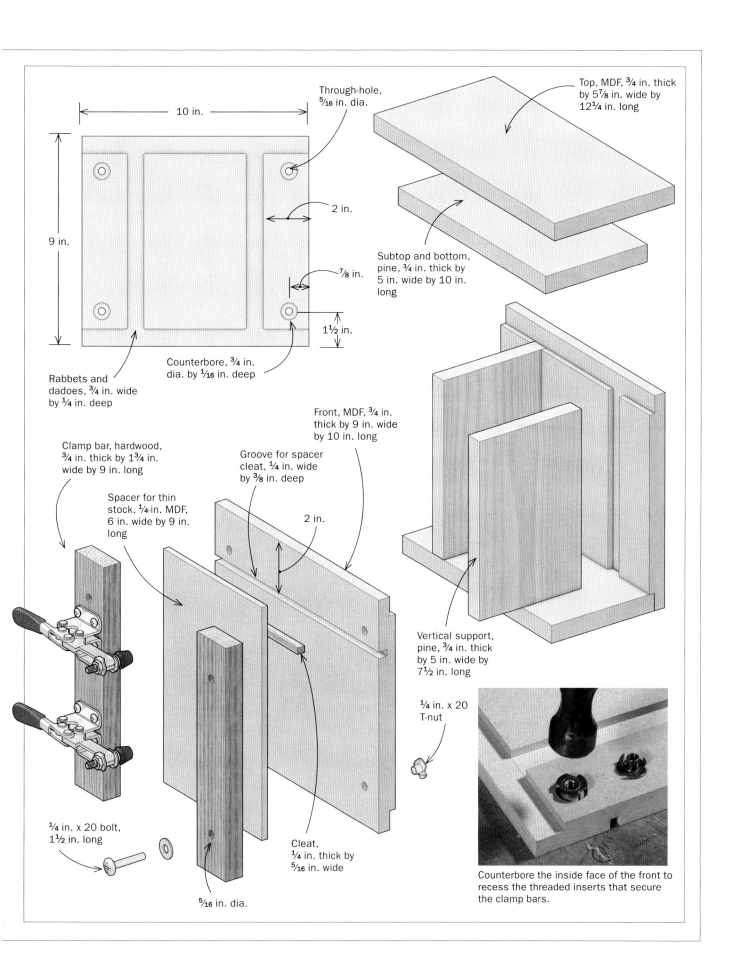

Through-hole, ⁵⁄₁₆ in. dia.

10 in.

2 in.

9 in.

⁷⁄₈ in.

1½ in.

Counterbore, ¾ in. dia. by ¹⁄₁₆ in. deep

Rabbets and dadoes, ¾ in. wide by ¼ in. deep

Top, MDF, ¾ in. thick by 5⁷⁄₈ in. wide by 12¼ in. long

Subtop and bottom, pine, ¾ in. thick by 5 in. wide by 10 in. long

Front, MDF, ¾ in. thick by 9 in. wide by 10 in. long

Clamp bar, hardwood, ¾ in. thick by 1¾ in. wide by 9 in. long

Groove for spacer cleat, ¼ in. wide by ³⁄₈ in. deep

Spacer for thin stock, ¼-in. MDF, 6 in. wide by 9 in. long

2 in.

Vertical support, pine, ¾ in. thick by 5 in. wide by 7½ in. long

¼ in. x 20 T-nut

¼ in. x 20 bolt, 1½ in. long

⁵⁄₁₆ in. dia.

Cleat, ¼ in. thick by ⁵⁄₁₆ in. wide

Counterbore the inside face of the front to recess the threaded inserts that secure the clamp bars.

HALF-BLIND DOVETAILS

Even after cutting them for years, it seems that the first joint is slow and tentative and I begin to wonder just how long it's going to take to get through them all.

A half-blind dovetail, by its nature, is designed not to be seen. Though I confess that, like every other woodworker, the first thing I do when inspecting a piece of furniture is to pull open a drawer and check for dovetails. Not only is it an indicator of the skill, quality, and care with which a machine or woodworker made it, a nicely proportioned and well-executed joint is also a beautiful thing. Half-blind dovetails are a little more time-consuming to make, but not that much more difficult than through-dovetails. The main difference lies in creating the pins. Rather than sawing through the stock, you can saw only a triangle of the side walls before running into the scribe lines. And while you can use a router to do away with most of the waste, the flush-trim bit won't work here. Instead, a straight bit is needed, which introduces the risk of accidentally cutting into the pins when routing. Even after the routing is complete, there's still some chisel work left to do. For that reason, routing isn't much more efficient than drilling and chopping, so I want to show you that method as well. If I have a lot of drawers to do, I tend to break out the router; for just one or two, I typically head to the drill press instead. Even after cutting them for years, it seems that the first joint is slow and tentative and I begin to wonder just how long it's going to take to get through them all, only to find that the process speeds up once I regain my sea legs and begin to get more confident and purposeful with my actions.

SCRIBE AND SAW THE PINS

Scribing the drawer front is fairly straightforward. When aligning the tails board for scribing, the end of the tails should hit the scribe line on the end of the drawer front (1). I typically apply tape only inside of the scribe line since I won't be sawing any farther than that (2). Continue vertical lines down from the pins (3) and pull out your dovetail saw. This is the trickiest step because you need to saw adjacent to the tape and hit the vertical line in the face while making sure that you don't inadvertently saw past your scribe lines (4). The method I use is to start with the saw almost level and establish a kerf along the tape, stopping the cut at the scribe line. From there, I drop the handle to continue the cut down the face. By establishing the cut along the end grain first, I don't have to keep an eye on both faces at once. The saw will take care of just half of the pin wall, leaving the remainder for the chisel to handle (right).

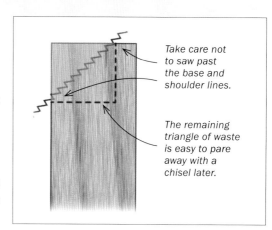

Take care not to saw past the base and shoulder lines.

The remaining triangle of waste is easy to pare away with a chisel later.

TWO WAYS TO REMOVE THE WASTE

DRILLING AND CHOPPING IS NOT A BAD WAY TO GO

The aim of drilling first isn't to remove the waste as much as it is to try and sever as much of the end-grain fibers as you can. This way the majority of the waste pops out with a single strike of a mallet (**1**). From there, chisel down to the baseline (**2**) and pare back to the shoulder. To clear the end grain in the corners, I use a pair of skew chisels (**3**) or a fishtail chisel (facing page). Finally, pare the walls to complete the task the dovetail saw started (**4**). Pay special attention when cleaning out the corners. If the joint doesn't fully seat (**5**), that's usually where the problem lies.

ROUTING WORKS AS WELL

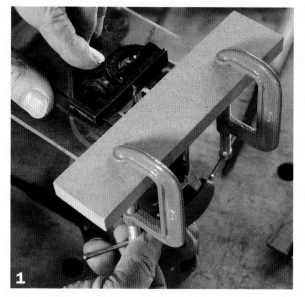

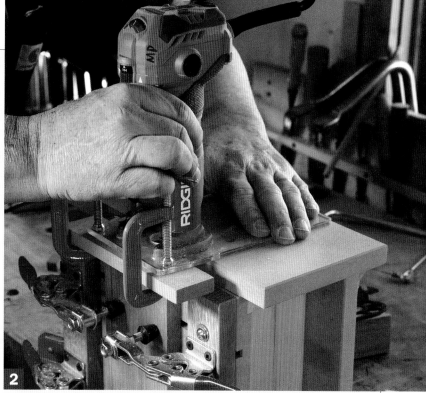

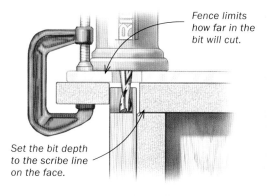

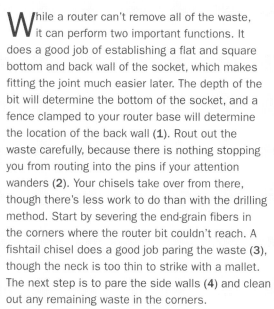

Fence limits how far in the bit will cut.

Set the bit depth to the scribe line on the face.

While a router can't remove all of the waste, it can perform two important functions. It does a good job of establishing a flat and square bottom and back wall of the socket, which makes fitting the joint much easier later. The depth of the bit will determine the bottom of the socket, and a fence clamped to your router base will determine the location of the back wall (**1**). Rout out the waste carefully, because there is nothing stopping you from routing into the pins if your attention wanders (**2**). Your chisels take over from there, though there's less work to do than with the drilling method. Start by severing the end-grain fibers in the corners where the router bit couldn't reach. A fishtail chisel does a good job paring the waste (**3**), though the neck is too thin to strike with a mallet. The next step is to pare the side walls (**4**) and clean out any remaining waste in the corners.

AN EASIER HALF-BLIND DOVETAIL

Another way to achieve the effect of a half-blind dovetail with a little less work is to cut a normal through-dovetail on the drawer front and add a veneer to the face after the drawer is glued up. In theory this is simple, but it's also a bit of a pain, and while the dovetailing is faster, I don't seem to save any time overall. One advantage is that you can stretch a nicely figured piece of wood across multiple drawer fronts for continuous grain (**1**). To keep the veneer from sliding out of position during glue-up, drive in some pins and clip them just proud of the surface (**2 & 3**). Use a caul to apply even pressure across the drawer face (**4**) and trim it flush once the glue dries (**5**).

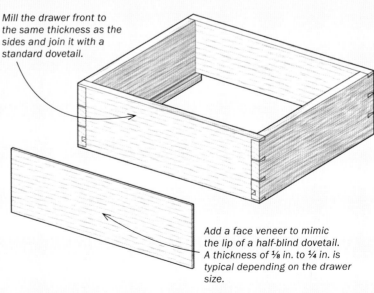

Mill the drawer front to the same thickness as the sides and join it with a standard dovetail.

Add a face veneer to mimic the lip of a half-blind dovetail. A thickness of ⅛ in. to ¼ in. is typical depending on the drawer size.

A DOVETAILED DRAWER

This is where the understanding of specific techniques runs head-on into the notion of developing a coherent strategy to put them to use for best effect.

We've covered through- and half-blind dovetails separately, but now I want to show how to use them in tandem to make a drawer. In addition, we need to address the sizing of the parts and the order in which you go about making the drawer. In short, this is where the understanding of specific techniques runs head-on into the notion of developing a coherent strategy to put them to use for best effect. So while on one level this section is about making a drawer, it really speaks to the heart of what this book is about. We can talk about the big picture as much as we want, but putting the ideas into action is where the true understanding begins.

The half-blind dovetail at the front gets all of the attention but it's straightforward enough. It's the through-dovetails at the back of the drawer that are unique here and warrant a closer look. The process begins with sizing the parts, which takes us back to the "Building Strategies" chapter and the concept of working from the outside in. To make a dovetailed drawer, step one is to build a case. The opening will determine the width and length of the drawer front, and that in turn will begin to determine the size of the remaining parts. After that, with a good working plan in hand, the path is easily navigated.

ONE MARKING GAUGE SETTING FOR ALL OF THE PARTS

Sizing the parts and scribing the shoulder lines set the foundation for the work to follow. Begin by fitting the drawer front to the case. It should be snug side to side, just fitting into the case (**1**). Vertically, there should be enough of a gap to accommodate seasonal movement in the future. Rip the sides and back to the same width and crosscut the back to the same length (**2**). The length of the sides is determined by the overall depth of the drawer minus the thickness of the lap at the drawer front. Set a marking gauge to the thickness of the sides (**3**) and scribe shoulder lines on the sides and back (**4**). Scribe a shoulder line just on the inside face of the front (**5**) and finish up by scribing for the end of the tails on the end grain of the drawer front (**6**).

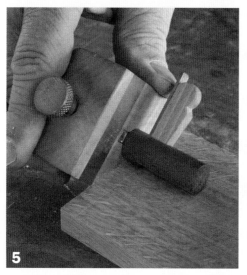

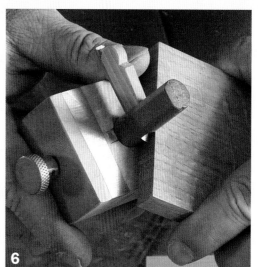

MAKE WAY FOR THE BOTTOM

A key feature in a traditional dovetailed drawer is a bottom that slides in place from the rear. This has the advantage of allowing for seasonal movement; it also makes construction easier because you can install the drawer bottom after assembly. The key is a drawer back that is cut short to align with the top of the grooves in the drawer sides, and this affects the dovetail pattern on the sides. You need to skip the half-pin socket at the bottom corner of the drawer side. As a reminder, I mark an "X" on the drawer side (**1**). The half-blind dovetails are straightforward (**2**), but the dovetails at the back will look a little odd due to the lack of a half-pin at the bottom corner (**3**). After the parts are dovetailed, cut a groove in the sides and front for the drawer bottom (**4**). Dry-fit the back and make a mark at the top of the groove (**5**), and then trim the back to width. Mill the bottom thicker than the groove and bevel the bottom to fit with a block plane (**6**).

AN ADJUSTABLE SLIDING DOVETAIL

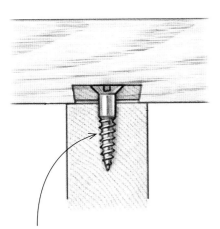

Tighten or loosen the screw to adjust the fit of the key in the slot.

Sliding dovetails can be an effective way to hold parts, but getting the fit right can be a challenge. Shorter dovetails on something like a drawer stretcher are fine, but longer joints like those for shelves or tabletops can seize up as you're trying to assemble the parts. If you loosen the fit to let the part slide more easily, you reduce its holding power. A traditional solution for this problem is to use a tapered sliding dovetail. This creates a joint that is loose at first, allowing you to slide it easily, but that tightens up as you drive it home. It is a wonderful joint but it can be cumbersome to execute. I found that an easier solution is to use a floating dovetail key that is screwed in place. I learned this technique from Christian Becksvoort, who uses it to attach moldings to a case side. I found that it not only works for moldings, but for tabletops as well. The idea is to make the key a little thinner than the socket, which lets you adjust the tightness of the fit by loosening or tightening the screws as you go. With this method, I can assemble parts without a problem and still end up with an assembly that holds tight.

ONE BIT FOR THE SLOT AND KEY

I use a two-sided edge guide when routing the dovetail slots because I typically need to rout in from two directions. The extra fence keeps the router from possibly wandering away from the fence (**1 & 2**). The next step is to make the key. Start with stock that is wide enough to handle safely at the router table and, using the same bit that you used for the slot, rout the tapered walls (**3**). Check for a snug fit in the slot (**4**), then rip off the keys from the block (**5**). The key should be thinner than the depth of the slot and slightly recessed from the bottom. You can plane the bottom of the key to fine-tune the fit. To install the top, insert the keys into one half of the top and clamp it in place while screwing the keys in place to keep them aligned with the slots (facing page). On this particular table, a spline connects the halves and they can be locked in place by driving pins into the spline (**6**). Plans for the table can be found in *The Why & How of Woodworking*.

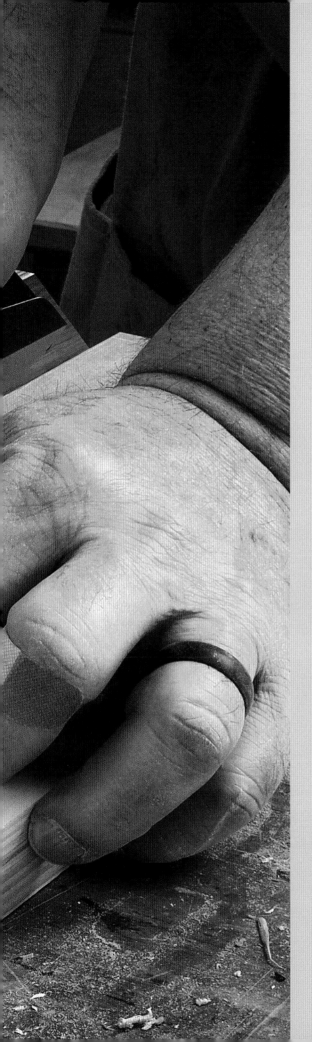

CHAPTER 5

MITERS

A miter is a funny thing. Basically a butt joint on the bias, it's a joint that is simple in concept but sometimes tricky to execute. It's a versatile option for joining parts at a right angle (or any other angle for that matter). You can join parts flat, as when making a picture frame, or vertically when making boxes or dividers. Each orientation requires its own approach to cutting and fine-tuning the fit. The end grain of a 45° miter is halfway between a butt joint and an edge joint, so its glue strength falls somewhere in between as well. A perfectly fitted miter can be strong, but any slight gap will cause it to fail. For that reason, there are some occasions—frames and larger boxes mainly—where I like to reinforce the joint, usually with cross-grain splines. These add a good deal of strength as well as some visual interest to the joint.

There are some benefits to using miters. The first is that you can create continuous grain from piece to piece with an almost invisible glueline separating them. This is really nice for the sides of boxes and adds to the harmony of the piece. It is also a nice effect on picture frames. Though the grain on the face of each part is meeting at a right angle, it still connects the parts visually and creates a nice border around a mirror, photo, or work of art.

The second benefit is that grooves and profiles can be cut prior to cutting the parts to length, because the mitered corner will conceal any joinery. This makes picture frames and mitered moldings on furniture much easier to handle. I also take advantage of this benefit when making boxes, where I can cut the grooves and rabbets, as well as sand and pre-finish the inside faces, before cutting the miters.

PICTURE-PERFECT MITERS

I only make frames on occasion and don't have room for another sled, so I get by with a simple mitering template.

Making a dedicated sled for picture frames is not a bad idea, especially if you plan on gearing up to make a lot. However, since I only make frames on occasion and don't have room for another sled, I get by with a simple mitering template that I can attach to my sled when I need it. The template itself can be nothing more than a triangle of plywood or MDF. The only critical aspect is that the leading corner must be exactly 90°. This may sound a little intimidating, but I usually have pretty good luck using the factory edges of a piece of plywood. It might be a little dinged up, but if it measures square, it's easy to clean up later. This is one example of how the frequency in which you perform a task will often determine how you go about handling it. While the technique I use to make a frame is pretty simple, the sled I use to miter boxes is more involved and speaks to how many more boxes I make than frames.

A SIMPLE FRAME

While frame profiles can get impressively elaborate (just stop by any framing shop), I get by with a simple Arts and Crafts-inspired frame. The wide, flat face highlights the ray fleck of quartersawn oak, and a shallow rabbet creates a nice shadowline and mimics the stepped look of the mat surrounding the image. Tilting the blade a few degrees when cutting the rabbet creates a subtly angled face.

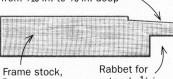

Rabbet, ⁷/₈ in. wide, tapers from ¹/₁₆ in. to ¹/₈ in. deep

Frame stock, ⁷/₈ in. thick by 3 in. wide

Rabbet for artwork, ½ in. wide by ½ in. deep

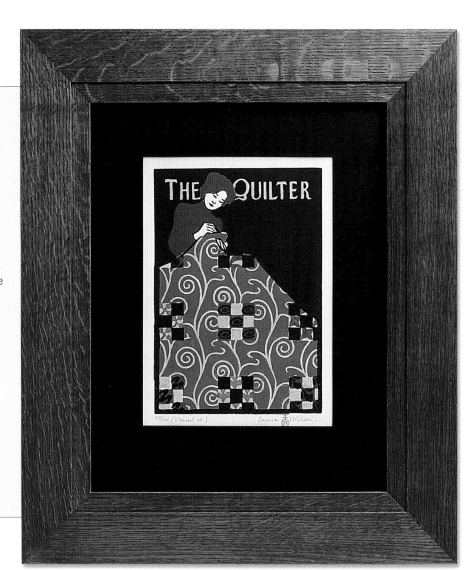

A MITER TEMPLATE FOR FRAMES

When making a picture frame, or mitered molding, I add a triangular template to my sled. To create the template, begin by making a square. I'll start by checking the factory edges of the MDF or plywood. if I have a square corner (**1**), I'll reference that when cutting the opposite faces. If I need to create a square corner, I'll strike a line and use an edge guide in tandem with an L-fence to make the cut. To create the triangle, make a diagonal cut corner to corner. First draw out the diagonal, and then saw off most of the waste. Clamp an L-fence to your rip fence just above the blade and flush with the outside edge. Use an edge guide with sandpaper adhered to the bottom and a handle attached to the top. Align the guide with the layout line (**2**) and slide it along the L-fence to make the cut (**3 & 4**). You'll see this technique show up throughout the book to handle a variety of tasks, and it's one of those simple things that I think you'll put to use often.

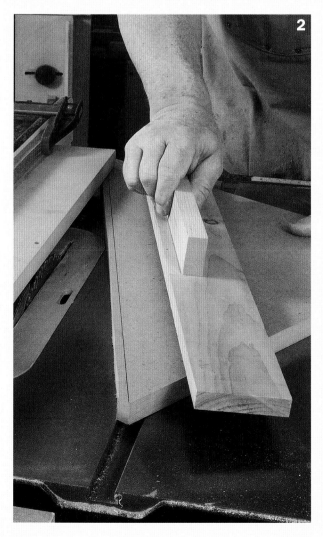

1

ALIGNING THE MITER TEMPLATE

Once you have a template with a square leading corner, the next task is to position it correctly on your sled. Start by placing the template on the sled with its point aligned to the kerf and its base snug against the fence. Trace each side of the template lightly with a sharp pencil (**1**). Then flip the template and check its alignment with the pencil lines. Ideally the template should still line up with the pencil lines. If the angle is off, however (**2**), it's still an easy fix. Add a shim or tape to the low corner of the template. The idea is to reduce the gap by half (**3**). Erase the pencil line and try again. It shouldn't take too many tries to dial in the correct angle. Secure the template in position with double-sided tape (**4**), and then drive in screws if you wish.

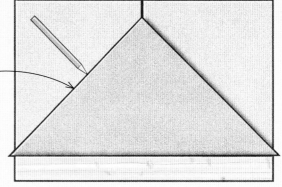

1. Center the template on the sled and trace its outline.

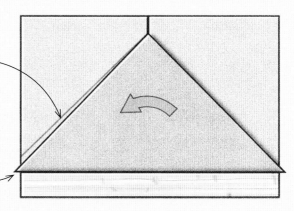

2. Flip the template over and check its alignment to the pencil lines.

3. If the template isn't parallel to the line, shim the low corner and repeat the process.

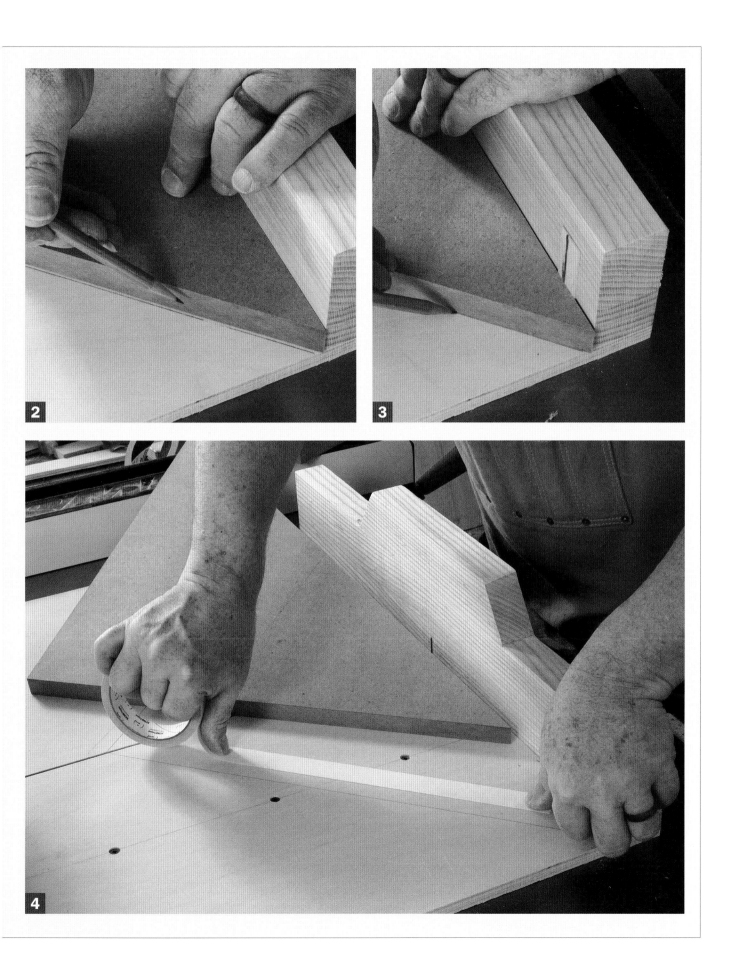

PUTTING THE MITER TEMPLATE TO USE

When using the jig, you'll make the first cut on the left side of the template and the second cut on the right. I avoid end stops by first cutting all of the parts to exact length while keeping the ends square. When sizing a frame, it's not the inside or outside dimensions that matter, but the dimension at the rabbet on the back of the frame (below). While it may not seem particularly precise, I simply align the end of the stock to a pencil mark on the sled. To locate the mark, align the corner of the stock with the sawkerf and strike a line along the end (**1**). Repeat the process with the stock on the second side of the template. To cut the miters, start on the left side for the first cut (**2**), and then move to the right side for the second (**3**). To check your work, pair up the parts and compare their lengths (**4**). Typically a light skim cut at the saw is all it takes to even things up.

DETERMINING THE FRAME SIZE

3. The point where the diagonal lines intersect the outside edge of the frame indicates the length to cut the stock.

1. Measure the object to be framed and mark its dimension along the rabbet.

2. Extend diagonal lines from the marks across the width of the frame.

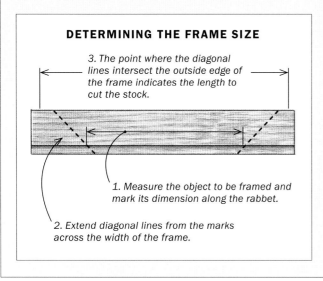

SAVE THE OFFCUTS FOR GLUING UP

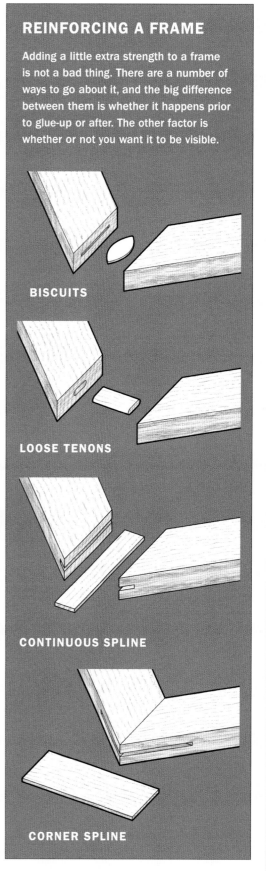

REINFORCING A FRAME

Adding a little extra strength to a frame is not a bad thing. There are a number of ways to go about it, and the big difference between them is whether it happens prior to glue-up or after. The other factor is whether or not you want it to be visible.

BISCUITS

LOOSE TENONS

CONTINUOUS SPLINE

CORNER SPLINE

If you've ever flipped through a woodworking catalog, you're probably aware that there are a lot of ways to go about gluing up a picture frame and a lot of clamping systems on the market to aid you in the task. I have no doubt that at least some of the products work really well, but since I don't glue up frames very often, I haven't had a reason to invest in one. However, I do have a simple, effective method that utilizes your offcuts as clamping cauls. The key when clamping is directing clamping pressure across the joint. By taping the triangular offcuts to the ends of the frame parts, you create the perfect seat for the clamp pads.

A HANDPLANE HANDLES SMALL BOX MITERS

A simple shooting board is the key to mitering small boxes with a handplane. If you keep extra stock on hand, you're never too far away from a quick storage container or a last-minute gift.

My wife, Rachel, needed a box to hold some thread and needles, a thimble, and some bird scissors. She had threatened to use an empty Altoids tin if I wasn't quick about it, which had the proper effect of putting the project at the top of my list. The box, in turn, had to fit inside a larger container. I also thought it would be nice if the box could tuck inside the lid when it was open so that you weren't searching for it when you went to put things away. From a design standpoint, this might sound a little constraining and, though I may complain, I usually find that the more parameters I'm given, the easier it is to come up with an idea. Its intended use dictated both how big and how small the box needed to be. In order to maximize interior space, it needed thin walls as well. Finally, the fact that a perfectly good Altoids tin substitute was looming on the horizon meant that time-consuming joinery was off the list. So miters it was. Mitering small parts on the tablesaw can be tricky and a little stressful, but a handplane could make quick work of them. The key was coming up with a way to hold the stock when mitering. Wide, thin stock needs to be well supported to keep it from flexing, so the best option is to lay it flat and tilt the handplane instead. A shooting board with an angled fence handles the job well and is easy to make.

FIT THE BOX TO THE CONTENTS

While it makes sense that a box should be large enough to hold its intended cargo, I find it important that it's not overly big. Objects rattling around inside a box that's too big seem more like random occupants than intended guests. On the other hand, a deck or two of playing cards that just slip inside a case offer a simple air of luxury (and a quick-to-make, well-received gift).

A SHOOTING BOARD FOR SMALL BOX MITERS

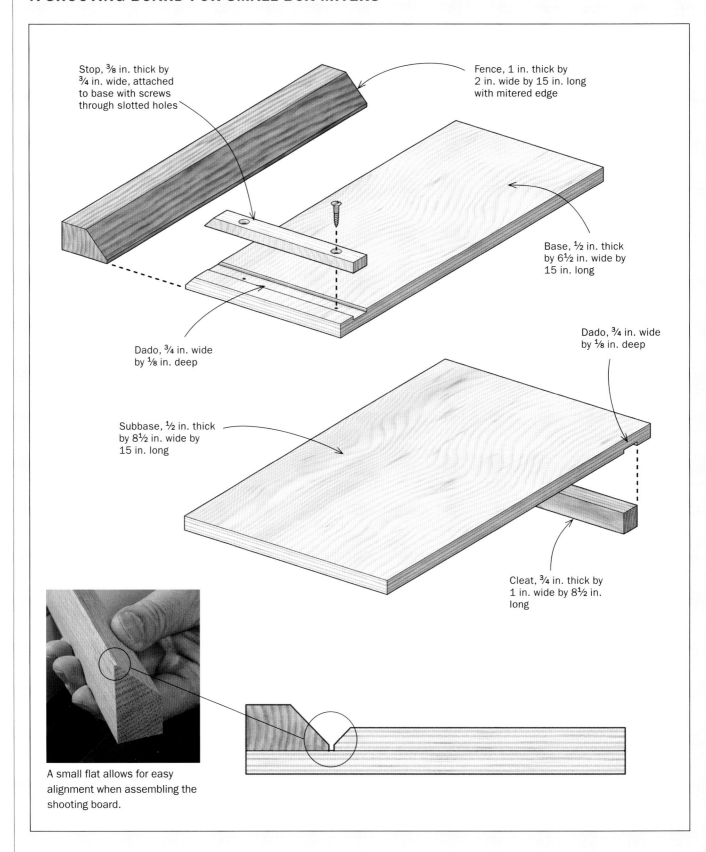

Stop, ³⁄₈ in. thick by ³⁄₄ in. wide, attached to base with screws through slotted holes

Fence, 1 in. thick by 2 in. wide by 15 in. long with mitered edge

Base, ¹⁄₂ in. thick by 6¹⁄₂ in. wide by 15 in. long

Dado, ³⁄₄ in. wide by ¹⁄₈ in. deep

Dado, ³⁄₄ in. wide by ¹⁄₈ in. deep

Subbase, ¹⁄₂ in. thick by 8¹⁄₂ in. wide by 15 in. long

Cleat, ³⁄₄ in. thick by 1 in. wide by 8¹⁄₂ in. long

A small flat allows for easy alignment when assembling the shooting board.

While this is perhaps a complex-looking jig, it's actually really quick to make. It consists of a plywood subbase dadoed for a cleat, on which rests a bed that is outfitted with a mitered edge and a shallow dado for a stop. An angled fence is attached adjacent to the bed. A miter ripped along an edge of the fence allows it to be glued at the appropriate angle (**1**). Rip a miter on the side of the bed as well (**2**). Leave a small flat at the point of the miter on both parts (see facing page). This ensures that the parts are parallel when gluing and nailing them to the subbase (**3**). The fence acts as a zero-clearance support and prevents chipout when planing. It gets worn out over time, so I attach the fence with screws through oversize holes that allow me to adjust it for a fresh cut on occasion (**4**). Finally, glue the cleat to the bottom of the subbase (**5**).

MITERING A SMALL BOX

Cut the sides of the lid and box to final length prior to planing the miters. I make the box sides just over ⅛ in. thick. The top and bottom are thinner at ³⁄₃₂ in., and I cut them oversize and trim them flush once they are glued in place. Start with the lid. When using the shooting board, reference the side of the plane against the angled fence, and then slide the workpiece tight against the sole ahead of the blade and make the cut (**1**). Continue feeding the stock toward the plane rather than tilting the plane toward the workpiece, which will throw off the angle and cut into the sled. Use the remaining flat as a guide when planing (**2**). The aim is to create a complete miter without shortening the workpiece. To glue the lid, first pre-finish the inside faces with shellac and use a straightedge to align the parts while applying a strip of tape to the backs (**3**). Apply glue to the mitered ends (**4**) and roll up the box using the tape as a clamp (**5**). Because the top and bottom are thin, they can be glued directly to the sides (**6**). Once the lid is dry, use it as a guide when sizing the box parts. They should fit snugly but comfortably in the lid (**7**). You may need to sand the box to fit the lid once it's glued, but you shouldn't be too far off.

Top and bottom, ³⁄₃₂ in. thick; cut oversize and trim to fit after gluing.

Sides, ⅛ in. thick

Start by making the lid of the box, then size the body to fit.

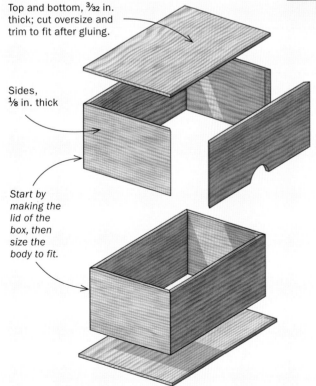

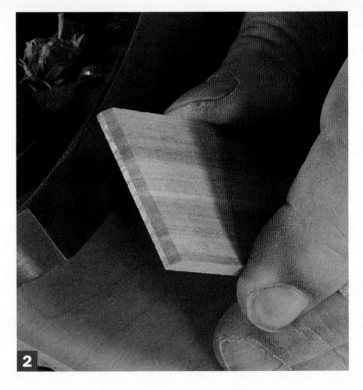

A TABLESAW SLED FOR MITERED BOXES

For anything but the smallest boxes, I turn to the tablesaw to cut the miters. I do it often enough that I've built a dedicated sled for the purpose. In fact, I've rebuilt the sled a number of times, and the current version works well for me. It's not a lot different from a typical crosscut sled, but the differences count. It has a pair of stop blocks that I can set up for each side of the box. This way I can alternate between the stops and end up with a rectangular box that has continuous grain around all four sides. In addition, you can make a small or large square box by using just one stop for all of the sides. So with a single setup, you can make a batch of boxes in three different sizes.

Before we get into it, I want to take a minute and talk about stock. There's a notion that because a box is a small object, it's a good place to use up scraps. While this can be true if you've held onto a nicely figured piece of wood to use as a future box top, it doesn't really hold up in terms of box parts in general. Milling up stock for box sides probably takes more time and lumber than you'd expect. In fact, I'd say that the majority of time spent on making a box is focused on preparing the stock. So with that in mind, I recommend milling extra stock while you're at it. That way if you ever need a last-minute gift, you're ready to go.

A DEDICATED SLED FOR MITERED BOXES

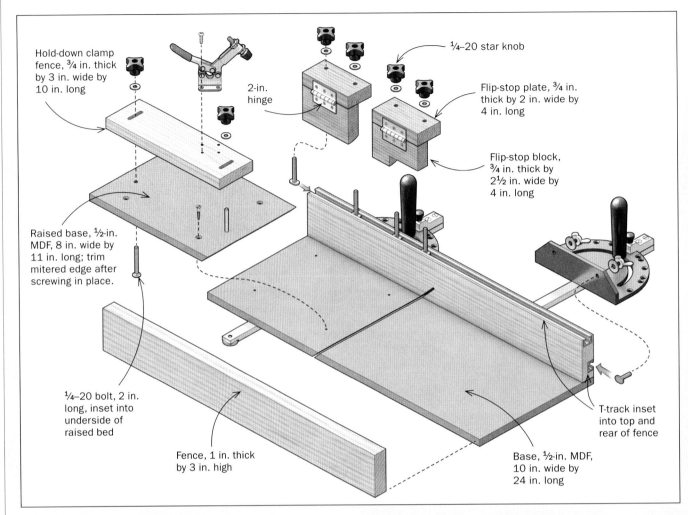

Hold-down clamp fence, ¾ in. thick by 3 in. wide by 10 in. long

2-in. hinge

¼–20 star knob

Flip-stop plate, ¾ in. thick by 2 in. wide by 4 in. long

Flip-stop block, ¾ in. thick by 2½ in. wide by 4 in. long

Raised base, ½-in. MDF, 8 in. wide by 11 in. long; trim mitered edge after screwing in place.

¼–20 bolt, 2 in. long, inset into underside of raised bed

Fence, 1 in. thick by 3 in. high

Base, ½-in. MDF, 10 in. wide by 24 in. long

T-track inset into top and rear of fence

A mitered box is a simple thing to make, yet a lot can go wrong if you don't take the time to set up properly. I've fine-tuned my approach over years of teaching, and I have an efficient and accurate way to go about it. At the heart of my approach is a miter sled. It secures the stock safely and has a pair of stops that allow me to cut all four sides of a rectangular box without changing the setup. Building it required just a handful of inexpensive hardware.

The sled doesn't have to be very deep, but it should be wide enough to support the stock through the cut. I bolt the miter gauges to a T-track in the back of the fence instead of screwing them in place (**1**), which allows me to slide the fence sideways for a fresh zero-clearance cut after the kerf has been widened with use. This helps minimize chipout when mitering the box parts. There's also a T-track along the top of the fence that makes adjusting the stops easy. To mount the T-track, run continuous grooves along the top edge and back of the fence. Inset a full-length piece of T-track on the top, but on the back use a pair of shorter tracks, staying clear of the blade area.

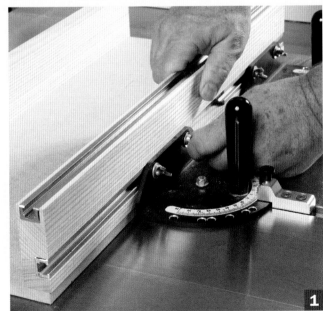

An important feature of the sled is its split-level base: I screw a piece of MDF to one side of the base to elevate it above the other. This allows the offcut to drop away from the blade when cutting a miter instead of being trapped beneath it. My saw tilts left, so I mount the piece of MDF to the right of the blade.

Once the sled is mounted to the miter gauges, tilt the blade to 45°, raise it slightly above the base, and make a cut. Next mount the raised base, which should be sized to cover half the sled base and extend slightly beyond the kerf. Before screwing it in place, drill holes for the bolts that secure the clamping fence, counterboring them on the underside to recess the bolt heads (**2 & 3**). Next raise the blade to trim the raised base flush with the kerf (**4**).

Each of the stop blocks consists of two blocks of wood that are hinged together. The top piece is drilled for bolts that mount to the T-track (**5**). The swinging portion of the stop is beveled on the bottom inside corner to allow clearance when lifting it.

I add a hold-down clamp to secure the parts and keep fingers away from the blade. The clamp is screwed to the adjustable fence that is bolted to the raised base through slotted holes. This lets the sled accept stock of varying widths. To set the fence, slide the fence snug to the workpiece and tighten the star knobs.

A FAST, ACCURATE MITERED BOX

Start with stock long enough to yield all four sides of the box and rip any necessary grooves or rabbets. I also sand the inside face and wipe on a quick coat of shellac. This pre-finishes the box and keeps any glue squeeze-out from sticking. Slide the stock in place and adjust the hold-down fence snug to it to prevent the box parts from pivoting during the cut. Clamp down the stock and cut a miter on one end (**1**). Then rotate the stock and place the mitered end against the far stop to complete the box side (**2**). Cut a fresh miter on the end (**3**) and repeat the process using the near stop to cut a short end of the box (**4**). Alternating between long and short pieces will result in continuous grain on all sides of the box.

Raised bed allows offcut to drop down and away from blade.

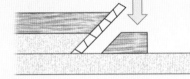

A pair of stops allows you to alternate long and short cuts, resulting in continuous grain from side to side without changing setups.

Layout marks help you to keep track of the orientation when gluing up the box.

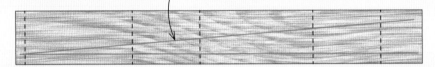

DIALING IN A PERFECT ANGLE

The best way to verify that your blade angle is correct is to miter four test pieces to the same length and tape them together. This multiplies any error and makes it easy to see any gaps. Adjust the blade angle until you have four tight corners and you're ready to go.

Three box sizes from a single setup. By setting the stops to make a rectangular box, you can pair up the sides to create a smaller and larger square box as well. If you plan to batch out a lot of boxes, this shortcut can come in handy.

DRESSING UP A BASIC BOX

While it may not be apparent at first, the way you go about deciding how to attach a top and bottom to a box constitutes a good portion of the design process. It will determine how the box looks, how easy it is to make, and how long it will last without splitting or popping the joints. This last factor has to do with how well you accommodate seasonal movement in the way you attach them. Although you may be able to simply glue a very thin lid on a small box (see p. 170), you're asking for trouble if you try that on a larger box with a thicker lid. You can get around the issue by building with plywood, but for solid wood you need to come up with a way to attach the lid (and bottom) securely while still allowing them to move.

An **INSET LID**, where a rabbet around the edges creates a tab to fit into a groove in the sides, is a straightforward approach. This joint exposes the full thickness of the sides bordering the lid. Because of that, it's important to mill your stock as thin as possible to avoid a clunky look. A thickness of $\frac{5}{16}$ in. to $\frac{3}{8}$ in. will look better than a $\frac{1}{2}$-in.-thick side on a smaller box. In addition, there is a visible gap between the raised portion of the top and the sides. While this gap is only needed on two sides, I aim to keep it even all the way around so it looks like an intentional design detail.

An **OVERLAY LID** has some advantages if you're after a cleaner look. In this case, the top has a groove around the edges that fits into a groove in the sides and allows the top to partially or completely conceal the sides. Because only a portion of the thickness of the top is visible, the lid appears thin but has the strength of a thicker one. This requires more work than the rabbeted lid, but it's worth it if that's the look you want.

A **DROP-IN PANEL** is a third option. A panel sized to fit snugly in a rabbet along the top edges of the sides is a clean way to top off a box. A solid-wood panel wouldn't work for this option because it would need room to expand and contract. One way around this problem is to make a more stable panel, such as a veneered piece of plywood or MDF. I like to use a kumiko panel, which is made using a Japanese latticework technique that can be sized for a snug fit without worry about movement. A variation on a drop-in panel would be a removable top that is rabbeted to fit the box. In this case a solid-wood panel wouldn't pose a problem.

AN INSET TOP

Visible gap between the lid and box along edges

Leave room for expansion between the lid and sides, and at the bottom of the groove.

Lid is rabbeted to fit the groove in the box sides.

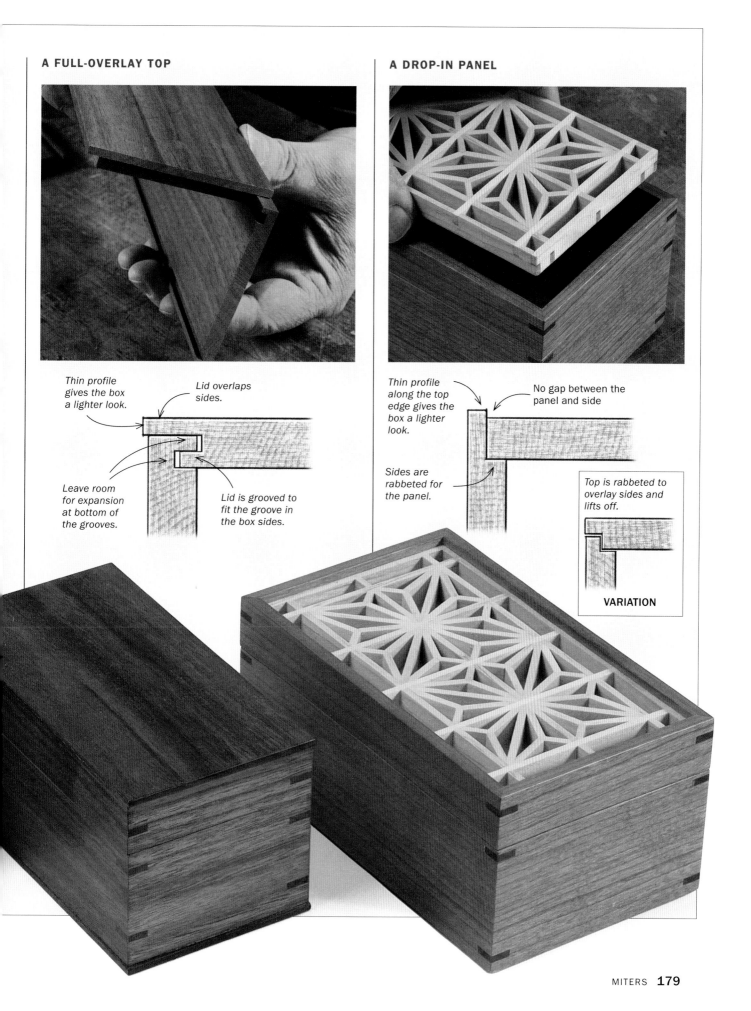

A FULL-OVERLAY TOP

Thin profile gives the box a lighter look.

Lid overlaps sides.

Leave room for expansion at bottom of the grooves.

Lid is grooved to fit the groove in the box sides.

A DROP-IN PANEL

Thin profile along the top edge gives the box a lighter look.

No gap between the panel and side

Sides are rabbeted for the panel.

Top is rabbeted to overlay sides and lifts off.

VARIATION

A SLED FOR CORNER SPLINES

The jigs and fixtures I make share a common theme in that they tend to be quick and simple to make. This sled is no exception. The aim when cutting a slot for a spline is to hold the box at a 45° angle as you run it across the blade. There are different ways to go about it, but this particular sled consists of a V-shaped bed sandwiched between two runners that slide in the saw's miter slots. To size the bed, set the runners in the miter slots and trim the bed halves to fit in between them (**1**). Glue the bed, checking that the halves are square (**2**), and miter the corner where they meet (**3**). This creates a contact surface to hold the bed at the correct angle when adding the runners. I find the easiest way to align the parts when gluing is to use the tablesaw itself. Once more, set the runners in the miter slots and glue and clamp the bed in between (**4**).

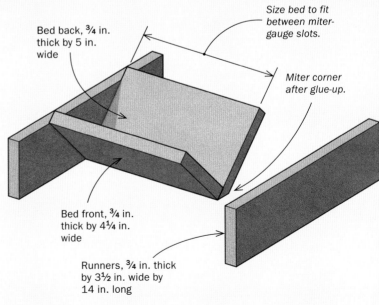

Bed back, ¾ in. thick by 5 in. wide

Size bed to fit between miter-gauge slots.

Miter corner after glue-up.

Bed front, ¾ in. thick by 4¼ in. wide

Runners, ¾ in. thick by 3½ in. wide by 14 in. long

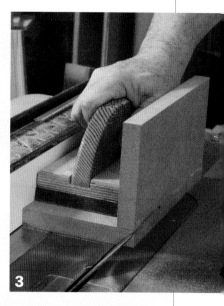

GLUE THE SPLINES AND SAW OFF THE LID

Gluing in the splines doesn't have to be a neat affair. I start with ½-in.-wide strips ripped to a snug fit and then cut them into oversize triangles. This is one occasion where I don't worry about squeeze-out (1). If the splines stick out too much, I trim them closer at the bandsaw before heading to a benchtop belt sander to flush them up and clean up any dried glue. You can use a block plane to flush the splines, but be sure to work in from each corner to avoid chipping off the point of the splines. I like to saw off the lid at the bandsaw (2). A sharp blade and slow feed rate should leave a smooth surface that doesn't require a lot of cleanup. For a perfect fit between the top and bottom, I use sandpaper glued to a flat surface to sand the edges where they meet (3). This is much easier than trying to chase any gaps by sanding one side at a time. To minimize cross-grain scratch marks, I sand at a diagonal using light pressure and a circular motion. I like to finish the box at this point using shellac followed by steel wool and wax. Skip the wax on the interior because the smell will last for a long time.

ADD A MITERED LINER

An easy way to register the lid to the base is to install a mitered liner. I make the liners using the same method as for the small box on p. 166, and size each side to the box (**1**). If the fit is too snug, it can be difficult to slide the parts back out of the box, and you may be tempted to leave them in place. However, I find that the miters will open at some point and I think it's worth the effort to get them out, pre-finish them, and glue them together (**2**). Then sand the liner as needed to fit. Finish the outer surface where the liner extends above the box sides (**3**). On a liner with dividers, I cut a shallow dado in the parts. Start by planing the continuous divider to fit (**4**), and then fit the remain dividers as a pair in order to avoid bowing the center divider (**5 & 6**). Another method, which I covered in *The Why & How of Woodworking*, is to cut V-grooves and miter the ends of the dividers to fit.

AN L-FENCE FOR MITERED CASEWORK

A miter joint in plywood is actually stronger than one in solid wood. This is because the alternating plies provide a good amount of long-grain glue surface in the joint. Proof of that can be seen in the mitered cases of this wall unit by Anissa Kapsales, a good friend and great woodworker. She glued the ½-in. plywood backs in place for added strength but skipped any splines or loose tenons in the miters.

While a miter joint in casework is simple in concept, it can be the most challenging miter to cut. The parts are usually big and not necessarily flat, which can throw off the accuracy of the cut. The other challenge is figuring out a way to glue the case together. Bob Van Dyke, another friend and mentor (it's good to have woodworker friends), came up with this technique that makes both cutting and gluing fast and accurate, and I'd be lost without it now. The key is an edge guide that rides along an L-fence during the cut and also acts as a clamping caul later.

AN EDGE GUIDE THAT DOUBLES AS A CLAMPING CAUL

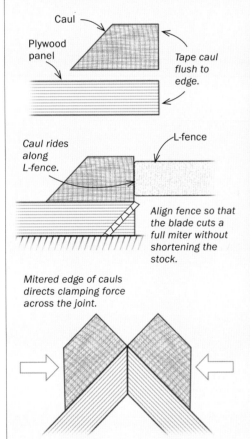

Caul

Plywood panel

Tape caul flush to edge.

Caul rides along L-fence.

L-fence

Align fence so that the blade cuts a full miter without shortening the stock.

Mitered edge of cauls directs clamping force across the joint.

Start by cutting all of the sides to final length. Then tape a caul flush to the ends of the panel to be mitered (**1**). Tilt the sawblade to 45° and position an L-fence so that the blade cuts a full miter along the edge without shortening the panel. Register the edge guide against the L-fence as you cut the miter. A push pad helps to keep the stock flat against the saw table (**2**). Leave the edge guides in place to act as cauls to direct clamp pressure across the joint when gluing up the case (**3**).

CHAPTER 6

SHAPING

When we think of shaping, there's a good chance that something as sinuous as a Maloof rocker may come to mind, but even a detail as inconspicuous as a small chamfer can have an impact on the look or feel of a piece of furniture. It's often the subtle details like a slight taper on a leg or a subtle arch on a rail that add up to give a piece its personality. And that's not to mention the overt effect of dramatic curves and shaping, which can transform the essence of a piece to something bordering on sculptural. Whether we use eye-catching swooshes or hardly noticed details, we have powerful tools at our disposal when bringing a piece of furniture to life. Becoming familiar with the different techniques, and using them enough to be able to predict their effect on a piece, are the keys to designing with intent and controlling the outcome you're after.

For subtle shaping and refining details, nothing beats a block plane. This humble tool is a powerful addition to your design kit. When creating curves, there are three basic methods: sawing, laminating, and bending. Sawing curved parts out of square stock, the first option, has the advantage of allowing you to cut joinery while the parts are still square. The downside is that the grain won't necessarily flow with the curves, and tight curves can present short-grain problems that can weaken the parts.

Creating curves using bent lamination, the second option, is the process of gluing thin strips of stock together while clamping them to a curved form. The payoff here is grain that follows the curve, which not only looks good but also creates strong parts and a predictable bend. And you can use just about any wood with this process. The downside is that there may be visible gluelines on the edges of parts or where you cut through the laminations when doing further shaping.

The third way to create curves is by steam-bending parts, a process whereby parts are heated by steam in an enclosed chamber and then bent around a form and allowed to dry. This is a fast and flexible way to bend, but it works best with a small variety of woods, preferably air-dried, and you risk breaking parts as you bend them.

Between them, these three methods provide a powerful way to give your work some originality.

DIAL IN DETAILS WITH A BLOCK PLANE

The block plane is probably the one hand tool that inspires the least amount of fear, but maybe the least amount of excitement as well. Even if we're not at the level of taking gossamer-thin shavings with a smoothing plane, there's a good chance we're knocking the corners off the edges of a board with a block plane without a second thought. However, if that's all the consideration you give to your block plane, you're probably missing out on the capabilities that make it one of the most important design tools in your kit.

Although larger, longer planes handle flattening and smoothing, the block plane excels at shaping. That chamfer we cut on the edge or end of a board changes the geometry of the board. And therein lies this little plane's power as a design tool. It's the details of a design that bring a piece to life, and those details are often best handled with the block plane. While it's great for a simple task like breaking an edge, it can also create roundovers and bullnose profiles. It can refine the appearance of parts by making them look thicker or thinner. It can exaggerate a curved arch, or even give a straight edge the appearance of a curve. You can straighten up shadow lines around doors and drawers, and create corners that are friendly to the touch with just a couple of passes. These subtle changes can have a big impact on the refinement of your work, and they offer you a greater level of control over the final product.

Even if all you want to do is break a sharp corner, a block plane will make a difference. Sandpaper can handle the task quickly, but it will yield a rounded corner rather than the flat chamfer created by a block plane. The difference between the two is revealed in how light reflects off the corner. A rounded profile will have a softer look because the light is dispersed as it reflects off the rounded surface. By contrast, the light will reflect evenly off the flat surface of a planed chamfer, creating a crisp highlight or shadow line. While the difference may be subtle, when you multiply the effect by every edge of a project, clean chamfers will add a crisper look overall. There is nothing wrong with a rounded corner if that is the effect you are after, but having the ability to create a crisp corner offers you a second choice...and more control over your design.

The wider you make a chamfer, the greater the impact it will have on the look of a piece. And the location of the chamfer will determine the effect you create. A tabletop is a good example. Adding a chamfer to the edge can make the top appear thinner or thicker. Because you view a tabletop from above, adding a heavy chamfer to the bottom corner of the edge will make the top look thinner. But a heavy chamfer along the top increases the visual width of the edge

SANDING VS. PLANING

This is a really good example of how small details can add up to create a big impact on a piece. It's easy enough to knock off a sharp corner with sandpaper (1). Not only does it leave a corner more friendly to the touch, but it also creates a softer look overall (2). A light chamfer from a block plane also takes off the edge (3), but the resulting facet reflects the light and leaves a crisper look (4). On its own, this is a subtle difference. However, when you multiply it by the numerous edges that make up any piece, it can give your work a sense of order and precision.

CHANGE THE LOOK WITH A CHAMFER

Any chamfer, even a narrow one, can affect the look of a piece. Make it wide, and the impact is even more dramatic. On a tabletop edge, you can use a wide chamfer to create the appearance of a thinner top, or even make it look thicker. You can create these different looks because a tabletop is typically viewed from above, and by changing what the viewer sees when looking at the top from a high angle, you change how they perceive it. An edge with no chamfer appears consistent with its actual thickness. If you add a heavy chamfer to the bottom corner, only a portion of the edge is in view and the tabletop appears thinner. Conversely, adding a heavy chamfer to the top corner creates the appearance of a thicker top because the eye perceives the combination of the wide chamfer and edge as a single unit.

Visual width of edge when viewed from above

No chamfer

An unchamfered edge offers an accurate idea of the true thickness.

Chamfer on bottom

Just a portion of the edge is in view and the top looks thinner.

Chamfer on top

The wide chamfer increases the visual width of the edge, giving the impression of a thicker top.

and makes it appear thicker. This is because the eye takes into account the width of the chamfer as well as the thickness of the edge, and the total is greater than the width of a square edge with no chamfer.

Although I mostly use chamfers that are even in width along their length, sometimes an intentionally uneven chamfer is a good thing. If a tapered leg that narrows toward the bottom looks a little heavy, a chamfer on the inside corner that widens at the bottom can lighten the look. Alternatively, on a straight leg, cutting a tapered chamfer that is wider at the top can lighten the leg's top while maintaining the visual mass at the bottom for a more grounded effect. The key to creating a tapered chamfer is to control the length of the passes with the block plane. The aim is to start with a short stroke at the wider end of the chamfer and make progressively longer strokes until you are making a full-length pass. This will create a straight taper along the workpiece. If the chamfer isn't wide enough, repeat the steps.

Creating a double-tapered chamfer is just as easy as a straight taper. This is a useful technique for fine-tuning curves in a design. If the curve of an arched apron is too shallow, for example, adding a chamfer that is wider in the middle than on the ends will exaggerate the appearance of the curve.

The wider you make a chamfer, the greater the impact it will have on the look of a piece.

CREATE A TAPERED CHAMFER WITH GRADUATED STROKES

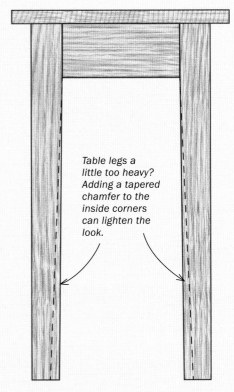

Table legs a little too heavy? Adding a tapered chamfer to the inside corners can lighten the look.

PLANING SHORT TO LONG

While a consistent chamfer is typically the goal, a tapered chamfer can be used to change the appearance of a part by altering its visual width. A table leg is a good example. If after tapering your table legs, you're left with a look that's a little heavier than you expected, you can correct it with a chamfer that gets wider at the bottom of the leg. The key to a consistently tapered chamfer is to keep track of your strokes. Start short, and then take longer passes, lengthening the passes in even increments until you take a full-length pass. To increase the depth, repeat the process.

The key to creating a tapered chamfer is to control the length of the passes with the block plane.

To create a double taper, start with a short stroke in the center of the arch. Then follow with progressively longer passes that are also centered on the arch. By skewing the block plane, you can plane to the inside edge of most shallow curves. For tighter curves, you can use a spokeshave in the same manner.

There are times when an asymmetric double taper is useful as well. When making a cabinet on stand with legs that flared toward the bottom, I wanted the appearance of a narrower waist toward the top of the legs. To achieve the look, I created a double-tapered chamfer with its center near the top of the leg. In that case, rather than taking even-length passes on each side of the center point, I divided the length above the center point into four sections, and then divided the length below the center into four equal sections as well. The sections above the center were much shorter than those below and created the appearance of a tighter curve at the top of the leg and a longer, shallower curve below.

ACCENTUATE CURVES WITH DOUBLE TAPERS

Enhancing an arch with a double taper can help you fine-tune curves in a design or even add a curve to a straight edge. A double taper on the bottom edge of this stretcher lightens the look in the center, giving it a little lift. Start with a short pass at the center of the board and follow with longer passes to create the double taper.

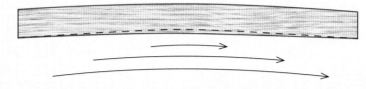

ADD A CURVE TO A STRAIGHT EDGE

I wanted the legs on this cabinet to have a very subtle curve to them. I first tried to saw a curve into the faces, but the effect was too dramatic. Instead, I ended up cutting a straight taper on the outside faces, and then I planed a double chamfer on the outside corners to give the appearance of a curved leg. Rather than centering the widest part of the chamfer along the length, I located it about a quarter of the way from the top. This gave the appearance of a curved leg that flared out slightly at the top.

FROM A CHAMFER TO A ROUNDOVER

The key to consistent curves is starting with accurate chamfers. While it may sound counterintuitive, starting with a flat chamfer is the easiest way to get to a roundover. Start by drawing the profile on the end of the stock, and then mark a diagonal line tangent to the curve. Extend layout lines from the diagonal along the face and edge of the board (**1**) and use them as a guide for chamfering. Try to maintain a consistent angle when planing. The aim is a chamfer that hits each line and is a consistent width along its length (**2**). The next step is to plane off the points of the primary chamfer to create secondary chamfers that further define the profile (**3**). Finally, set your block plane for a lighter cut and work your way across the profile, removing the flats and creating the final roundover (**4**).

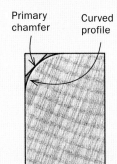

Primary chamfer   Curved profile

The angle of the primary chamfer for a quarter-round profile is 45°.

Plane along the corners of the primary chamfer to create secondary chamfers.

A REFINED BULLNOSE

Repeat the roundover on both corners to create a bullnose profile. Use a circle template or compass to lay out the profile on the end of the stock, and then start with a pair of primary chamfers (below) and continue establishing the profile. After planing the secondary bevels, set your block plane for a light shaving and work across the profile to create a smooth curve (right).

Although a router bit may be the first thing that comes to mind for rounded profiles, I find that a block plane is usually faster and always more versatile. It can easily handle any shape from a quarter-round to a bullnose, or something in between.

With the block plane, every curved profile begins with a primary chamfer. The width and angle of this chamfer will determine the shape and size of the curve. For a simple roundover, it's easiest to draw the curve onto the end of the stock, and then draw a 45° line tangent to the curve. This will be the primary chamfer. Draw lines down the face and edge of the board where the diagonal line intersects them. Plane to the lines to create the chamfer. The next step is to plane away the points of the primary chamfer, creating secondary chamfers. Technically these are 22.5° chamfers, but I just tilt the plane until it's angled halfway between the primary chamfer and the edge or face of the board and call it close enough. Next, lighten up the depth of cut and continue to plane off the points of the facets until you're left with a rounded edge. On long-grain edges of a board I usually leave the last tiny facets; the corner appears round, but you can feel the facets as you run your fingers down the edge. On end grain, I'll often need to follow with fine sandpaper to get rid of the fuzzy texture. To create a bullnose profile, repeat the quarter-round on the adjacent edge.

On both the quarter-round and bullnose profiles, there's a smooth transition between the edge and face of the board that can look soft or mushy. For a crisper look,

Although a router bit may be the first thing that comes to mind for rounded profiles, I find that a block plane is usually faster and always more versatile.

A CURVE WITH CORNERS

A rounded edge is a nice detail, but a smooth transition can yield a soft look to the edge. A solution is to create a curved edge profile that intersects the surface with a hard corner. This arris curve creates crisp shadow lines that help define the profile. It's a detail that can be found in Shaker furniture, such as on the edge of a chimney cupboard top (**1**). I use this profile a lot in my work. The key is to create a curve with a larger diameter than the thickness of the stock. That sounds complicated, but all you need to do is to start with chamfers that are shallower than 45°. These shallow chamfers create the hard transition between the curved edge and flat faces (**2**). Plane the profile as you would a normal roundover, but be sure to leave a crisp edge between the profile and the face of the board (**3**).

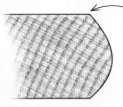
A curve with a diameter larger than the thickness of the board will create a hard transition, or arris, where it intersects the adjacent face.

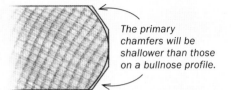
The primary chamfers will be shallower than those on a bullnose profile.

A bullnose profile (top) creates a soft transition between the face and edge of a board. An arris curve (bottom) creates a hard shadow line that adds definition and interest to the profile.

I use an arris curve, leaving a sharp edge, or arris, where the curved edge and flat face intersect. The sharp curve creates a distinct shadow line where the surfaces meet that adds more visual interest than a regular bullnose profile.

To cut an arris curve, draw the profile on the end of the board. Then lay out the primary chamfers. In this case, they will be shallower than 45°, because you are creating a curve with a diameter larger than the thickness of the stock. Create secondary facets, and then smooth the profile with lighter cuts, making sure to leave a hard transition between the edge and the face.

One of my favorite edge treatments for tabletops is an asymmetric arris curve—like an underbevel, but with a curve that brings it to life. Again, start by drawing the curve and then the tangent diagonal to establish the primary bevel. When shaping this profile, it's important to plane the entire edge to avoid leaving a flat above the curve. You can make this profile fairly blunt for a heavier look or more undercut to create a thinner edge.

BEVEL WITH A BELLY

Adding a shallow curve to a beveled edge is a nice way to add some interest to a design. It can be found on both the table edge as well as the outer faces of the legs on this table. Tackle the profile as you would any other. Begin by establishing the primary chamfer (1), and then work your way around the curve. Be sure to leave crisp corners at the edges (2).

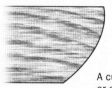

A curved bevel, or asymmetric arris curve

Define the profile with one shallow primary chamfer.

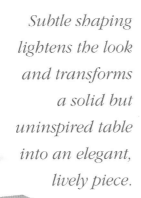

BRINGING A BASIC TABLE TO LIFE

Subtle shaping lightens the look and transforms a solid but uninspired table into an elegant, lively piece.

Most aspects of making this little table have been covered elsewhere in this book, everything from basic joinery to making a dovetailed drawer, choosing and using the lumber effectively, and having a sound milling strategy. I even talked about shaping the tabletop profile in the last chapter. You'd think that there wouldn't be a lot left to cover by now. In this particular chapter, I'll talk specifically about shaping the legs, but I'd like to take a minute to address a larger concept that ties all of those disparate elements together.

When focusing on the construction of a piece, it is easy to lose sight of how exactly you go about bringing it to life. When does a table become more than a combination of legs, aprons, and a top? When does it begin to have its own personality? We tend to simplify this idea into a question of "style," as in "what style are you going to make it in?" While this does point to the question at hand, it speaks to a larger issue as well. Every established furniture style relies on a combination of details and forms that defines it. When we choose to incorporate those elements into our work, we impart a certain identity to what we make. When we try to convey a more personal view, the key is still in the details we choose. Each of those details is similar to a spice in a soup. Randomly tossing things in can lead to a mess, but experimentation is vital to understanding how certain details will affect the overall look of a piece. While I know talented makers who take great design leaps with each piece they build, my approach tends to be more measured. There's no right way to go about it, but I like to start with familiar elements and then add one or two new ideas to the mix in every piece I make. This gives me an idea of how a new detail can affect the whole and how it enhances or conflicts with existing elements. A detail that doesn't mix well isn't necessarily bad; it just may point to a new direction to follow in order to make it work.

On this table, a decision to stray from a simple tapered leg to one that incorporated a shoulder and subtle curves ended up transforming what was intended to be a Shaker-style side table into something with its own unique personality. Once the legs were shaped, they began to dictate changes to details in the other components as well, such as the short overhang and curved bevel of the top and the arched bottoms of the aprons. Those details, in turn, made their way into future projects.

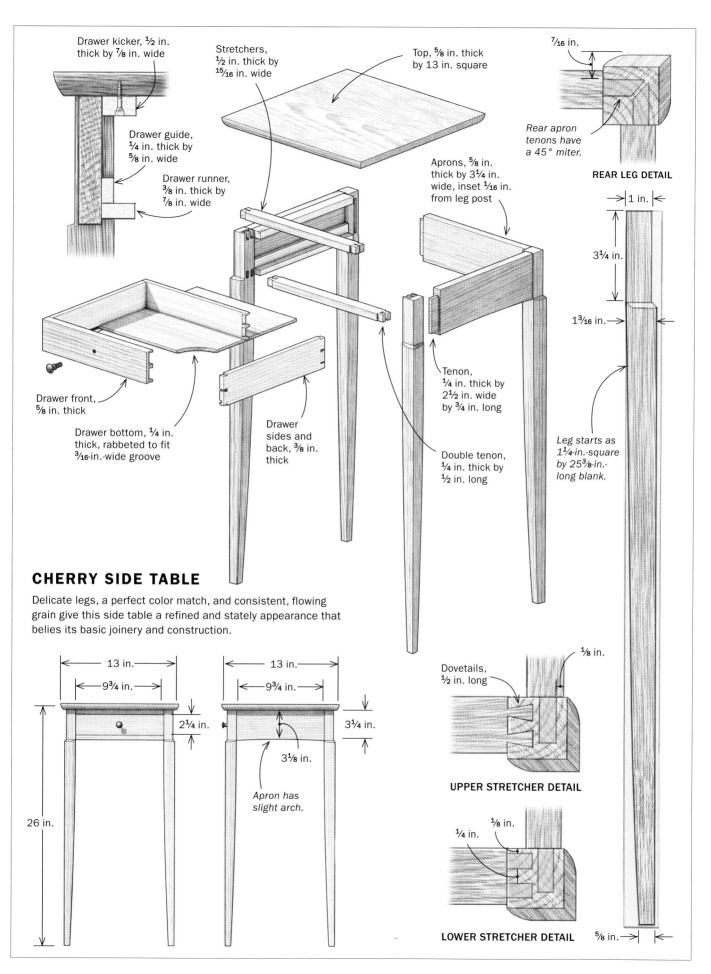

Drawer kicker, ½ in. thick by ⅞ in. wide

Stretchers, ½ in. thick by ¹⁵⁄₁₆ in. wide

Top, ⅝ in. thick by 13 in. square

⁷⁄₁₆ in.

Drawer guide, ¼ in. thick by ⅝ in. wide

Rear apron tenons have a 45° miter.

REAR LEG DETAIL

Drawer runner, ⅜ in. thick by ⅞ in. wide

Aprons, ⅝ in. thick by 3¼ in. wide, inset ¹⁄₁₆ in. from leg post

1 in.

3¼ in.

1³⁄₁₆ in.

Drawer front, ⅝ in. thick

Tenon, ¼ in. thick by 2½ in. wide by ¾ in. long

Drawer bottom, ¼ in. thick, rabbeted to fit ³⁄₁₆-in.-wide groove

Drawer sides and back, ⅜ in. thick

Double tenon, ¼ in. thick by ½ in. long

Leg starts as 1¼-in.-square by 25⅜-in.-long blank.

CHERRY SIDE TABLE

Delicate legs, a perfect color match, and consistent, flowing grain give this side table a refined and stately appearance that belies its basic joinery and construction.

13 in.

9¾ in.

13 in.

9¾ in.

2¼ in.

3¼ in.

3⅛ in.

Apron has slight arch.

Dovetails, ½ in. long

⅛ in.

UPPER STRETCHER DETAIL

26 in.

⅛ in.

¼ in.

LOWER STRETCHER DETAIL

⅝ in.

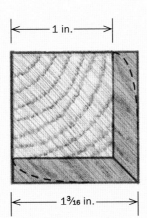

← 1 in. →

← 1³⁄₁₆ in. →

1

The legs on this table are tapered with a little twist. To lighten the look, I trimmed the upper portion where the legs meet the apron, creating a narrow post. For a little extra flair, I added a gentle curve to the tapers and rounded the outside faces. The inspiration came from the classic cabriole leg, which also combines a square post at the top with a serpentine profile below.

I started by making a full-size template from ¼-in. MDF. Once the joinery was cut, I traced the profile onto the leg. Then I defined the angled shoulder at the tablesaw and used the bandsaw to cut the leg post (1) and profile the legs (2). The curves are so subtle that I didn't need to tape the waste from the first cuts back onto the legs to make the second cuts more stable, a common practice for traditional cabriole legs.

For a seamless transition from the legs to the aprons, I rounded the outside faces of the legs so the shoulder would end where the legs

2

meet the aprons. To lay out the profile on the shoulder, start by drawing a subtle curve from the intersection of the post and shoulder to the outside corner of the leg (**3**). With your fingertips as a guide, draw a line from each corner of the leg post down to the bottom (**4**). These lines will define the inside corner of the leg. Then use a spokeshave set for a heavy cut (a block plane would work) to establish a primary chamfer (**5**). Make a series of chamfers to define the curve, using the layout line on the shoulder as a guide (**6**). Smooth the face with sandpaper, but keep a crisp edge on the inside corner.

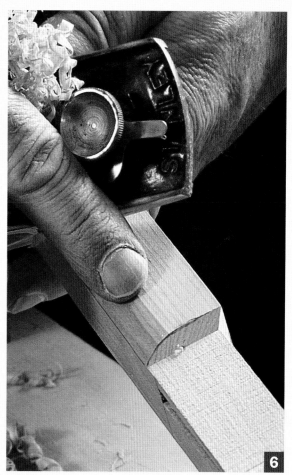

The advantage of creating curves by sawing is that you can usually handle your joinery tasks first while the parts are still square. This helps to ensure accurate joints and a square glue-up.

SAWING A CURVE HAS ITS ADVANTAGES

Each step of the process, from layout to sawing to smoothing, has its own methods and options depending on the situation you're facing.

O f the three ways to create curves—sawing, laminating, and bending—sawing is usually the easiest. Just strike a line, saw the curve, and smooth it. The other advantage is that you can typically cut joinery while the part is still square, which makes the job a lot easier (see p. 217 for tenoning a curved part). The downside of a sawn curve is that it cuts through the grain, which can possibly weaken the part and result in an unruly grain pattern on the surface.

Each step of the process, from layout to sawing to smoothing, has its own methods and options depending on the situation you're facing. To saw a curve, you first need to draw it; you'll find some tips on this on the following pages. For the most part, it makes sense to make a template of the shape you want and then use it to transfer the shape to the workpiece. Making a template has a number of advantages: It allows you to fine-tune the shape without the risk of ruining a part, it lets you lay out multiple parts, and it can be saved for future use. A template can also aid in smoothing the sawn profile: Clamp it to the workpiece and use it to guide a router bit, or use a template to make a routing sled to use at the router table.

Sawing is typically handled at the bandsaw, unless the workpiece gets too large. In that case, a jigsaw may be a better choice. Either way, the goal is to get as close to your layout line as you can without cutting into it. When you meet this goal, smoothing the curve will be easier.

SMOOTHING BY HAND

Hand tools are a fast and effective way to go about refining curves. While there are times when a router makes more sense, I usually start with a hand tool. And on a wide surface like the backrest of a chair, hand tools are the only way to go about it without getting into really crazy router setups. A block plane can handle both outside and even gentle inside curves. A spokeshave, however, is ideally suited for curves of just about any shape. Rather than grab it by the handles, I like to pinch it between my thumb and index finger, which offers more control over the angle of cut (above). I follow the spokeshave with a card scraper (right), which does a good job of removing any tearout or chatter marks and readies the piece for final sanding.

DRAWING CURVES BIG AND SMALL

To cut a curve, you first need to draw it accurately. Often this presents a bigger challenge than the actual shaping of it. For every type of curve, there seems to be a different method to match it. These are the tools I use to handle curves big and small, and changing curves as well. A basic compass (**1**) is a good choice for arcs and circles up to 6-in. in radius. For larger-radius arcs, I have a pair of trammel points that clamp to a piece of hardwood (**2**). One trammel head is fixed, while the other has a fine-adjustment screw. Look for a trammel set where you can replace one of the points with a pencil holder.

For very subtle curves, I pinch a thin piece of stock between the jaws of a bar clamp (**3**). It creates a fair curve, and you can make small, accurate adjustments by tightening or loosening the clamp. Drafting templates come in handy for very small circles (**4**), and a set of french curves (**5**) or ship's curves are an inexpensive addition to your drawing kit, and a good way to tackle changing curves. I often draw curves on the computer as well, gluing a printout onto a piece of ¼-in. MDF to create a template (**6**). I bandsaw to the line and smooth the profile with a spokeshave or block plane.

USING A ROUTING TEMPLATE

Shaping the profiles on the side of a cabinet (see p. 112) is a good job for a routing template. The template is made from ½-in.-thick MDF, which provides a good reference for a bearing-guided bit. Use the template to trace the profile onto the stock (**1**), and then saw out most of the waste. I used a Forstner bit at the drill press to drill out the tight corners at the ends and connected the holes with a jigsaw (**2**). Once the waste is removed, clamp the template back in place (**3**). If you cut into your pencil line by mistake, just slide the template up to create a clean profile. No big deal. Next use a router equipped with a pattern bit to rout the profile. On a profile with tighter curves like this foot cutout, it's best to rout it one half at a time to avoid routing into the grain. Start with the router at the highest point in the curve and rout toward the end (**4 & 5**). Then flip the stock over and remount the template to complete the profile (**6**).

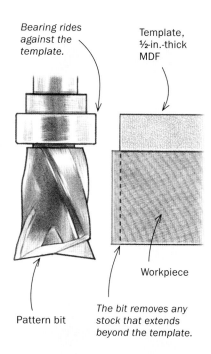

Bearing rides against the template.

Template, ½-in.-thick MDF

Workpiece

Pattern bit

The bit removes any stock that extends beyond the template.

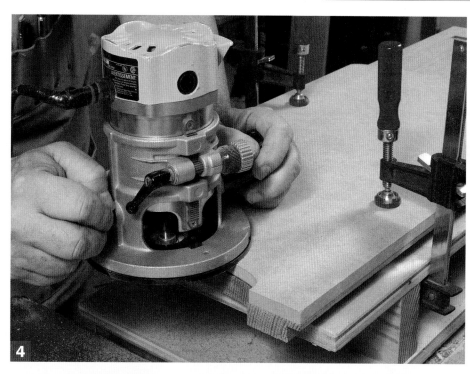

4

5

6

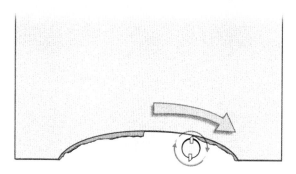

Start at the center of the curve and rout half of the profile. Flip the stock to complete the curve.

CURVES AT THE ROUTER TABLE

For smaller parts, I like to head to the router table and use a template jig that the workpiece clamps into. A profile cut into the jig base guides the router bit. Attached to the base is a rear fence and an end stop that help to align the part in the jig. Hold-down clamps screwed to the fence keep the workpiece in place and offer a good handhold when routing. Before routing the profile, the part needs to be marked and most of the waste removed. To trace the profile onto the workpiece, temporarily clamp it in place (**1**), and then flip the jig over and trace the profile (**2**). Bandsaw the waste close to the pencil line (**3**) and clamp the workpiece back in place. Adjust the bit height so that the bearing contacts the jig base (**4**) and take a slow left-to-right pass (**5**). On shallow curves, you can rout the entire profile in a single pass. For tighter curves, make a half template and rout the profile in two passes.

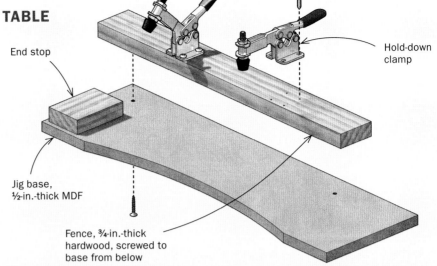

End stop

Hold-down clamp

Jig base, ½-in.-thick MDF

Fence, ¾-in.-thick hardwood, screwed to base from below

1

2

3

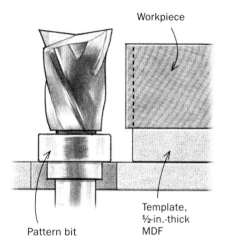

Workpiece

Pattern bit

Template,
½-in.-thick
MDF

USE A HALF-TEMPLATE ON TIGHT CURVES

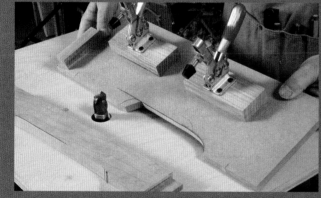

To avoid routing into the grain on profiles with tight curves, make a template with just half of the profile sawn into it (above). Clamp the stock in place and rout half of the profile, and then flip the stock in the jig to complete the cut. It's not uncommon to have a slight bump where the two halves of the profile meet, but a scraper or sandpaper should take care of it.

BUILD WITH CURVES IN MIND

I'll be honest, as much as I like this little cabinet now, it came close to being shelved, or even scrapped, on a number of occasions. The case was left over from a dovetail demonstration and it was an odd size. It was too big to sit on a table and too deep to turn on end for a wall cabinet. It was also too shallow for a case on stand, but it was close enough in size that I ended up gluing strips to the front and back edges of all of the pieces to deepen the case while still salvaging the dovetails. The minute I did that, it became more of a prototype than a "real" piece of furniture, so the pressure was off. I actually have more than a few pieces of that pedigree living in my house. I tend to think of them as "studies," or rough quick sketches in preparation for some future project. With that in mind, I saw it as an opportunity to combine some ideas such as sliding doors and rope handles that had found their way into various smaller projects, as well as to try out a little different style of base. It was something that got built in the background in between class prep, commissions, and writing articles, but somehow I kept coming back to it and crossing another task off the list.

The base was an unknown entity for me. I had a rough idea of what I wanted—the sled feet, for example, a sturdy but lighter look, and some subtle curves to give it just a little spring. I mocked up a base out of pine that got me close to the target before I started milling lumber, but I still wanted some room to refine the design as I was building. It wasn't really a matter of not knowing what I wanted so much as something I had to sneak up on. So the legs and stretchers all started heavier than I knew I wanted them. The feet were quite a bit oversize as well. In addition, I joined the legs to the feet in such a way that it allowed me to change the profile of the feet

LEAVE ROOM TO REFINE THE DESIGN

A deep two-stepped haunch allowed me to attach the legs to the feet and still have the flexibility to dial in the design as I built (**1**). Once the base was together, I was able to try out different foot designs by masking them out with tape (**2**). Even though the final design varied quite a bit from the original idea, there was still enough stock to make the change (**3**).

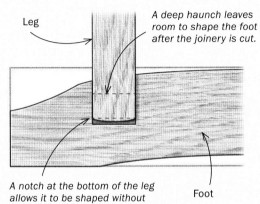

Leg

A deep haunch leaves room to shape the foot after the joinery is cut.

A notch at the bottom of the leg allows it to be shaped without creating a gap in the joint.

Foot

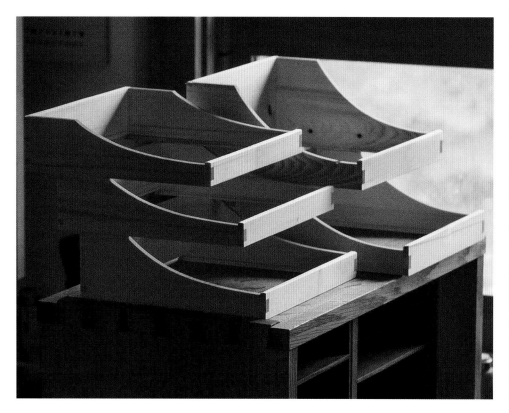

Drawers that put pottery on display. Stacked up, they look a little odd, but the low fronts essentially transform the drawers into slide-out shelves that help to show off the contents and offer a nice surprise when the doors are slid open.

I had imagined some dramatically arched feet, but better sense prevailed and I ended up going with a subtler shape.

without creating gaps in the joinery. Initially, I had imagined some dramatically arched feet, but after laying out the profile on the blank with blue tape, better sense prevailed and I ended up going with a subtler shape. I also added an arched stretcher connecting the feet that ties the base together both structurally and visually.

The case is divided with mitered partitions and is meant to hold various teapots and cups. To make them more visible once the doors were opened, I ventured away from traditional drawers and went with something closer to slide-out shelves instead. I made them by scalloping the sides and connecting them with a narrow rail at the front. The full-height rear portion of the drawer sides keeps the drawers from tipping down as you pull them out.

The project ended up being an interesting little piece. It sits in my office at work, and whenever I happen to glance at the cabinet, it reminds me to stop and gather my thoughts for a moment before jumping into the next task.

STRONG CURVES FROM STRIPS OF WOOD

The bent-lamination process is simple in concept: Cut a board into strips and glue them back together while clamped to a curved surface. This process requires more effort than sawing a curve into a part, but it has its benefits. Because the grain follows the curve, the resulting parts are very strong and the grain on the faces looks more natural. If you keep your strips in order when gluing, the gluelines on the edge almost disappear. You also use less stock than you do when sawing a curve out of square stock. Along with the benefits come some challenges, too. First, you need a way to create the thin strips with smooth faces, and second, you need a bending form to clamp them to (and a lot of clamps!). The other challenge comes when you are cutting joinery in curved parts. It's not unreasonably difficult, but you do need a sound strategy in order to end up with gap-free joints.

MAKE A BENDING FORM

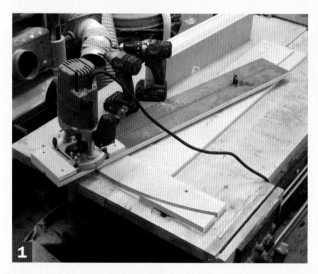

1

2

There are different ways to go about building a bending form, but for narrower parts like rockers and curved backrests, I make mine by stacking layers of MDF. Rather than gluing up a bunch of layers and then trying to cut a curve into them, I start by shaping a single layer. One technique that yields a perfect curve is to attach my router to a long base and use it like a compass (**1**). My base has a sliding center point that lets me adjust it for curves of different diameters. I then trace the curve from the first layer to a second, bandsaw off most of the waste, and screw it to the first layer. At the router table, use a flush-trimming bit to rout the second layer flush with the first. Then repeat the process one layer at a time until you have the width you need (**2**).

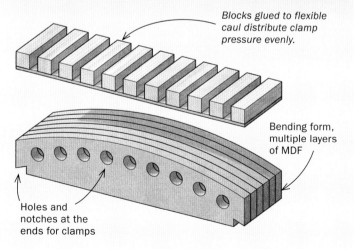

Blocks glued to flexible caul distribute clamp pressure evenly.

Bending form, multiple layers of MDF

Holes and notches at the ends for clamps

SAW IT APART AND GLUE IT BACK TOGETHER

Whenever possible, I try to get all of the strips from a single board. This yields the best grain match on the edges of the glue-up. Mark a triangle on the end grain before sawing to help align parts later. I typically aim for ⅛-in.- to ³⁄₁₆-in.-thick strips depending on the curve (1). To get an idea whether your strips are the correct thickness, bend one over the form using hand pressure; it should conform to the curve without a lot of force. To create a smooth face on each strip, joint the blank between every cut. To smooth the second face, I run them through my planer. If yours can't plane stock that thin, a thickness sander is great if you happen to have one (I don't), and a handplane does the job as well. Cut the strips ½ in. wider than the finished part and roughly 6 in. longer. The extra length helps you to clamp the strips to the form. Use a glue with a rigid glueline to prevent the parts from creeping over time. Unibond 800 (2) and epoxy are both good choices. I hold the parts in place with stretch wrap on the ends to help keep them aligned when clamping (3). Start clamping from the center (4), using a caul to distribute the pressure, and work your way toward the ends (5).

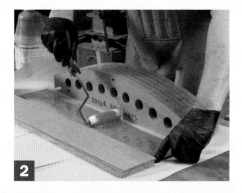

A LITTLE CLEANUP IS REQUIRED

Coming out of the clamps, the blank can look a little scary. To cut the blank to width, start by scraping one face as clean as you can get it with a card scraper. Position the scraped face against the bandsaw fence to trim the opposite face (**1**). Then run the just-sawn face across the jointer to clean it up and give you a good reference face (**2**). You can cut the piece to width at the tablesaw, but it takes a little coordination when cutting a curved part. Instead, I prefer to use the planer when I can (**3**). In that case, I trim the part slightly overwidth at the bandsaw before running it through the planer.

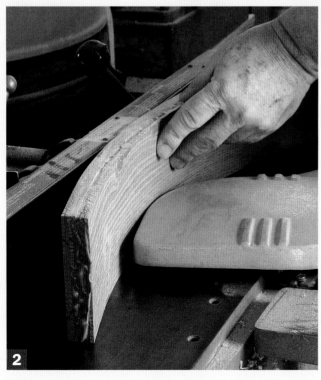

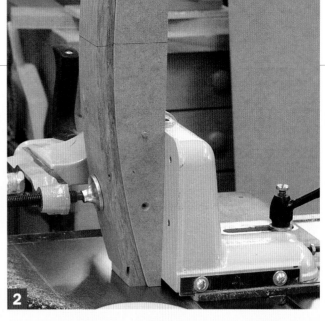

JOINERY ON CURVED PARTS

Joining curved parts is a challenge but not impossible. I find that making a curved caul that matches the radius of the workpiece helps to secure it in the correct position when machining. Mark a centerline on the workpiece and caul for consistent alignment. The first step is to trim the part to length. Clamp the caul to the crosscut-sled fence and use it to support the stock when trimming the ends (**1**). When cutting tenons on a curved piece, I find it easiest to use a tenoning jig, clamping the caul in place along with the workpiece (**2**). To trim the shoulders, use the caul once again at the crosscut sled. In addition, clamp a stop block to the fence and register the end of the tenon against it when cutting the shoulders (**3**). You'll need to invert the caul to cut the second set of shoulders (**4**). To cut mortises along a curve, I screw a pair of curved cauls to my mortiser fence and clamp jaw. Align the center of each mortise with the centerline on the jaws and cut the mortise (**5**). This technique can also be used with a router guided by a fence.

BENDING THIN STOCK

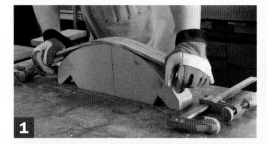

When the part comes out of the steambox, try bending it around the form with hand pressure (1). If it starts to split, it may need to steam longer, or you may need to stop and set up a compression strap (see pp. 220–21). Otherwise, clamp one end to the form (2) and bend it slowly using consistent pressure. Finally, clamp the other end in place (3). Leave it in the form for a week or transfer it to a drying form (see p. 222).

STEAM-BENDING CURVES

A small steamer like this one from Earlex is an inexpensive way to get started.

Of the three ways to create curves, steam-bending offers the most natural results. A steam-bent part is a solid piece of wood, with no sawing or gluing required. Because of that, you can bend stock with a small cross section and still end up with a very strong piece. Steam-bending, as the name implies, is a process of introducing heat and moisture into the wood, making it temporarily pliable so that it can be bent over a form and clamped in place while it dries. The two major pieces of equipment are a steambox (along with a source of steam) and a bending form. Although steam-bending is similar in concept to making a bent lamination, fewer clamps are needed because you don't have to worry about gaps in the laminations; you just need to get the piece to conform to the bending form. Some woods are more conducive to steam-bending: Tough, open-pored woods like ash and oak are ideal, though woods such as cherry, maple, and walnut can also be used. While every woodworker agrees that air-dried wood is best for bending, many get by with kiln-dried lumber. Noted chairmaker Brian Boggs goes through the extra step of first steaming kiln-dried stock and then soaking it in water for three days before finally steaming it again and bending it.

A SIMPLE STEAMBOX

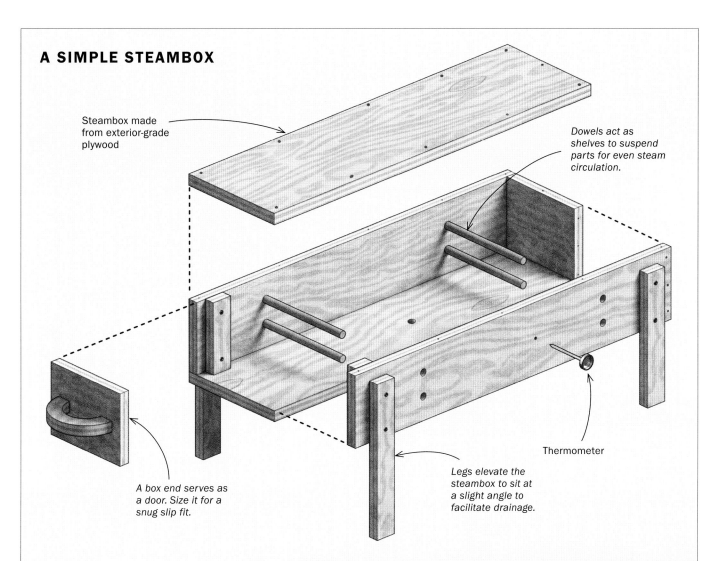

Steambox made from exterior-grade plywood

Dowels act as shelves to suspend parts for even steam circulation.

Thermometer

A box end serves as a door. Size it for a snug slip fit.

Legs elevate the steambox to sit at a slight angle to facilitate drainage.

A steambox can be a down-and-dirty affair. You just need an enclosed space that is ideally not a lot larger than the pieces you need to steam. I make mine from exterior-grade plywood, which holds up better to the wet conditions than regular plywood. Legs are screwed to the sides of the box, with a pair at one end shorter than the others so that the tilted box allows the accumulated water to drain. Strips of wood elevate the workpieces and allow the steam to circulate around the parts. A handle on the end panel makes a nice door, though I've been known to simply screw a square of plywood to the end of the box. A general rule is to steam parts for an hour per inch of thickness, but the timing can vary depending on the species and drying method of the wood. I usually err on the side of longer steam times since I typically use kiln-dried stock.

A COMPRESSION STRAP HELPS PREVENT SPLITTING

1

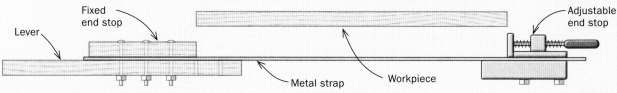

Fixed end stop

Lever

Adjustable end stop

Metal strap

Workpiece

When using thin stock or creating shallow curves, you can usually get by with bending the stock directly over the form and clamping it in place. However, for thicker parts and tighter curves, a compression strap can mean the difference between split parts and a successful bend. A compression strap consists of a flexible metal strap with blocks at each end. When the stock is placed between the blocks, the wood on the inside of the bend is forced to compress, which it does without consequence. Without the strap, the wood on the outside of the curve tends to stretch, resulting in split parts. You can make your own strap or buy one from online suppliers.

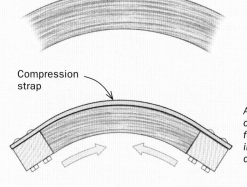

On a normal bend, the wood fibers on the outside of the curve stretch and can split.

Compression strap

A compression strap constrains the wood and forces the fibers on the inside of the curve to compress.

MAKING A BEND

Clamp the bending form to a sturdy surface and adjust the blocks on the compression strap so that the piece fits comfortably between them (**1**). Then use a wrench to tighten the adjustable block snugly against the stock (**2**). Clamp one end of the stock against the bending form (**3**) and slowly bend it around the form (**4**). Finally, clamp the end in place (**5**). Leave the part in the strap for an hour or so. Then remove it and clamp the part directly to the form while it dries, or transfer it to a drying form to maintain the curve.

A REAL-WORLD APPLICATION

The base of this cabinet contains both subtle and more pronounced curves (**1**). The legs have a slight flair along the bottom third, so I didn't need to steam the entire part. Instead, I replaced the door of the steambox with one that had holes in it, into which I was able to insert the ends of the legs (**2**). Because the leg curve was only slight, I skipped the compression strap and clamped the legs directly to a pair of two-sided forms that acted as both bending forms and drying forms (**3**). That way, I was able to bend all four legs at once. The arched stretchers had tighter curves (**4**), so I put a compression strap to use when bending them. A bar clamp acted as a drying form to hold the curve while the stretchers dried (**5**).

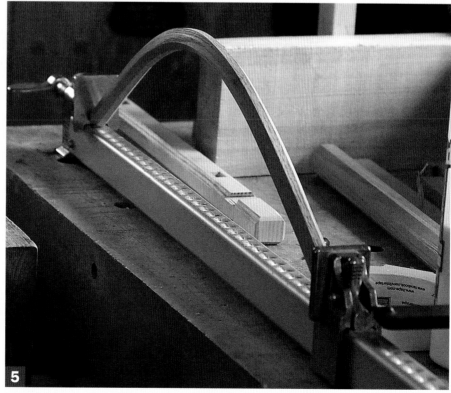

CHAPTER 7

PUTTING IT ALL TOGETHER

While earlier projects in this book fit nicely into a specific joinery category, most of the things we are apt to make probably won't. The reason for that is pretty simple. The challenges that most projects present are best addressed by using joinery in combination. To this point, I've covered basic joinery families, their utility, and a variety of strategies for executing them. The next step is to formulate a plan to put them to best use in order to address the specific challenges a project may present.

The small bookshelf illustrates how dovetails and mortise-and-tenons work well in combination. Once you begin to view a dovetail as a good method for joining parts at corners, and a mortise-and-tenon joint as a way to allow one part to extend past another, it's easy to begin to plan their use when designing a new project. The tansu-style cabinet takes the concept even further and applies it to a more ambitious case piece. With its routed double mortises, it is also a good example of how a project can prompt a novel way to make a familiar joint. The arched entry table also combines dovetails and tenons, but in a slightly different way. A dovetailed drawer box perches atop a tenoned timber frame-style base for a fresh take on a table with drawers. Shaping also plays a big part in bringing the piece to life with its dramatic arched stretchers and subtle tapering.

A pair of chairs round out the chapter, starting with a versatile dining chair design. The basic chair introduces angled joinery, as well as the challenge of mortising oddly shaped parts. It also shows how details like a pierced back splat and crest rail can enliven a design while keeping it anchored within a specific style. Finally, a rocking chair begins where the dining chair leaves off by adding sculpted armrests and laminated rockers.

Although some of these projects may seem intimidating at first glance, a closer look will reveal that each is comprised of a basic set of joints and techniques that are not difficult to master.

A BOOKSHELF WITH DOVETAILS AND TENONS

I've made a few pieces that, while definitely influenced by the Arts and Crafts style, have a sort of chunky, friendly, storybook quality to them. I usually make them for our home, and they're nice to live with. These pieces remind me a little of flea-market finds I've collected over the years that have an indeterminate age and style, and no inherent value as an antique, but still seem to find a use and end up hanging around for a while. This bookshelf definitely fits in that category, and it's fun to build.

It's a nice sampler with a pair of dovetailed corners and a single mortised shelf—just enough joinery to give you a quick workout without tying you down to a long-term project. The edge of the shelf also provides an opportunity to try your hand at some simple chip carving.

The vertical dividers are joined with Dominos, which makes sizing them easy (see p. 108). Another option would be to cut stopped dadoes in the shelf and bottom, and stub tenons on the top and bottom of the dividers so that they could be slid in place from behind after the case was assembled. The desktop organizer on p. 52 offers a good example of this technique. Sometimes the task at hand will demand a particular solution, while at other times, the decision isn't quite as clear. In that type of situation, I have a sense that the method I chose is probably related to the tools and methods I happened to be using on other parts of the project. So where one approach may come to mind one day, a different approach to the same challenge may seem like a better way to go the next.

A project with just two dovetailed corners may seem a little odd, but I actually use that form quite a bit in my work. It shows up in other wall cabinets, but it's also common in floor-standing pieces. The ash cupboard on pp. 222–23 looks quite a bit different from this bookshelf, but it

ENSURING A SQUARE CASE

The key horizontal components in the bookshelf are the shelf and the bottom. Even though they are joined to the sides in different ways, it's important that their shoulder-to-shoulder dimensions match. This is where the routing method I use to clean out the waste between dovetail pins comes in handy. Not only do I use it for the dovetails (**1**), but by keeping the bit set to the same depth, I can rout the waste between the tenons as well (**2**). As long as the parts were cut to the same length to begin with, the shoulder distance should match (**3**), resulting in a case that comes together square without a lot of fuss (**4**).

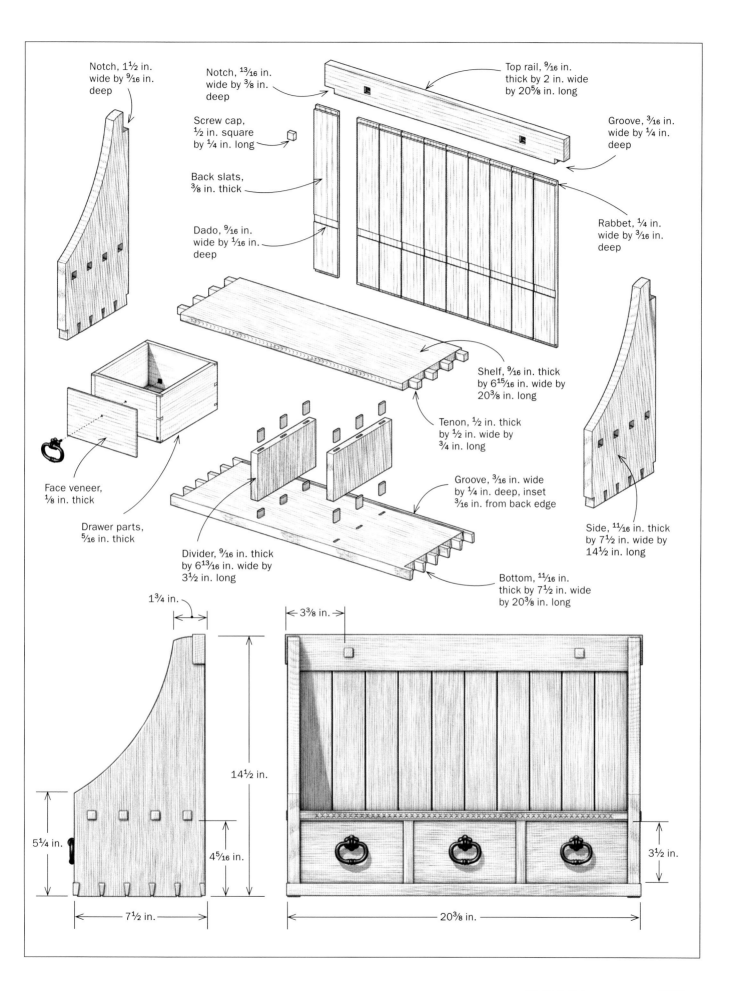

Notch, 1½ in. wide by 9/16 in. deep

Notch, 13/16 in. wide by 3/8 in. deep

Screw cap, ½ in. square by ¼ in. long

Back slats, 3/8 in. thick

Dado, 9/16 in. wide by 1/16 in. deep

Top rail, 9/16 in. thick by 2 in. wide by 20 5/8 in. long

Groove, 3/16 in. wide by ¼ in. deep

Rabbet, ¼ in. wide by 3/16 in. deep

Shelf, 9/16 in. thick by 6 15/16 in. wide by 20 3/8 in. long

Tenon, ½ in. thick by ½ in. wide by ¾ in. long

Face veneer, 1/8 in. thick

Drawer parts, 5/16 in. thick

Divider, 9/16 in. thick by 6 13/16 in. wide by 3½ in. long

Groove, 3/16 in. wide by ¼ in. deep, inset 3/16 in. from back edge

Side, 11/16 in. thick by 7½ in. wide by 14½ in. long

Bottom, 11/16 in. thick by 7½ in. wide by 20 3/8 in. long

1¾ in.

3 3/8 in.

14½ in.

5¼ in.

4 5/16 in.

3½ in.

7½ in.

20 3/8 in.

A DRESSED-UP FRAME-AND-PANEL BACK

Coming up with solutions for problems you might face, even if it's not the "right" way to go about it, is a big part of building.

shares the same basic construction. There the form is turned upside down so that the dovetails join the top of the case, while the tenons at the bottom allow the case sides to extend beyond the bottom shelf to create a base for the piece.

One feature I really like is the shiplapped back. Though it will be concealed by books for the most part, it's a prominent feature and likely to be more visible than a typical case back, so I wanted to dress it up a little. It consists of slats that are rabbeted not just on their sides but also on the top and bottom edges. This allows them to fit into grooves in the top rail and case bottom. As an extra touch, the slats have a shallow dado at the shelf location, which allows the slats to overlap the shelf, concealing the gap between the shelf and slats. I had never seen this exact detail used before, so it was fun to brainstorm it, try it out, and have it work. That sort of creative engineering is something I enjoy about woodworking, and while it might be overkill in this situation, it's in my tool kit now and I can imagine putting it to use again on future projects. I digress, but the notion that you can read enough, watch enough videos, or take enough classes so that you'll be prepared for any scenario you might encounter in your shop is, on the one hand, not feasible, and, on the other, beside the point. Coming up with solutions for problems you might face, even if it's not the "right" way to go about it, is a big part of building. And it's one of the most rewarding aspects of the craft.

4

5

The back panel starts as a normal shiplapped back with each slat having rabbeted edges. From there, gang up the pieces three or four at a time and use a push pad to rabbet the ends of each slat as well (**1 & 2**). I use a dado blade partially concealed by an L-fence to cut the rabbets. Size the rabbets on the ends so that the remaining tab fits comfortably in the groove in the top rail and case bottom (**3**). The slats extend to the bottom of the case so the shelf needs to be ripped narrower on the back edge (**4**). To help conceal the joint, cut a shallow dado in the slats at the location of the shelf. The dado allows them to overlap the shelf a little and avoid a visible gap between the back of the shelf and the slats (**5**). It's a little thing, but it makes a nice detail. The top rail locks all of the slats in place (**6**). The slats butt up flush with the case sides, so to prevent a gap where they meet, I start by gluing the outer slats to the case sides and then install the remaining slats between them, using spacers for even reveals between the slats.

6

ONES AND ZEROS: A TANSU-STYLE CUPBOARD

Tenons, dovetails, rabbets, and dadoes. These basic building blocks are simple enough on their own but powerful in combination. Like the binary code that underlies all things digital, a small number of joinery methods make up the heart of furniture making. Master those joints and the woodworking world is your oyster. This cabinet is a great example of how we can limit ourselves to just a few elements and still have a tremendous amount of freedom when building. Although at first glance the cabinet and the small bookshelf on p. 226 appear far removed from each other, the two pieces share the same basic construction, combining a dovetailed corner with through-tenons. It's a theme that can be played out in many forms. Dovetails are a good choice where parts meet at a corner, while through-tenons allow a part to extend beyond the corner. In this case, dovetails are used at the top, and the tenons at the bottom allow the sides to extend beyond the bottom shelf, creating a base for the cupboard. On the previous bookshelf, the dovetails are at the bottom, while the tenons at the shelf allow the sides to extend up and provide a nook for the books. As you become more accomplished, your focus will turn from simply executing the joinery to a larger understanding of how joints can work in concert to help you realize the projects you want to make.

Although we tend to think of woodworking in terms of making objects, on just about any piece tasked for storage, the aim is really about enclosing a space and then subdividing it into smaller spaces by adding doors, dividers, drawers, and shelves. For me, this aspect of design is the most enjoyable (and challenging) part of building because it determines not only the utility of a piece but also how it looks. My work is typically devoid of excess ornamentation so its structure is what gives a piece its identity, and the basic skeleton becomes a major design element. Shaker furniture has always been a big influence and inspiration. Its minimalist design combined with creative arrangements of doors and drawers, often in asymmetric patterns, breathe life into the work. The same wonderful creativity can be found in

TANSU-STYLE CUPBOARD

The dovetails at the top of the case present a strong design detail, but the remainder of the case joinery consists of mortise-and-tenons. Quartersawn ash gives a quiet sense of order to the piece.

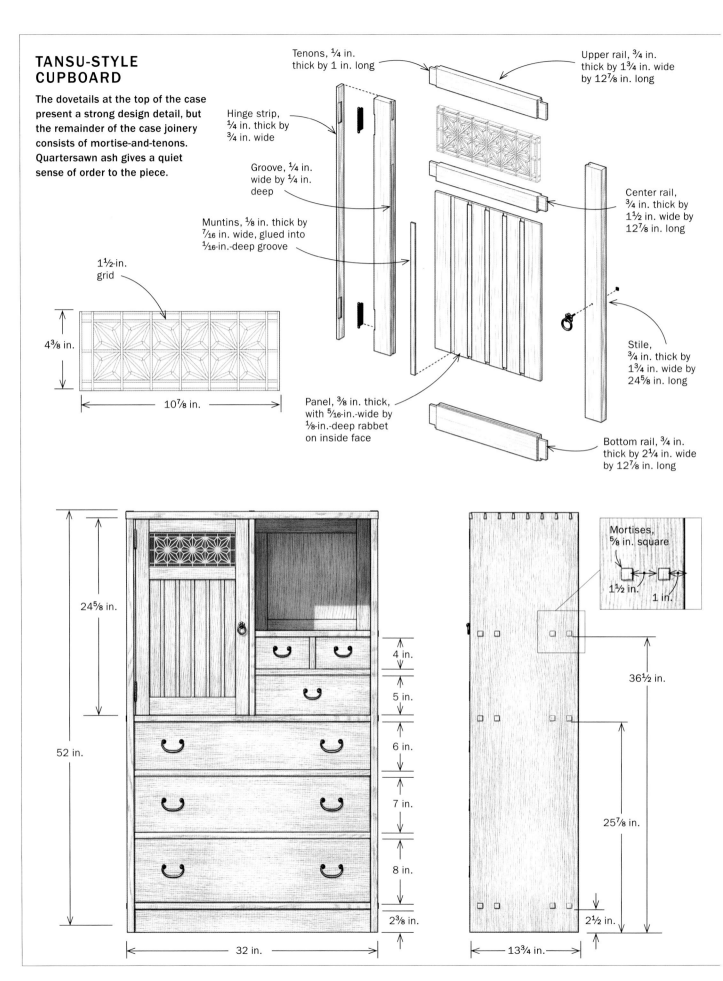

Tenons, ¼ in. thick by 1 in. long

Upper rail, ¾ in. thick by 1¾ in. wide by 12⅞ in. long

Hinge strip, ¼ in. thick by ¾ in. wide

Groove, ¼ in. wide by ¼ in. deep

Center rail, ¾ in. thick by 1½ in. wide by 12⅞ in. long

Muntins, ⅛ in. thick by 7/16 in. wide, glued into 1/16-in.-deep groove

1½-in. grid

4⅜ in.

10⅞ in.

Stile, ¾ in. thick by 1¾ in. wide by 24⅝ in. long

Panel, ⅜ in. thick, with 5/16-in.-wide by ⅛-in.-deep rabbet on inside face

Bottom rail, ¾ in. thick by 2¼ in. wide by 12⅞ in. long

24⅝ in.

52 in.

4 in.

5 in.

6 in.

7 in.

8 in.

2⅜ in.

32 in.

Mortises, ⅝ in. square

1½ in.   1 in.

36½ in.

25⅞ in.

2½ in.

13¾ in.

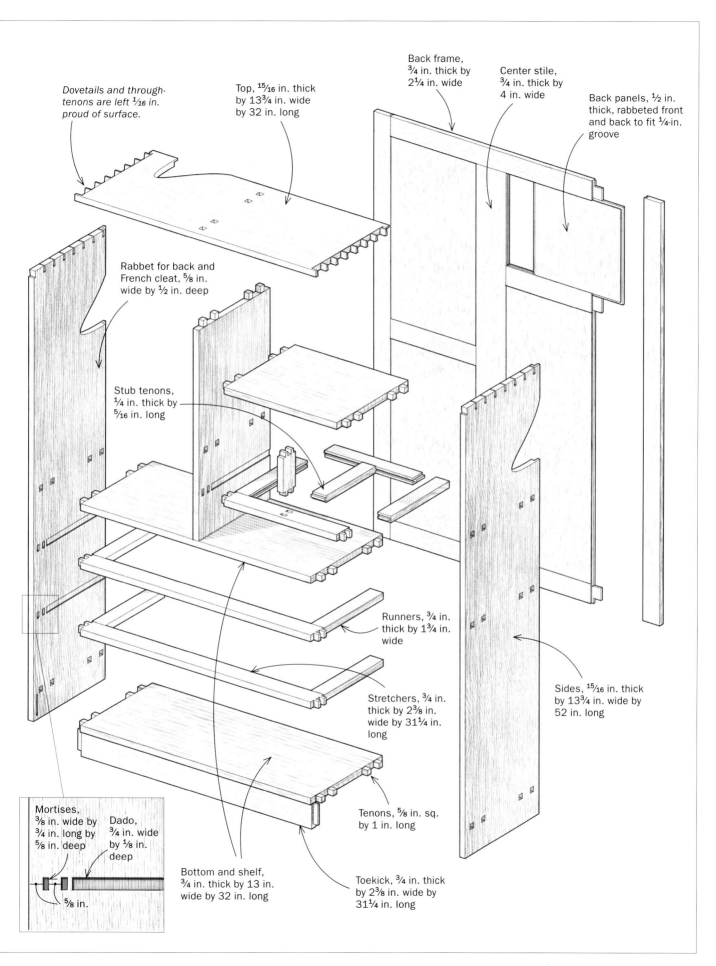

Dovetails and through-tenons are left 1/16 in. proud of surface.

Top, 15/16 in. thick by 13¾ in. wide by 32 in. long

Back frame, ¾ in. thick by 2¼ in. wide

Center stile, ¾ in. thick by 4 in. wide

Back panels, ½ in. thick, rabbeted front and back to fit ¼-in. groove

Rabbet for back and French cleat, ⅝ in. wide by ½ in. deep

Stub tenons, ¼ in. thick by 5/16 in. long

Runners, ¾ in. thick by 1¾ in. wide

Stretchers, ¾ in. thick by 2⅜ in. wide by 31¼ in. long

Sides, 15/16 in. thick by 13¾ in. wide by 52 in. long

Tenons, ⅝ in. sq. by 1 in. long

Mortises, ⅜ in. wide by ¾ in. long by ⅝ in. deep

Dado, ¾ in. wide by ⅛ in. deep

⅝ in.

Bottom and shelf, ¾ in. thick by 13 in. wide by 32 in. long

Toekick, ¾ in. thick by 2⅜ in. wide by 31¼ in. long

THROUGH-TENONS IN LARGE PARTS

While the tenon layout process is similar to that for the Arts and Crafts cabinet (p. 112), the situation is different enough to make it worth covering here. Rather than two horizontal tenons, this case has two pairs of square tenons. In addition, many of the tenons are located so far from the ends of a board that you can't use a marking gauge to lay out the top and bottom walls of the mortises. The good news is that you can use a spacer to lay out all four mortise walls.

An important concept to keep in mind is that this technique involves referencing off both edges of the boards when laying out the mortises and the tenons. This is the source of its accuracy, but it can also cause problems because any slight variation in the width of the parts will result in joinery that's off the mark.

Start by laying down tape at the locations of the mortises, and then pencil in the approximate horizontal location of the mortises. Set up a pair of marking gauges, one for the inside wall of the inner mortise and the other for the outer mortise (this is a good excuse to get a second marking gauge if you don't already have one). Scribe the inner wall of the mortises (**1**). Add a spacer the size of the intended mortise (**2**) between the gauge and the edge of the stock to scribe the outer wall (**3**). Be sure to scribe all of the mortises on the opposite face of the board as well (it's easy to miss one). Using the second gauge, repeat the process for the remaining mortises. Keep the gauge settings because you'll need them for the tenons. Now mark the top and bottom walls of the mortises using an edge guide with a cleat glued to one end (**4**). Size the guide for the row of mortises farthest from the end and trim it later for the remaining rows of mortises. Register the cleat against the end of the board and knife the mortise walls (**5**). Then place the spacer against the guide to knife the opposite walls (**6**). Peel away the tape to reveal an accurately located mortise (**7**). Finally, use the gauges and spacer block to scribe the tenon locations as well. If you plan to cut the tenons at the tablesaw (see p. 92), mark the face of the tenons as shown (**8**). If you plan to use a handsaw, tape and mark the end grain as you would a dovetail pin.

Hold the tenon board in place to check your work (**9**). If you worked carefully but the tenons are slightly offset from the mortises, double-check to see that the boards are exactly the same width. If they're a little off, all is not lost. I wouldn't worry about an offset of $\frac{1}{64}$ in. or less, but anything more and I'd go through the trouble of re-ripping the boards to the exact width and trying again.

DOUBLE-TENON DIVIDERS

I used double tenons to join the drawer dividers to the case sides (**1**), because the increased glue surface makes for a stronger joint. To maximize strength, the tenons are unshouldered top and bottom, and any gap will be concealed by the drawers. I covered a method for double tenons using a hollow-chisel mortiser and a standard blade at the tablesaw in the cabinet-on-stand project (p. 124), but I opted for a different route here. Although this method also uses a pair of spacers, this time it combines them with a router for the mortises and a box-joint blade for the tenons. The router is necessary because the case sides are too wide for the mortiser, so this is a good technique to know for big parts. Set up a plunge router with a fence in the same way you'd rout a conventional tenon and adjust it to cut the inside mortise of the pair (**2**). Then attach a spacer to the fence using two-sided tape (**3**) and rout the outer mortise (**4**). Finish by squaring the ends of the mortise with a chisel.

A box-joint blade set for a ⅜-in.-wide cut is used to cut the tenons; the wider blade eliminates all of the waste between the tenons so there's no need to clean up to the baseline later. You'll use the same gap spacer used for the mortises as well as a spacer to make the tenon (see p. 100 for sizing the spacer). Set up a stop to cut the outside of the tenon farthest from the stop (**5**). Then make a pass using the tenon spacer (**6**), followed by the gap spacer (**7**). The final pass is made with both spacers in place (**8**). To remove the remaining waste along the edges of the board, align it with the blade and make a cut (**9**). The final fit should be close right off of the saw, and it makes quick work of a fair amount of joinery.

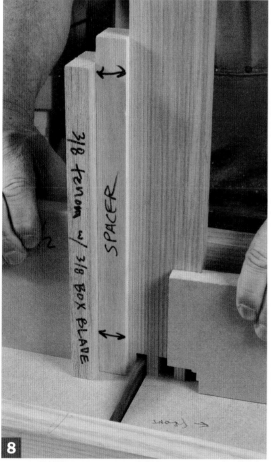

SIMPLIFYING A COMPLEX GLUE-UP

Glue-ups are typically stressful affairs under the best of circumstances, but the scale of this project and the number of components that need to come together make for a particularly challenging operation. Whenever I can, I try to break up an assembly into as many smaller glue-ups as possible. It's less taxing on my patience and on my clamp collection as well. There aren't a lot of steps we can separate the process into, but we can create two subassemblies that lessen the number of individual parts that need to come together in the final glue-up. One challenge in pre-gluing sections is keeping the parts in proper alignment. A really helpful technique is to dry-fit additional parts to the assembly in order to hold them in position. When gluing up the case top and shelf to the vertical divider (**1**), temporarily fit the sides in place (**2**). This does a good job of ensuring that the assembly is square and won't cause problems in the later glue-up.

Another challenge on a big glue-up is getting enough clamps in place to hold

By gluing two subassemblies together prior to gluing the entire case, the number of elements that needed to be joined was reduced from 12 to 8, which still made for a big glue-up, but one that wasn't quite so stressful.

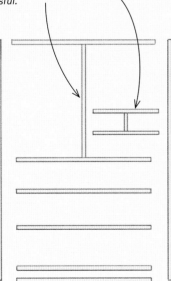

everything together while the glue dries (**3**). On a project with through-tenons like this, kerfing the tenons before assembly and driving in wedges (see p. 105) can help in a couple of ways. First, it does a really good job of locking the parts in place, preventing gaps in the future. Of greater benefit is that once the wedges are driven home, you can remove the clamps from the area and reposition them while wedging a different section of the assembly. This way, you can work around the assembly, clamping and wedging as you go (**4**). Although you do have a limited time to get the parts together, I find that wedging is effective even as the glue begins to set.

ADDING SUPPORT FOR THE DRAWERS

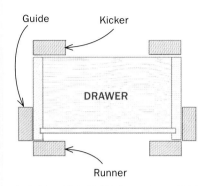

A drawer needs to be supported in a few different ways in order to slide smoothly. First, it needs a surface to run on. This could be a case bottom or a solid shelf, but where neither option is available, a runner is required. To keep the drawer from tipping down as it is opened, you'll need a kicker. In a case with stacked drawers, the runner for the drawer above acts as a kicker for the drawer below. Finally, you need to guide the drawer side-to-side. For full-width drawers, the case sides handle this job, but for side-by-side drawers a guide must be added between them. Ok, let's get to work.

Tasks that were simple on a smaller project required a different approach when scaled up.

tansu furniture as well. While indebted to both these styles, this piece also draws from an Arts and Crafts aesthetic, with its proud joinery and the offsets where components meet. Finally, there's a splash of kumiko gridwork to light up the cabinet like fireworks in a night sky. I find that the quieter a design is, the greater the impact a small detail can have.

I'd been wanting to make a cupboard of this type for a while, and it has its origin in a number of wall cabinets that I've built in the past. The cabinets were fun exercises in a creative use of space, and when I looked at them in retrospect, it seemed like they could be scale models of larger cabinets. With this book as an excuse, I could finally explore the idea.

A big challenge—and one that I hadn't anticipated—had to do with changing the scale of the design. The first task was to determine the overall size of the piece and the scale of the components within it. I had an idea of how large I wanted the cupboard to be, but once the elements were scaled to fit, I sometimes ended up with odd dimensions. A design that looks good on paper may yield a door too tall or a drawer too short in real life.

After I had finally locked down the design, the next challenge came from building in a larger scale than the earlier wall cabinets. Tasks that were simple on a smaller

The runners are joined to the drawer stretchers with a stub tenon that fits in a groove in the back edge of the stretcher (**1**). Because the grain of the runner runs perpendicular to the grain of the case side, you need to secure it in a way that accommodates wood movement. Here, I glued the front portion to the case side and screwed it to the case at the back through a slotted hole. In addition, I routed a shallow dado in the case side for the runner, which made alignment automatic. For a single drawer, I wouldn't bother, but on this project it was worth the added effort.

For the side-by-side drawers, a center runner and guide were needed as well. I ran a groove along the inside edges of the runners (**2**), which allowed me to install a wide center runner to support both drawers (**3**). To support the runner at the back, I tenoned a rear stretcher to the side runners (**4**). To finish the job, I'll glue a guide the thickness of the vertical divider to the center runner to guide both drawers.

A DRESSED-UP FRAME-AND-PANEL BACK

On a large floor-standing piece, the back plays an important role in helping to keep the case square over time. Although plywood is most resistent to racking, I tend to go with solid-wood options. A shiplapped back is a simple option, but a frame-and-panel back offers more rigidity (**1**). When the interior is visible, such as on a bookcase or a cupboard with doors, the back plays an aesthetic role as well. With that in mind, I took the extra step of adding rails that frame the two open areas in the upper portion of this case. Normally, I make the back slightly oversize and trim it to fit snugly in the case opening. Because of its size, I did the final fitting while the parts were dry-fitted. This made it easy to take a frame part off to trim it and try the fit again (**2**). The case back sits in a rabbet along the back edge of the case and is glued and screwed in place (**3**). The center stile looks overly wide from the back but appears as two separate stiles from the front (**4**).

The good thing about pen and paper is that you can work through a lot of designs, good and maybe not so good, before committing one to lumber.

project required a different approach when scaled up. Going into the project, I felt that the construction would go quickly and smoothly considering my familiarity with the joinery. However, the larger scale of the parts often had me rethinking my approach to each task. Not that this project was more difficult to build, but it is a different animal than what was essentially the same piece in smaller form.

In addition, while a wall cabinet with relatively thick components is a solid structure that I didn't have to worry about going out of square, a cupboard of this size could rack out of square sitting on an uneven floor due to its own weight. With that in mind, I reinforced the joinery by wedging the through-tenons that joined the case. I also replaced the single tenon I used on the drawer stretcher of the Arts and Crafts cabinet (p. 112) with a pair of vertical tenons. The added glue surface acts as a further precaution against the case sides bowing over time. Of course, the double tenons were pinned as well.

In all, I'm happy with this piece. There's a lot that's familiar about it, yet it has its own personality and charm. As with the wall cabinets, this larger form offers a nice canvas for exploring any number of designs, though the cost of materials and the time and effort required may have me at the drawing board for a while longer to make sure I've got a design worth investing in. The good thing about pen and paper is that you can work through a lot of designs, good and maybe not so good, before committing one to lumber.

ARCHED ENTRY TABLE:
BOLD CURVES AND SUBTLE TAPERS

This entry table is another example of how dovetails and mortise-and-tenons work well together both structurally and visually. It's also a good exercise in shaping with its defining arched stretchers, bold chamfers, and subtly tapered legs. An earlier version of this table made it into my first book, but I stopped short of offering plans or telling you how to build it. The truth of the matter is that I wasn't entirely happy with the table. It was a design that I liked but never felt that I had fully resolved. I'd built it five or six times, and each time I'd made small changes to the design. When I finally got to the point where I could say "Ok, there it is," I realized that I'd needed to get this far in my journey before I could begin to get to the heart of what wasn't quite right. In short, it felt just a little top-heavy to me. A narrower drawer box and top helped to a certain extent, but it was easy to go too far and have it look undersize for the base. The ultimate solution to the problem, though subtle, had a big impact on the finished look. Adding a ⅛-in. taper to the outside faces of each leg created a base with a slightly bigger cross section

It was a design that I liked but never felt that I had fully resolved.

TRESTLE TABLE

The stout oak base gives the table a solid stance, while arched rails give it a lift.

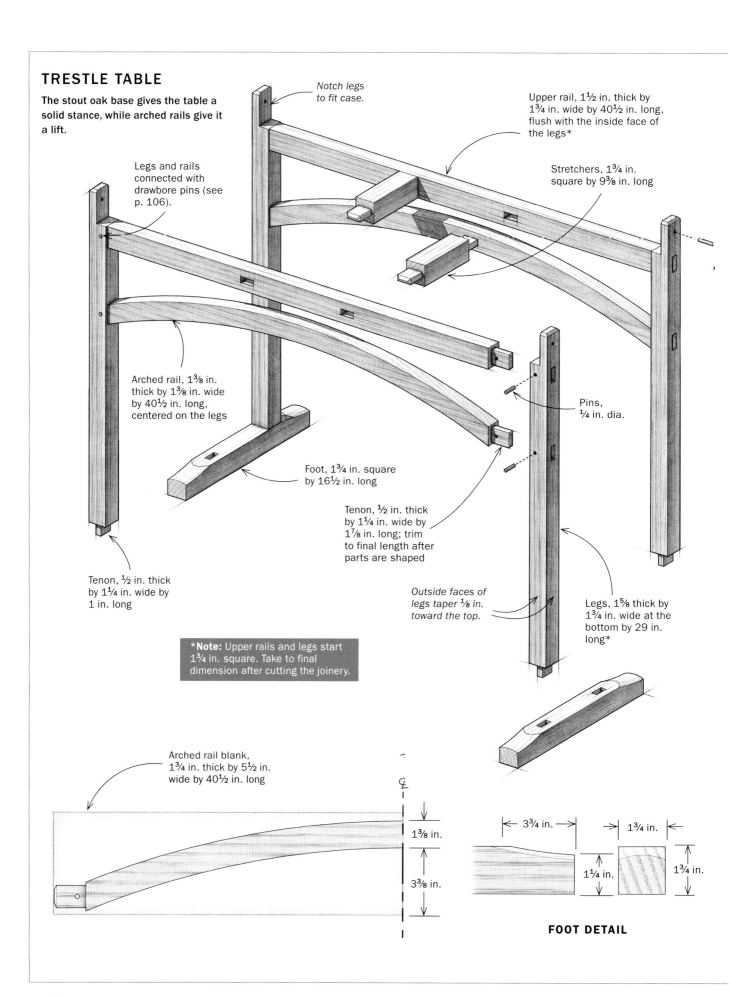

Notch legs to fit case.

Upper rail, 1½ in. thick by 1¾ in. wide by 40½ in. long, flush with the inside face of the legs*

Stretchers, 1¾ in. square by 9⅜ in. long

Legs and rails connected with drawbore pins (see p. 106).

Arched rail, 1⅜ in. thick by 1⅜ in. wide by 40½ in. long, centered on the legs

Pins, ¼ in. dia.

Foot, 1¾ in. square by 16½ in. long

Tenon, ½ in. thick by 1¼ in. wide by 1⅞ in. long; trim to final length after parts are shaped

Tenon, ½ in. thick by 1¼ in. wide by 1 in. long

Outside faces of legs taper ⅛ in. toward the top.

Legs, 1⅝ thick by 1¾ in. wide at the bottom by 29 in. long*

*Note: Upper rails and legs start 1¾ in. square. Take to final dimension after cutting the joinery.

Arched rail blank, 1¾ in. thick by 5½ in. wide by 40½ in. long

1⅜ in.

3⅜ in.

3¾ in.

1¾ in.

1¼ in.

1¾ in.

FOOT DETAIL

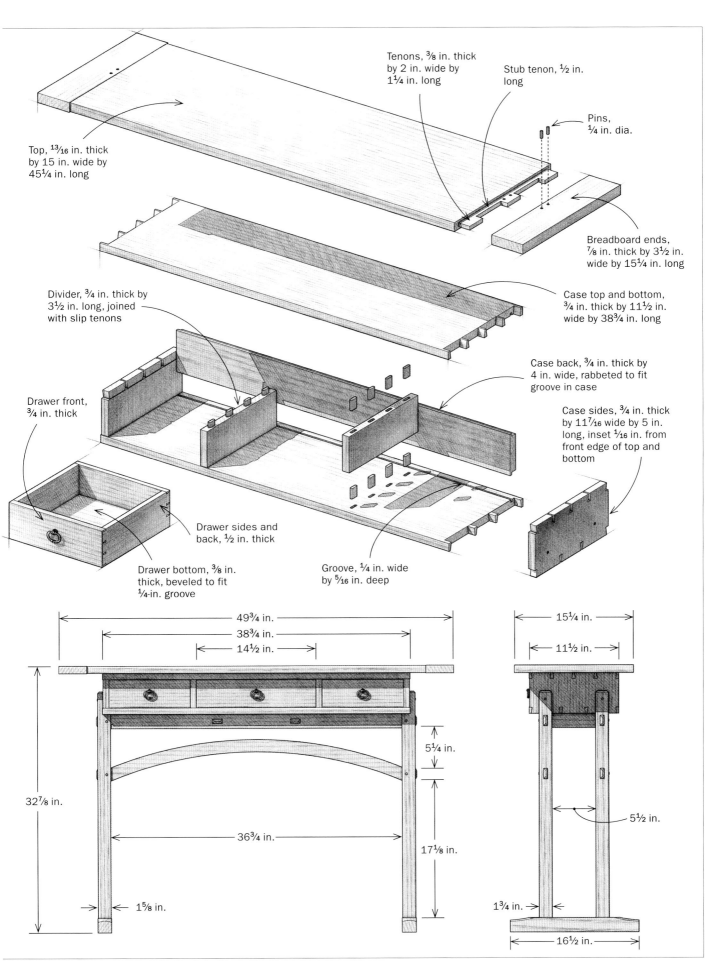

Top, $^{13}/_{16}$ in. thick by 15 in. wide by 45$^1/_4$ in. long

Tenons, $^3/_8$ in. thick by 2 in. wide by 1$^1/_4$ in. long

Stub tenon, $^1/_2$ in. long

Pins, $^1/_4$ in. dia.

Breadboard ends, $^7/_8$ in. thick by 3$^1/_2$ in. wide by 15$^1/_4$ in. long

Case top and bottom, $^3/_4$ in. thick by 11$^1/_2$ in. wide by 38$^3/_4$ in. long

Divider, $^3/_4$ in. thick by 3$^1/_2$ in. long, joined with slip tenons

Case back, $^3/_4$ in. thick by 4 in. wide, rabbeted to fit groove in case

Case sides, $^3/_4$ in. thick by 11$^7/_{16}$ wide by 5 in. long, inset $^1/_{16}$ in. from front edge of top and bottom

Drawer front, $^3/_4$ in. thick

Drawer sides and back, $^1/_2$ in. thick

Drawer bottom, $^3/_8$ in. thick, beveled to fit $^1/_4$-in. groove

Groove, $^1/_4$ in. wide by $^5/_{16}$ in. deep

49$^3/_4$ in.

38$^3/_4$ in.

14$^1/_2$ in.

15$^1/_4$ in.

11$^1/_2$ in.

5$^1/_4$ in.

32$^7/_8$ in.

36$^3/_4$ in.

17$^1/_8$ in.

5$^1/_2$ in.

1$^5/_8$ in.

1$^3/_4$ in.

16$^1/_2$ in.

TWO ARCHES FROM ONE BOARD

One downside of sawing curves is that it can lead to a lot of waste. On their own, each arched rail requires a 2-in.-thick by 5½-in.-wide board, with a good portion of it ending up in the scrap bin. However, a second arch can be had from the first board by gluing the waste below the arch onto the top edge of the blank. This will result in a glueline across one of the arches, and while it's typically not noticeable since the wood on each half comes from the same board, I tend to orient this arch at the back of the base.

Start by cutting the joinery while the blank is square and at full thickness. Cut the tenon cheeks with a dado blade and trace the arches on the face of the board to locate the tenons. Then cut the sides of the tenons at the bandsaw (**1**). Cut away the waste below the bottom arch, staying safely outside the pencil line (**2**). Glue the offcut to the top edge of the blank. (**3**). After the glue dries, flatten the blank again and plane it to final thickness. Trace the final arch profiles on the blank using the bandsaw kerfs to center the profile on the tenons (**4**). Saw out and smooth the arches and finish with a heavy chamfer on the corners. I really like the way white oak takes a hard shine with a sharp hand tool (**5**).

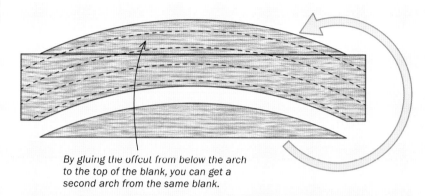

By gluing the offcut from below the arch to the top of the blank, you can get a second arch from the same blank.

TWO-PASS TAPER ON THE JOINTER

Set the jointer to cut half the depth of the final taper, in this case ⅟₁₆ in. With the top of the leg facing forward, take a single pass stopping halfway (**1**). A piece of tape on the fence marks the mid-point. Hold the leg in place as you turn off the jointer before lifting it. Then, keeping the same face down, rotate the leg so that the bottom of the leg is now facing forward. Press down on the rear end, pivoting the leading end off of the table, and take a full pass to complete the taper (**2**).

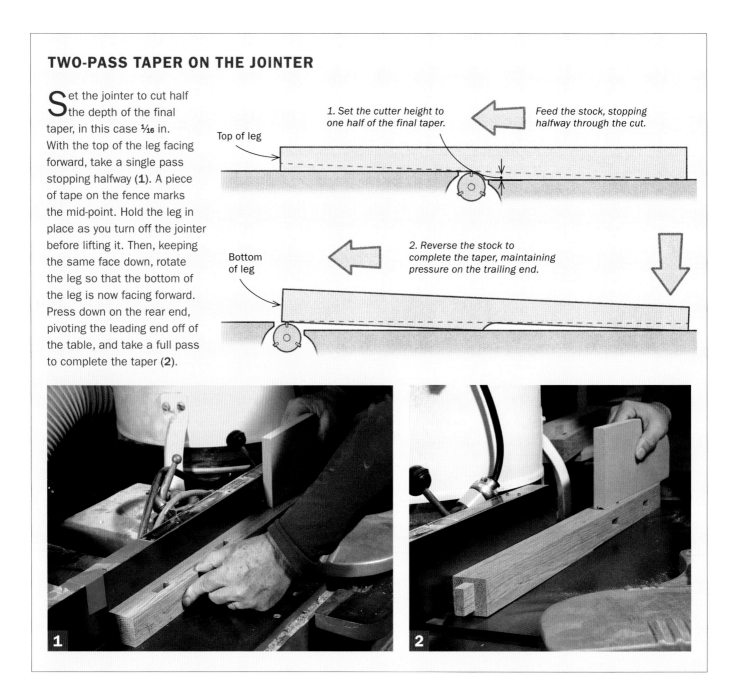

Top of leg

1. Set the cutter height to one half of the final taper.

Feed the stock, stopping halfway through the cut.

Bottom of leg

2. Reverse the stock to complete the taper, maintaining pressure on the trailing end.

1

2

Rule number one: Always make things as easy as possible for yourself because the craft is tough enough as it is.

than at the top. Perspective distortion, where things appear smaller from farther away, made the perfectly straight legs appear to be tapered toward the bottom, giving the table a top-heavy, unsteady look. Tapering the legs gradually toward the top makes them appear to be straight. The taper is not enough to be noticeable at first glance, but it seems to give the base a more solid stance. Having introduced curves and tapers into a number of projects since the time the first table was built, I had a better understanding of the effect they can have, which is what prompted this solution. While the arched stretchers are probably the first thing you notice about the table, the more subtle details play just as big a role in realizing the final design. This table's evolution shows that when starting out, the major elements in a design are the easiest to get a handle on. It's the small details, which take a little time to work out, that can mean the difference between a design you like and one you're really satisfied with.

CHAMFER THE TENONS AND SHAPE THE FEET

Because the outsides of the legs are tapered, it's nice to have the ends of the tenons parallel to the taper as well. The easiest way I've found to do that is to start by leaving the tenons long. I can then dry-fit the joint and, using a shim equal in thickness to the distance I'd like the tenon to protrude, trace the end of the tenon (**1**). While I'm at it, I also pencil a line on the tenon where it meets the face of the leg. I can use this line later as a guide when chamfering the end (**2**). To finish off the tenon, disassemble the parts and cut the tenon to length with a handsaw. Then chamfer the end, keeping just above the shoulder line (**3**). Taper the ends of the feet, and then plane an arris curve onto the tapered end (**4**). The curve echoes the arch of the stretcher, and though it's only a small detail, it helps to tie the different elements of the table together.

A DOVETAILED DRAWER BOX

Sandwiched between the base and the top is a dovetailed drawer box. The length of the top and bottom and the shortness of the sides made it difficult to dovetail in my usual way (see p. 138). Instead, I cut a shallow rabbet on the inside face of the tails board (**1**). This rabbet let me snug up the tails board to the case top and bottom when scribing, keeping it in perfect alignment (**2**). The vertical drawer dividers are attached with Domino slip tenons. To locate them, I cut a piece of MDF the width of the center drawer and added a fence to it, which I registered against the edge of the case piece (**3**). A centerline on the template and case pieces allowed me to align the parts for consistent spacing. To mortise the case, butt the base of the mortiser against the template (**4**) (see p. 109 for the full mortising sequence).

FIT THE BOX TO THE BASE

Because variations in the finished dimensions can sneak into the build by this point, I find it easiest to glue up the drawer box and then center it on the dry-fitted base to mark for the notches that allow it to seat against the upper stretchers. On just about any occasion where I'm scribing, I start by laying down some tape on the end grain first. Then I set the case in place and center it with a combination square before scribing the tops of the legs (above). It can be challenging to seat the case if the fit is snug. I find that tapping out the drawbore pins at the top of one set of legs allows enough clearance to seat the case. Once it's in place, the pins can be driven back in, tightening the assembly (right).

A GOOD FIRST CHAIR TO MAKE

I understand that the thought of making a chair can be intimidating. Yes, there are curves, but the aspect most likely to stoke fear is that the parts meet at an angle other than 90°. At first glance, a chair appears to be a somewhat free-form structure, and the notion of building without a reference point can leave you without a clear idea of where to begin. But don't worry about the angles (I have you covered there), and know that there is a logic to the geometry of a chair, especially a dining chair like this one.

Before we get too far along, a few words about this specific design. If you Google "Arts and Crafts dining chair," a lot of simple, similar designs pop up. While there's nothing wrong with that and my house is filled with examples of such chairs, when it came to building one myself, I wanted it to be, well, worth making. By that I mean something firmly in the Arts and Crafts style, but with its own flair. Although for many people the style is synonymous with rectilinear Stickley-style furniture, it actually encompasses a multitude of makers from many countries working in various media beyond wood, such as architecture, fiber arts, painting, glass, metal, and pottery. The biggest attraction for me is that there is a great variety of esoteric furniture designs that fall within the style, often bordering on the odd but wonderful nonetheless.

With that in mind, I went on the hunt for antiques that might provide inspiration. The piece that struck a chord with me was a clunky little chair that I believe was credited to L. & J.G. Stickley (younger brothers of Gustav), though I've never been able to locate it since. It had strangely shaped front legs and a heavy wooden seat, but what caught my eye were the backrest rails with their sinuous shape and piercings, as well as the single wide tapered back splat. Inspiration found, I went about designing my own chair, channeling that funky, clunky, friendly sensibility. Underlying the final design is a basic, sturdy chair form that can be dressed up in a variety of styles. Consequently, I think it offers a good lesson in a chair that you can make your own, as well as an example of how some simple shaping can transform a basic design into something unique to itself.

What makes the chair simple to build is that all of the joinery, with the exception of the rear legs, can be done while the parts are still square. So shaping the rear legs is a good place to start. After that, the only challenge is cutting the angled tenons on the side rails and lower side stretchers; I'll show how a simple wedge can handle that task for you.

Underlying the final design is a basic, sturdy chair that can be dressed up in a variety of styles.

ARTS AND CRAFTS DINING CHAIR

Quartersawn white oak, arched seat rails, and pierced back splat and backrest all combine to create a classic look.

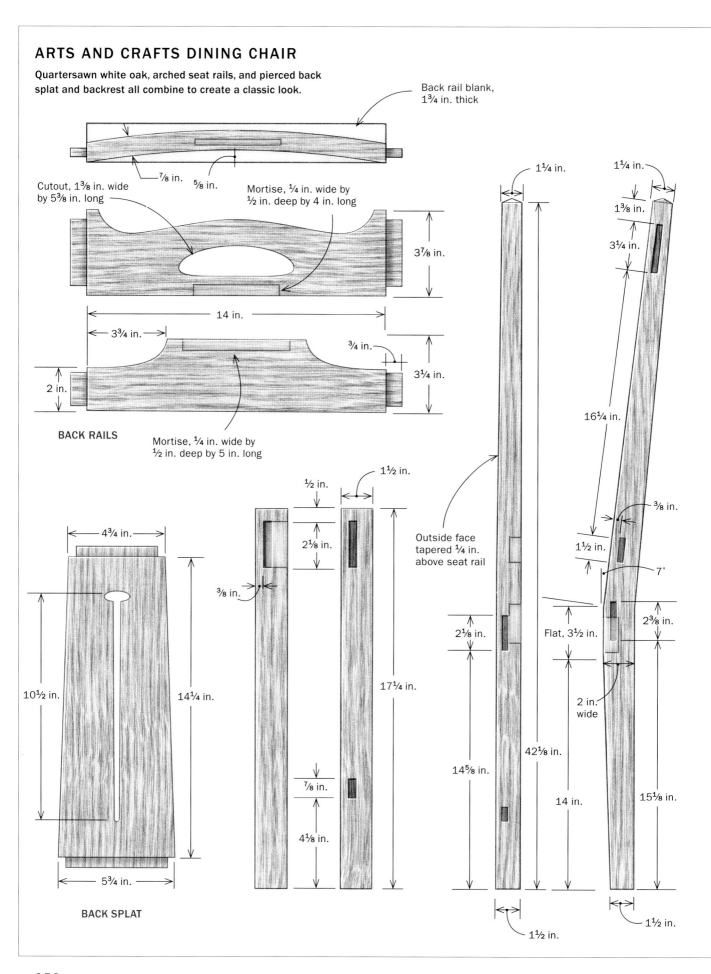

Back rail blank, 1¾ in. thick

⅞ in.

⅝ in.

Cutout, 1⅜ in. wide by 5⅜ in. long

Mortise, ¼ in. wide by ½ in. deep by 4 in. long

3⅞ in.

14 in.

3¾ in.

¾ in.

3¼ in.

2 in.

BACK RAILS

Mortise, ¼ in. wide by ½ in. deep by 5 in. long

1¼ in.

1¼ in.

1⅜ in.

3¼ in.

16¼ in.

⅜ in.

1½ in.

7°

½ in.

1½ in.

2⅛ in.

Outside face tapered ¼ in. above seat rail

3⁄8 in.

17¼ in.

2⅛ in.

2⅜ in.

Flat, 3½ in.

4¾ in.

14¼ in.

⅞ in.

2 in. wide

14⅝ in.

42⅛ in.

10½ in.

4⅛ in.

14 in.

15⅛ in.

5¾ in.

BACK SPLAT

1½ in.

1½ in.

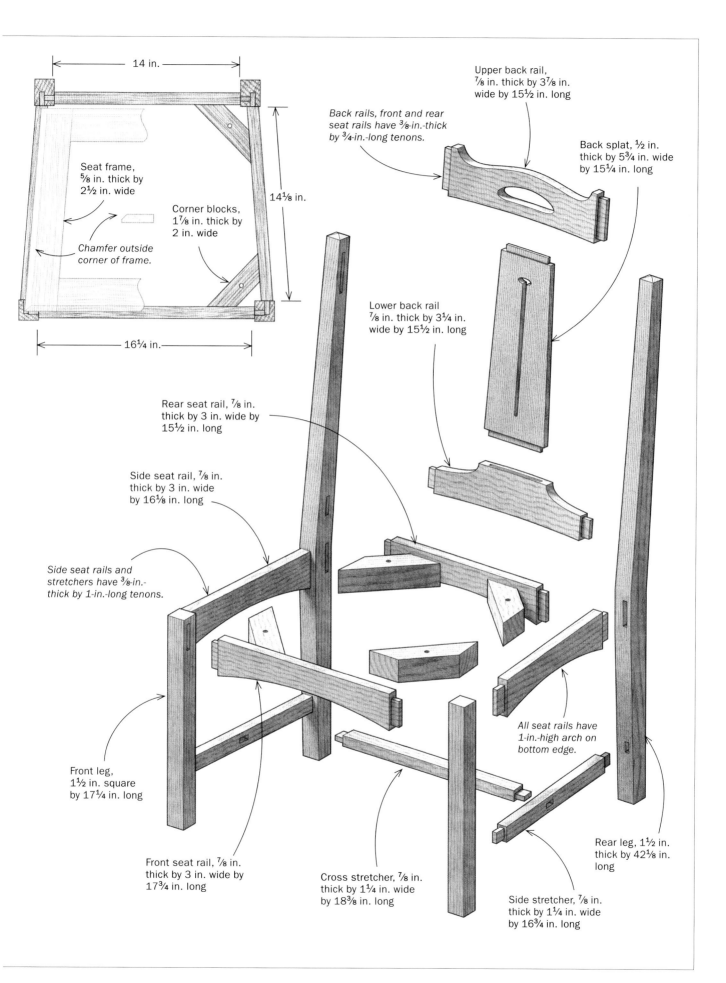

14 in.

Seat frame,
⅝ in. thick by
2½ in. wide

Corner blocks,
1⅞ in. thick by
2 in. wide

Chamfer outside
corner of frame.

14⅛ in.

16¼ in.

Upper back rail,
⅞ in. thick by 3⅞ in.
wide by 15½ in. long

*Back rails, front and rear
seat rails have ⅜-in.-thick
by ¾-in.-long tenons.*

Back splat, ½ in.
thick by 5¾ in. wide
by 15¼ in. long

Lower back rail
⅞ in. thick by 3¼ in.
wide by 15½ in. long

Rear seat rail, ⅞ in.
thick by 3 in. wide by
15½ in. long

Side seat rail, ⅞ in.
thick by 3 in. wide
by 16⅛ in. long

*Side seat rails and
stretchers have ⅜-in.-
thick by 1-in.-long tenons.*

*All seat rails have
1-in.-high arch on
bottom edge.*

Front leg,
1½ in. square
by 17¼ in. long

Rear leg, 1½ in.
thick by 42⅛ in.
long

Front seat rail, ⅞ in.
thick by 3 in. wide by
17¾ in. long

Cross stretcher, ⅞ in.
thick by 1¼ in. wide
by 18⅜ in. long

Side stretcher, ⅞ in.
thick by 1¼ in. wide
by 16¾ in. long

A TWO-SIDED ROUTING SLED

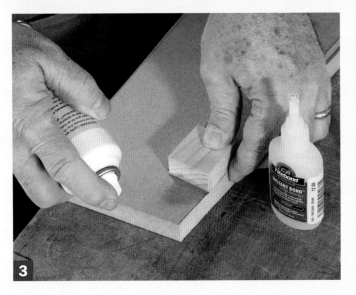

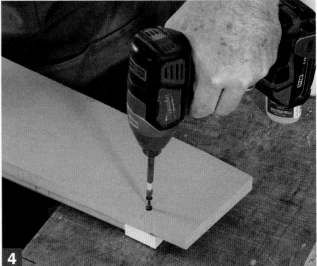

This sled is a step beyond a basic routing sled in that it allows you to rout two sides of a workpiece. It's easy enough to bandsaw and plane the rear legs by hand, but if you plan on making more than a single chair, it's worth the effort to make the sled. The first step is to make a template from plywood or MDF and trace it onto the base of the sled (**1**). Saw off most of the waste and then screw the template in place temporarily (**2**). Next add end stops to register the workpiece and provide areas to start and stop routing. Butt the blocks against the ends of the template and hold them in place with cyanoacrylate (CA) glue (**3**) while you drive in screws from below (**4**). Then head to the router table and use a bit with a bearing at the end to trim the sled flush to the template (**5**). Repeat the process for the opposite

edge of the template, this time adding stops along the back of the template.

To use the sled, first trace the profile onto the stock and saw just outside the line along the faces, but trim the ends exactly to the line so that it fits in the sled. Start by routing the front face of the leg. Clamp the leg in place so that the waste extends sightly beyond the edge of the sled and rout using a bit with a bearing at the shank (**6**). To rout the rear face, register the routed front face against the stop blocks on the opposite edge of the sled. While you're at it, you can clamp a second leg in place and rout both at once. If you have a batch of chairs to make, this definitely speeds the process.

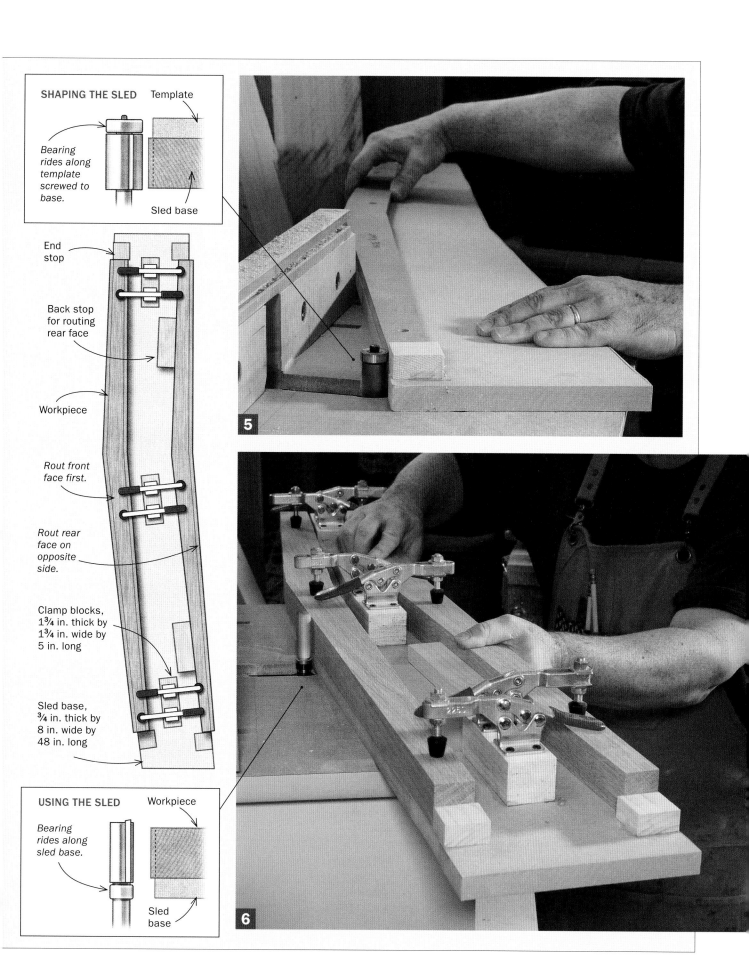

SHAPING THE SLED

Template

Bearing rides along template screwed to base.

Sled base

End stop

Back stop for routing rear face

Workpiece

Rout front face first.

Rout rear face on opposite side.

Clamp blocks, 1¾ in. thick by 1¾ in. wide by 5 in. long

Sled base, ¾ in. thick by 8 in. wide by 48 in. long

USING THE SLED

Workpiece

Bearing rides along sled base.

Sled base

5

6

A WEDGE SIMPLIFIES ANGLED JOINERY

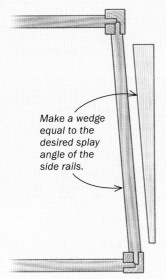

Make a wedge equal to the desired splay angle of the side rails.

Most chairs tend to be wider at the front than the back, which requires angled side stretchers. There are a few ways to handle the resulting angled joinery. I like to cut straight mortises in the front and rear legs, and then cut angled tenons on the side stretchers. To help me with that task, I first make a wedge equal to the splay angle of the side rails. To determine the angle of the wedge, make a full-size top-view drawing of the chair. Then, from the outside corner of a front leg, draw a line perpendicular to the front rail. This line along with the angled side rail determines the angle of the wedge you need. To use the wedge, first lay it flat on the crosscut sled, holding it in place with two-sided tape (**1**). Then lay the side rails flat on the wedge to cut the angled ends (**2**). To cut the angled tenons, mount the wedge on a tenoning jig. I use a box-joint blade to cut both the sides and shoulders of the tenons in one pass. Set the blade to cut the cheek farthest from the jig (**3**). Then insert a tenon spacer (**4**) (see p. 100), to cut the second cheek (**5**). I find it easiest to scribe and cut the ends of the tenons by hand.

JOINERY BEFORE CURVES

All of the shaping of the back rails is handled at the bandsaw, but it's easiest to cut the joinery while the parts are still square. Start by cutting the mortises for the back splat. Then use a tenoning jig and box-joint blade to cut the cheeks and shoulders of the tenons (**1**). Leave out the wedge but use the same tenon spacer that you used for the side rails. Next cut the piercing in the top rail. Drill a hole at each end of the cutout and connect the holes with a jigsaw (**2**). Now saw the curve of the rails at the bandsaw (**3**). Finally, cut the profiles of the rails. Tape the offcut to the bottom of the rail for support. If your bandsaw blade can't handle the tight curves, make a series of relief cuts first. This lets the blade cut a tighter radius (**4**).

The thing about a chair, a dining chair at least, is that you are often tasked with making more than just one. Once you begin to work in multiples, the calculus changes in terms of efficiency and the amount of setup and jig making you're willing to endure to speed the process. Making the rear legs of the chair is a good example of this. I show a somewhat involved router sled to handle the operation quickly, though it's not a lot of work to make just a pair of legs, and I'd probably skip it in that case.

Another situation where you may or may not want to involve a router is when shaping parts. The piercing in the back splat is an example of where a routing template comes in handy, though you can cut it with a jigsaw. Conversely, I show sawing the profiles of the backrest and the arched seat rails by hand, though you could certainly introduce router templates there as well.

One closing piece of advice is that even if you plan to make a set of chairs, start by making just one. That way, you can fine-tune the design and figure out your process before jumping into a big project.

Once you begin to work in multiples, the calculus changes in terms of efficiency and the amount of setup and jig making you're willing to endure.

PUT THE PLANS ASIDE AND MEASURE AS YOU GO

I wrote about the concept of "working from the outside in" in the "Building Strategies" chapter. It's a very powerful way to help ensure precise-fitting parts without having to do a lot of measuring, and we can put it to use when sizing the remaining parts of this chair. Save cutting the front rail to length until after the back and side rails are assembled. Any variation in the angle of your wedge will affect this dimension, so it's easiest to dry-fit the chair and take the measurement from it (**1**). The same is true for the lower stretcher assembly. Start by blocking up the side stretchers so that they are centered vertically on the mortises in the legs, and mark their shoulders (**2**). Use the wedge to cut the angled tenons on the ends. The rear tenon will have an angled vertical shoulder as well to match the taper of the rear leg. Start by cutting the shoulder square at the tablesaw and pare to the layout line with a chisel. Assemble the side stretchers and mark the shoulders of the center stretcher (**3**). The back splat can also be measured from the dry-fitted chair. Cut the tenons using a dado blade and sneak up on the shoulders for a snug fit (**4**).

A PIERCING BRINGS THE BACK SPLAT TO LIFE

The piercing can be drilled and sawn like the crest-rail cutout, or you can make a routing template (**1**). Blocks tacked to the bottom keep the splat centered. I use a ¼-in. straight bit with a ⅜-in. guide bushing, so the template needs to account for the offset (**2**). Rout in shallow passes, clearing out the chips as you go (**3**). To taper the sides, clamp an L-fence to your rip fence and position it above the blade and flush with the outside edge. Use a long push pad with sandpaper on the bottom and align it with a layout mark (**4**). The push stick runs along the L-fence to guide the cut (**5**).

FINAL SHAPING AND ASSEMBLY

Details, details. Small things can have a big impact on the overall look of a piece. There are a few final tasks to take care of now that the joinery is complete. A taper on the upper outside edge of the rear legs lightens the look of the chair (1). Your eye may not notice it, but I think it would look a little clunky if it weren't there. Arches along the bottom of the aprons also take away some of the visual mass and help to impart an Arts and Crafts sensibility to the chair (2). Pyramids at the top of the rear leg posts are also a classic detail of the style (3). A block plane leaves hard, shiny facets on the white oak end grain. Sometimes I like perfect geometry (OK, most of the time), but I don't mind a little more rustic, less-than-perfect look here. On this chair, assembly starts with the back and front assemblies (4). (On the rocker that follows it made more sense to start with the sides.) Before bringing everything together, take a minute to pin the joints (5). Add the side rails and the H-stretchers during final assembly (6). After the glue has had a chance to dry for half an hour or so, I removed the lower clamp and drove wedges in the cross-stretcher ends (7). The last step is to install the corner blocks (8). Start by gluing them in place using a V-caul on the outside of the leg. Once the glue is dry, add a couple of screws. In addition to creating an attachment point for the seat, they do quite a bit to strengthen the chair.

ROCKING CHAIR: CLASSIC STYLE MEETS COMFORT

The basic construction of this rocking chair doesn't differ a great deal from the previous dining chair. The big changes involve adding armrests and rockers, and that's what I'll focus on here. I went with a bent-laminated curve for the rockers, and it's a good place to give it a try if you haven't yet. The back rests could also be made using the technique, though it does make the joinery a little more challenging (go to p. 217 to see how to cut mortises and tenons in curved parts). One significant improvement over the original was in the way that the arms attach to the rear leg posts. Instead of screwing though the back of the leg into the armrest and plugging the hole, I opted for a double tenon. However, considering the original is still holding up well after one hundred years or so, I admit that a screw is a perfectly good way to go about it if you want to save yourself some work.

Honestly, I had bigger plans for this chair design. I'd spent the previous 20 Connecticut winters in front of my woodstove, sitting in an old rocking chair that I'd picked up at a flea market (bottom right). In the Arts and Crafts style, the chair was a little beat up, but the joints were tight and the finish was holding up well enough. The only rehab it got was a new cover on the spring-cushion seat. There was no maker's mark, and though it was an original chair from the era, there had most likely been some concessions to ease of production and sales price as well. The leg posts were a little thin, and the back slats were a little narrow and spaced just a bit too far apart. In short, there was nothing particularly special about it except for the fact that it was really comfortable to sit in.

A new rocking chair had been on my project list for a while, and because it can be tough to get the ergonomics right when starting from scratch, I decided to use my older rocker as a starting point. My first thought was that it would be a good base for coming up with a unique design more in tune with the current path I was on. But a funny thing happened as I began to

A new rocking chair had been on my project list for a while, and because it can be tough to get the ergonomics just right, I decided to use my old rocker as a starting point.

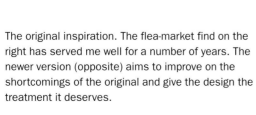

The original inspiration. The flea-market find on the right has served me well for a number of years. The newer version (opposite) aims to improve on the shortcomings of the original and give the design the treatment it deserves.

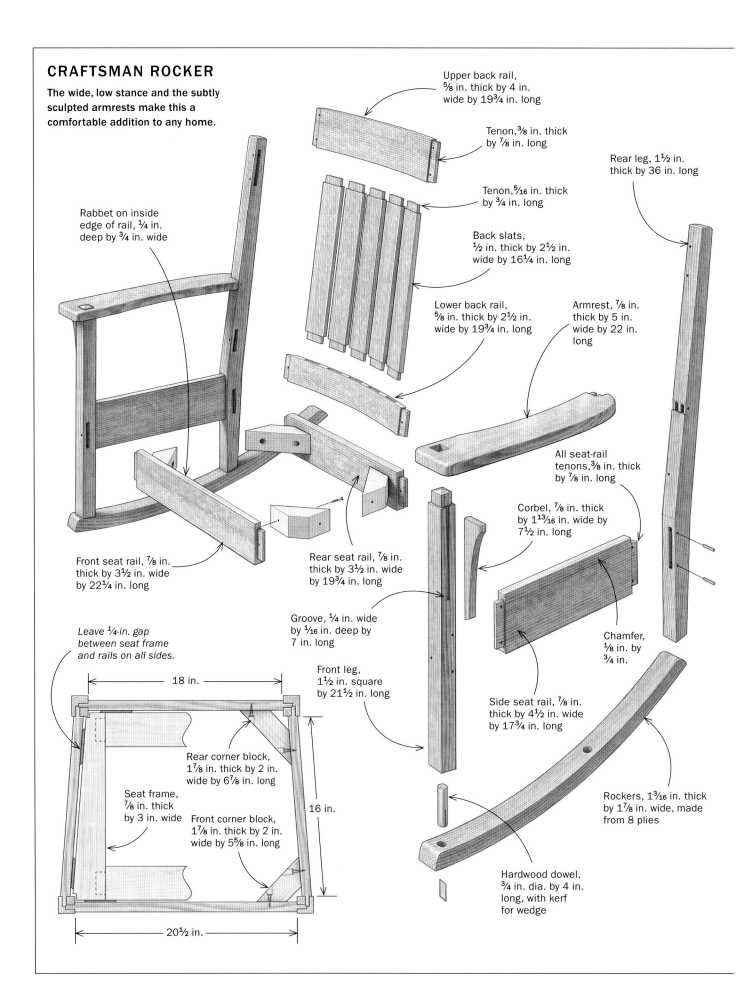

CRAFTSMAN ROCKER

The wide, low stance and the subtly sculpted armrests make this a comfortable addition to any home.

Upper back rail, 5/8 in. thick by 4 in. wide by 19¾ in. long

Tenon, 3/8 in. thick by 7/8 in. long

Rear leg, 1½ in. thick by 36 in. long

Tenon, 5/16 in. thick by ¾ in. long

Rabbet on inside edge of rail, ¼ in. deep by ¾ in. wide

Back slats, ½ in. thick by 2½ in. wide by 16¼ in. long

Lower back rail, 5/8 in. thick by 2½ in. wide by 19¾ in. long

Armrest, 7/8 in. thick by 5 in. wide by 22 in. long

All seat-rail tenons, 3/8 in. thick by 7/8 in. long

Corbel, 7/8 in. thick by 1 13/16 in. wide by 7½ in. long

Front seat rail, 7/8 in. thick by 3½ in. wide by 22¼ in. long

Rear seat rail, 7/8 in. thick by 3½ in. wide by 19¾ in. long

Groove, ¼ in. wide by 1/16 in. deep by 7 in. long

Front leg, 1½ in. square by 21½ in. long

Chamfer, 1/8 in. by ¾ in.

Leave ¼-in. gap between seat frame and rails on all sides.

18 in.

Rear corner block, 1 7/8 in. thick by 2 in. wide by 6 7/8 in. long

Seat frame, 7/8 in. thick by 3 in. wide

Front corner block, 1 7/8 in. thick by 2 in. wide by 5 5/8 in. long

16 in.

20½ in.

Side seat rail, 7/8 in. thick by 4½ in. wide by 17¾ in. long

Rockers, 1 3/16 in. thick by 1 7/8 in. wide, made from 8 plies

Hardwood dowel, ¾ in. dia. by 4 in. long, with kerf for wedge

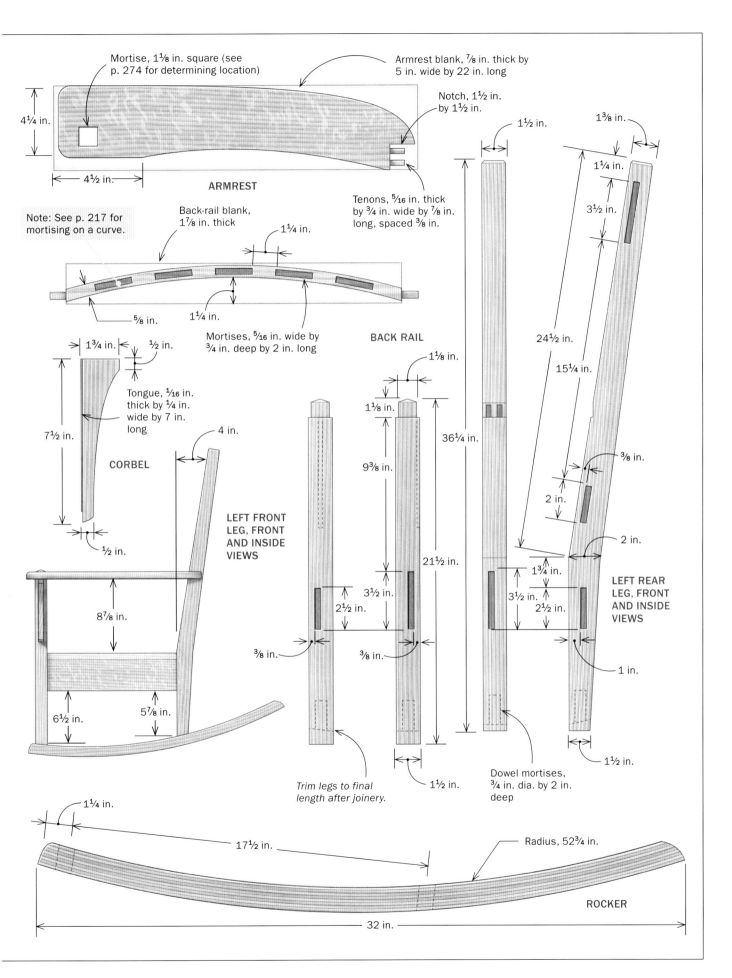

Mortise, 1⅛ in. square (see p. 274 for determining location)

Armrest blank, ⅞ in. thick by 5 in. wide by 22 in. long

Notch, 1½ in. by 1½ in.

4¼ in.

4½ in.

ARMREST

Tenons, 5⁄16 in. thick by ¾ in. wide by ⅞ in. long, spaced ⅜ in.

Note: See p. 217 for mortising on a curve.

Back-rail blank, 1⅞ in. thick

1¼ in.

⅝ in.

1¼ in.

Mortises, 5⁄16 in. wide by ¾ in. deep by 2 in. long

BACK RAIL

1½ in.

1⅜ in.

1¼ in.

3½ in.

24½ in.

15¼ in.

⅜ in.

2 in.

2 in.

LEFT REAR LEG, FRONT AND INSIDE VIEWS

1¾ in.
3½ in.
2½ in.

1 in.

1½ in.

1¾ in.
½ in.

Tongue, 1⁄16 in. thick by ¼ in. wide by 7 in. long

7½ in.

CORBEL

½ in.

4 in.

1⅛ in.

1⅛ in.

9⅜ in.

36¼ in.

21½ in.

3½ in.
2½ in.

⅜ in.

⅜ in.

1½ in.

Trim legs to final length after joinery.

LEFT FRONT LEG, FRONT AND INSIDE VIEWS

8⅞ in.

6½ in.

5⅞ in.

Dowel mortises, ¾ in. dia. by 2 in. deep

1¼ in.

17½ in.

Radius, 52¾ in.

ROCKER

32 in.

JOINING THE ARMRESTS TO THE LEGS

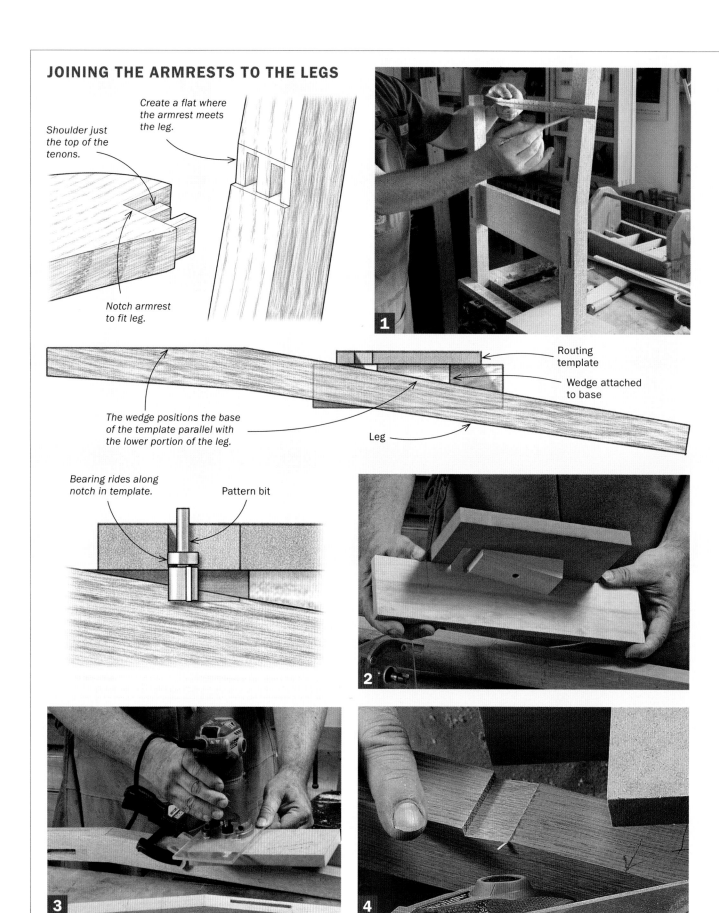

Shoulder just the top of the tenons.

Create a flat where the armrest meets the leg.

Notch armrest to fit leg.

Routing template

Wedge attached to base

The wedge positions the base of the template parallel with the lower portion of the leg.

Leg

Bearing rides along notch in template.

Pattern bit

Installing the armrests begins with creating a flat on the face of the rear leg post where the armrest meets it. This flat simplifies the joint by eliminating the need for angled shoulders. Dry-fit the chair sides to locate the flat. Hold a straightedge on the shoulder of the front leg post tenon and mark where it intersects the rear leg (**1**). You can saw and chisel the flat or make a quick router jig. The key to the jig is a wedge that positions the base of the jig parallel to the bottom portion of the leg (**2**). A bearing-guided bit rides in a notch in the base to create the flat (**3**). The flat should be flush with the leg at the top edge, but I set the bit a little deeper so that I can surface the leg front without creating a gap at the top of the armrest where it meets the leg (**4**). To cut the mortises, set the fence to cut the mortise farthest away. After mortising, insert a spacer between the leg and the fence (**5**) to cut the second mortise (**6**). You can use the same spacer to set the distance between the tenons at the tablesaw (**7**). In addition, you'll need to make a spacer to cut the tenons (see p. 100). By using both spacers in combination, you can cut all four tenon cheeks (**8**). To rout the shoulder at the top of the tenons, clamp a piece of stock along the baseline and use a bearing-guided bit (**9**).

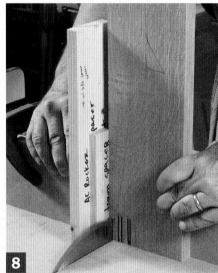

MORTISING THE ARMREST FOR THE FRONT LEG POST

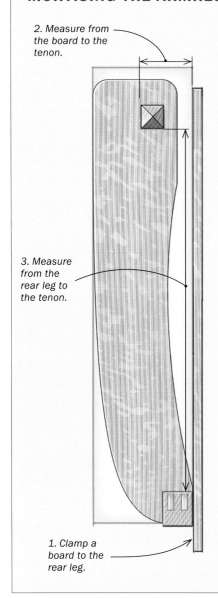

2. Measure from the board to the tenon.

3. Measure from the rear leg to the tenon.

1. Clamp a board to the rear leg.

develop a design. Instead of moving away from the original style of the chair, I found myself fixing what I didn't like about it. I beefed up the parts where they needed it, added more slats to fill out the backrest, fancied up the armrest supports, and took more care with the lumber selection. In the end, it wasn't a departure at all from the old chair: On the contrary, it was closer to the heart of the design than the original chair itself. You could say that there wasn't really any creative design involved at all, but while it may not have my fingerprints, I feel the chair is better served than if I had made a conscious effort to make it something else. In the end, I consoled myself with the thought that now that I had gotten to the essence of the design, maybe I could take the next chair further forward on that path. At the moment both rockers sit side by side in front of the woodstove, though Rachel tends to claim the new chair while I still sit comfortably in the old one.

2

3

4

5

6

With the rear joinery of the armrests cut, the next step is to locate and cut the mortise for the front leg post. Laying out the mortise is a little tricky because the front leg is at a diagonal to the rear leg, but you can take advantage of the fact that the inside edge of the armrest is flush with the inside face of the rear leg. This allows you to clamp a straightedge to the rear leg and take your dimensions from that. Place a rule against the rear face of the leg-post tenon and measure from the outside face of the tenon to the straightedge (**1**). Also, mark where the rule hits the straightedge and measure from that point to the rear leg. This measurement will give you the location of the mortise walls farthest from the edge and end of the armrest (see drawing). Set a marking gauge to one of the dimensions to scribe the first wall (**2**), and then, using a spacer the exact width of the tenon (**3**), lay out the opposite wall (**4**). Before changing the gauge setting, be sure to lay out the mortise on the bottom face of the armrests. Repeat the process for the second set of walls (**5**) and cut the mortise by first drilling out most of the waste and then chopping halfway in from each face (**6**). As always, save the shaping until the joinery is cut (**7**).

7

ADDING THE ROCKERS AND ASSEMBLING THE CHAIR

ROCKER DRILLING CAUL

Caul positions the rocker to drill holes in line with the legs.

1¼ in.

6½ in.

5⅞ in.

3 in.

4⅛ in.

17½ in.

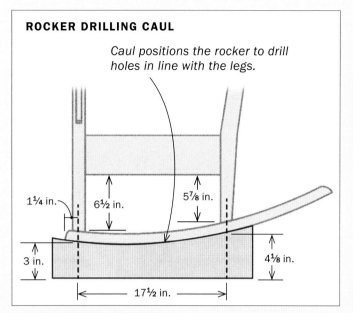

The rockers are a bent lamination (**1**) (see p. 214). Making them is not difficult; the challenge lies in attaching them to the legs. A tenon cut into the bottom of the legs would work, but you'd need to deal with the angled, curved shoulders of the tenon. I got around that problem by using what is essentially a slip tenon. Holes are drilled in both the rocker and the bottom of the leg and a dowel joins everything together. The trick is getting the holes in the right location at the correct angle. Start by drilling the rockers. Make a caul to support the rocker at the correct angle in relation to the leg posts and use a Forstner bit to drill completely through the rocker at the leg locations (**2**). Next cut the legs to final length. Dry-fit the chair sides and make a mark where the legs meet the rocker. Hold the rocker in place and trace the curved profiles (**3**), and then cut the legs to final length at the bandsaw and fine-tune the profile with a file. Do

your best to get a flush fit, but don't worry too much about it as it's tough to make it perfect. Then clamp the rocker in place and use it as a drilling guide to drill the legs (4). Glue an oak dowel into each leg using epoxy (5). Cut a kerf half the length of the dowel for a wedge before you install each dowel. Assembly begins with the side units (6). Clamp the legs, rail, and armrest together, and then add the rocker, wedging it in place (7). Then glue up the backrest and bring the chair together (8). Afterward, pin the joints and add the corner blocks.

METRIC EQUIVALENTS

INCHES	CENTIMETERS	MILLIMETERS	INCHES	CENTIMETERS	MILLIMETERS
⅛	0.3	3	13	33.0	330
¼	0.6	6	14	35.6	356
⅜	1.0	10	15	38.1	381
½	1.3	13	16	40.6	406
⅝	1.6	16	17	43.2	432
¾	1.9	19	18	45.7	457
⅞	2.2	22	19	48.3	483
1	2.5	25	20	50.8	508
1¼	3.2	32	21	53.3	533
1½	3.8	38	22	55.9	559
1¾	4.4	44	23	58.4	584
2	5.1	51	24	61	610
2½	6.4	64	25	63.5	635
3	7.6	76	26	66.0	660
3½	8.9	89	27	68.6	686
4	10.2	102	28	71.7	717
4½	11.4	114	29	73.7	737
5	12.7	127	30	76.2	762
6	15.2	152	31	78.7	787
7	17.8	178	32	81.3	813
8	20.3	203	33	83.8	838
9	22.9	229	34	86.4	864
10	25.4	254	35	88.9	889
11	27.9	279	36	91.4	914
12	30.5	305			

INDEX

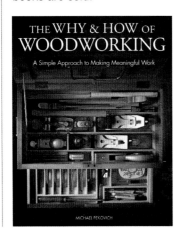
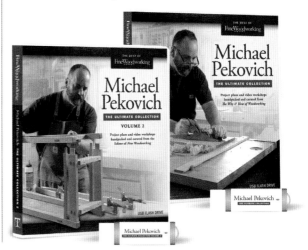